I0759935

Colman's
Mustard
30
min

MAKE THINGS. FROM WOOD.

Easy woodworking skills and designs for the modern maker

Written by Annabelle June Buckland
Illustrated by Kathrine Buckland

DAVID & CHARLES
— PUBLISHING —

www.davidandcharles.com

Contents

O
O
X
O
X

Introduction

Hi, I'm Annabelle and I make things. From wood. You can too.

I'm a self taught woodworker – I dipped my toes into woodworking several years ago and instantly fell in love. I never actually considered myself to be a creative person. I was always drawn to creative endeavours, but I wasn't naturally talented at anything. It took me a long time to realise you don't have to be any good – you can be terrible and still have fun. So my creative journey began. I learnt instruments (badly), I upcycled clothes (badly) and I woodworked (badly). But woodworking was the one thing that really stuck with me; it suddenly became all I ever wanted to do. But as someone with no prior knowledge or experience – and no one to guide or teach me in real life – I relied solely on books, blogs and YouTube to teach me, along with a lot of trial and error. And who would've thought that the more you do something, the better you get at it? And now, several years later, here I am writing this book and hoping you'll join me.

If you're a beginner interested in woodworking it can feel like an intimidating world to enter. When I first started out, there were two things I struggled to overcome. First was the fear of injury from scary power tools. The second was feeling totally overwhelmed trying to learn the basics from the endless amounts of information out there. My hope with this book is to give you the basic knowledge you need, all in one place, to give you the confidence to get started on your woodworking journey. And if you've already taken your first steps into woodworking, I hope this book can support you as you continue on that journey. Most importantly, I want you to realise that woodworking is an accessible and fun hobby that anyone can get into. Woodworking shouldn't be about perfection. There's nothing more joyful to me than bringing a vision to life with my hands – how finessed you want to become at the art is up to you. You might be someone who wants to create fun designs to fill your home with, or you might be someone who wants to dedicate your time to perfecting complex techniques. I'm here to say both are noble pursuits and neither is better than the other. Wood is beautiful. Creating art is beautiful. And, as we all know, beauty is different to each person. Woodworking is a way to bring your version of beauty into the world.

What to expect from this book

When creating this book, I took my mind back to the younger me and what I wish I'd been told. Not only that, but also *how* I wish I'd been told it, because too much of the information available left me more confused than when I started. I hope you'll find this book to be educational and accessible. We'll focus on a new tool or skill in each chapter, and you'll be able to jump straight in and start making projects immediately.

The information I share here is based on my years of experience, but it's not the Holy Grail. You'll get more than enough knowledge from this book to get you started, but, as with most pursuits, this isn't a journey that ends. You'll constantly learn new skills throughout your time, and luckily we live in the wonderful age of information, so there's plenty of places to continue your learning. If you need a little more support with any of the tools we cover in the book, you can head over to my YouTube channel to see video demonstrations.

WORX

Safety

When it comes to safety, I can't possibly provide you with every lesson you need – that's not my expertise. But what I can do is offer you the basics and remind you that safety procedures are well documented and shared via experts, tool manuals and manufacturers websites.

When it comes to safety in woodworking, the four main things you want to protect are:

Ears

Power tools are loud, and while this may not feel like an immediate risk, prolonged use will have an affect on your hearing. Look after your ears by wearing ear protectors when using power tools.

Eyes

Using tools correctly means nothing should be flying up at your face, but there's always a possibility that something can go wrong. If that happens, you want to ensure your eyes are protected. Best practice is to wear safety glasses whenever operating machinery.

Lungs

Doing any type of woodwork will produce dust, particularly fine dust that can linger in the air even if it's not visible to you. To protect your lungs you should wear a mask with filters designed for fine dust. You should also consider the environment you work in. If you're working inside, you'll need to ensure the room is well ventilated, and consider dust extraction. I'll talk a little more about dust management later.

Body

When I started woodworking, I was particularly concerned about my hands and fingers and I assumed gloves would be the best way to protect them. In reality, gloves are not safe to wear when operating power tools – if the fabric gets caught in the rotating mechanism it can pull your hand further into the tool. You should also avoid wearing baggy clothing and always tie long hair back.

The main way to protect yourself is simply following the manufacturer's instructions. Anecdotal evidence suggests the main cause of injury while woodworking is improper use of the tool. This includes beginners who haven't learnt the correct use, as well as experienced woodworkers who know what they're doing isn't right but are misguided by the confidence they've gained. Most of us have been there. Only ever use a tool for what it's designed for, and if something feels dicey, it probably is.

Other considerations

While I'll provide an overview of how to use each tool, it's important that you read and follow the user manual before working with any tool.

Another common reason for injury is working when you're tired or distracted. If you're feeling a little under the weather, it's best to leave the tools alone until you're feeling better. Make sure your work area is clear of distractions and that any other people in your vicinity know not to approach you while the power tool is on.

Power tools should be switched off and disconnected from power except for when you're actively using them. Whenever making adjustments to a tool, like installing a bit or adjusting the angle of a blade, it's especially important to ensure that it's switched off and disconnected from power.

Final thoughts

Before we jump in, there are a few things I want to share with you.

Firstly, mistakes happen. Projects won't always go to plan – that's normal. It doesn't make you a failure. One of the best parts of woodworking is evolving your design as you build it, revising your ideas and embracing your mistakes. Trust me, I make a lot of mistakes. It can be tempting to throw in the towel and feel like you have to start over again, but most of the time you can simply lean into the mistake and go with it. Even without mistakes, I regularly end up changing my plans halfway through a build. If you truly let your creativity flow, you'll come up with new ideas constantly. Allow yourself to be flexible. Change things up.

Secondly, you don't have to be good at something to enjoy it. I'll say that again: you don't have to be good at something to enjoy it. You may be a natural at woodworking, or you may find that, like me, the first few attempts aren't great. It's normal to be terrible at things when you first start. But if you let that dictate whether or not you continue the journey, you'll rob yourself of all the joy you could be experiencing. Let joy be the motivator, not perfection. Be brave enough to be terrible.

And lastly, you can do this. You. Can. Do. This. Seriously, you can. I don't care who you are, what creative experience you have (or don't have) or even your budget. Anyone can learn woodworking. Anyone can learn creativity. This isn't coming from someone with a natural ability. Quite the opposite. At the beginning, I didn't think I was creative or smart enough to get into woodworking. I'm also an incredibly slow learner, neurodivergent and riddled with anxiety. My woodworking journey has probably been slower than most. But I'm here. I make awesome things. And I have so much fun doing it. You can too. And I'm going to help you. So let's go!

Note – we have used metric measurements throughout this book, and the imperial conversions provided have been rounded to the nearest ⅛in/0.5cm. Use either metric or imperial throughout each project for reliable results. If you need more exact measurements, please use an online converter.

What is Wood?

Before we dive into the world of woodworking, let's take a moment to learn the basics of the very thing that allows us to bring our visions to life: wood. Okay, I know you know what wood is. Seed becomes tree. Tree becomes wood. But let's go over some of the terminology that you might hear.

Terminology

Timber/lumber – Timber and lumber are terms used to refer to wood that has been processed into the usable boards we need for woodworking. There are geographical differences in how these terms are used – in the UK, "timber" is used for both boards and felled trees; in the USA and Canada, "lumber" refers to usable boards, whereas "timber" is more commonly used to refer to standing or felled trees. To keep things simple, in this book (and in my life) I just call it wood.

Grain – the grain of the wood is the arrangement of fibres that make up a wooden board. Basically, it's the lines in the wood that make it pretty. When you hear the term "with the grain" or "along the grain", it means in the same direction as the lines. When you hear the term "across the grain" or "against the grain", it means perpendicular to the lines. The different sides of the wood are known as "end grain", "edge (or side) grain" and "face grain". The face grain is the more visible part of most projects.

Hardwood and softwood – all real wood falls into these two categories. As the name suggests, hardwood is generally much denser – literally harder. Softwood is less dense and therefore softer. Hardwood species – which include oak and walnut – take longer to grow and are more expensive; softwood – including species like pine and spruce – grows more quickly and is cheaper to buy.

Manufactured wood – in addition to natural hardwoods and softwoods, there's actually a third category: manufactured wood, also known as engineered wood. This includes plywood, MDF and chipboard. These are a composite of real wood along with other materials and adhesives. Usually cheaper than solid wood, manufactured wood can be a good option for a small budget. These wood types can be treated much the same as solid wood in terms of cutting, sanding and joining.

Workpiece – This simply refers to the piece of material that we're currently working on.

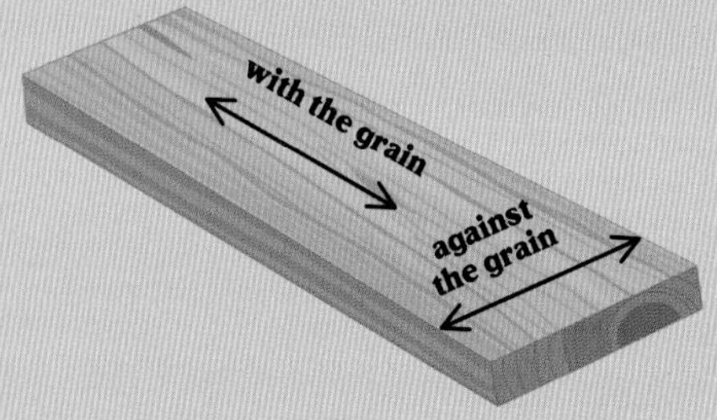

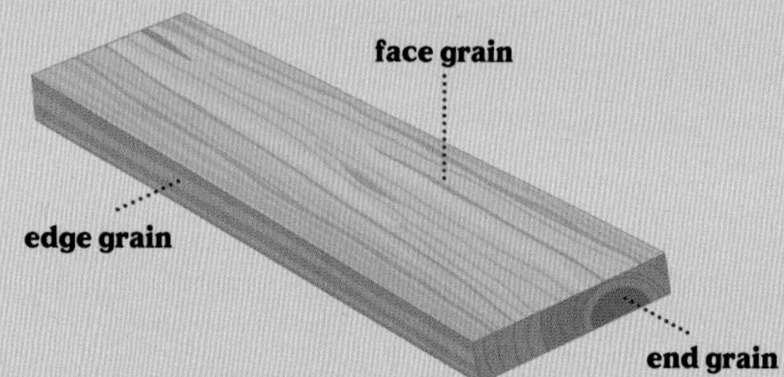

Square – In woodworking, "square" refers to the angle (rather than the shape). When the face of a piece of wood meets the edge at 90 degrees, the wood is square. When two pieces of wood are joined together to make a 90 degree angle, the angle is square. Square simply refers to materials that are straight and aligned at 90 degrees.

Waste – this refers to the unwanted side of a cut. If you have a length of wood at 30cm (12in) and you cut it down to 25cm (10in), the leftover 5cm (2in) piece is the waste piece or waste side.

Guide/fence/straight edge – these are all terms for a straight piece of material for either the wood or the tool to sit against, to help ensure a straight and square cut. On a mitre saw, the wood is held against a fence while the blade is brought down to make the cut. With a circular saw, a straight edge guide can be clamped onto the workpiece, and the saw is run along the edge of it to make the cut.

Planed wood – Planed wood has had thin layers of wood removed on all sides to create a flat, smooth and square finish. While you can plane wood yourself with a hand or electric plane, I prefer to buy pre-planed wood. We won't be covering planing in this book, but if it's something you'd like to try, there's an abundance of educational content out there to walk you through it.

Warping, twisting, cupping and bowing – these are terms used to describe wood that isn't straight and flat. Wood can twist in all sorts of ways.

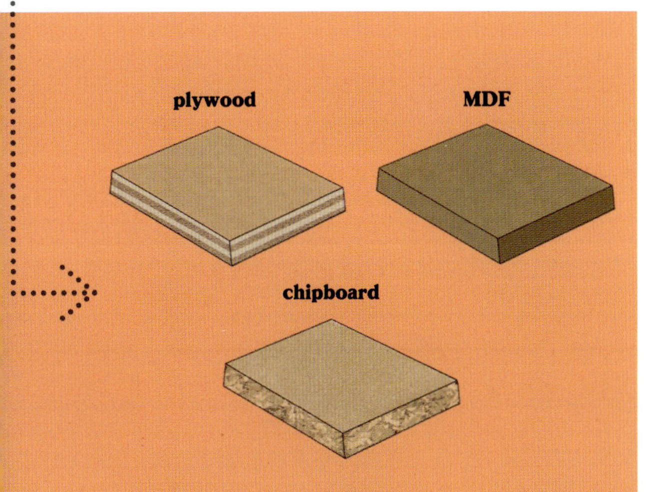

Choosing your wood

Generally, the choice of wood is down to personal preference. I use softwood for most of my projects. It's cheaper than hardwood, it's widely available and it's very light in tone, so you can stain it to whatever colour you want. Most projects can also be made using manufactured wood – I just prefer the look and feel of solid wood. There is a small handful of projects where the characteristics of the wood should take priority over preference. For example, it's best to use hardwood to make a chopping board. Not only would softwood not withstand all the chopping, but it also tends to be more porous, so bacteria from the food can get into the fibres.

The majority of the wood you'll find in stores – and the types I use for most of my projects – are pine (also called redwood) and spruce (also called whitewood), which are both softwoods.

Wooden boards come in a variety of widths and thicknesses, with the widest being around 10cm (4in). For wider projects, attach a number of boards side by side or use furniture boards (also known as timber boards), where narrower boards have already been joined together for you.

Here in the UK, wood is usually sold in lengths of 180cm (70in) and 240cm (94in) – this may vary depending on where you are in the world. Find wood that meets the width and thickness that you need, then cut it down to the required length. If you're unable to do this yourself, plenty of stores offer a cutting service.

Examples of warped wood:

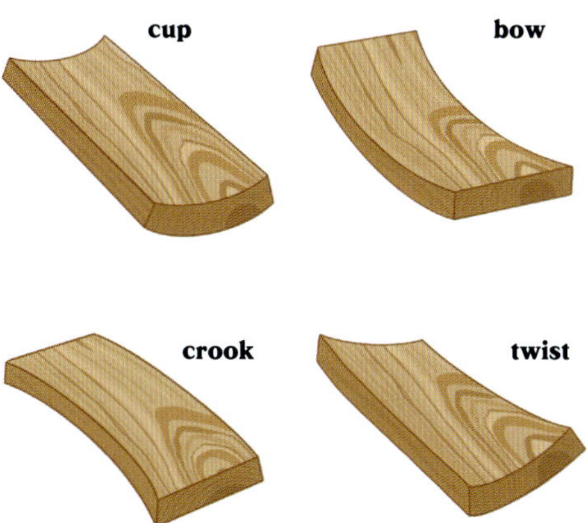

Where to buy wood

Buying wood can be daunting. When I started out, I was overwhelmed by all the different types, and I was certain everyone in the aisle was thinking "you don't belong here". But, spoiler alert, I belonged! We all do. Let's look at where and how to buy wood.

Hardware/DIY stores – wherever you are in the world, you'll have a hardware store that sells home DIY supplies, including wood. Head to the wood section, usually signposted as "timber" or "lumber" and divided into "sawn" and "planed" wood. Sawn wood is rough timber, often used for outdoor projects or where the wood won't be visible – think of it as a construction material. Planed wood (sometimes labelled "PSE" – planed square edge) is basically sawn wood that's been planed smooth and square, and it's the wood I use the most. You'll also find furniture boards in this section of the store, plus stripwood and moulding – thin strips of wood in a variety of shapes, often used for decorative purposes.

Check the wood for faults or defects (see the next section). Once you're happy, stroll up to the till with the casual confidence of someone who knows they belong there.

Buying online – I like buying online because I don't have to worry about fitting everything into my car. The only downside is you don't get to check the wood yourself, so it's likely there will be some boards that aren't in the best condition. If online is your best option, I recommend buying a little extra. That way, if some of the boards aren't usable, it won't leave you short. The wood will be categorised in much the same way as in store: sawn, planed (PSE), furniture boards, stripwood and moulding.

Timber yard/timber merchant – unlike hardware stores, timber yards specialise in wood, which means they'll have a larger variety of species, shapes and sizes. All the same rules apply as at the hardware store: find the wood you want, check for defects and saunter to the till.

Recycling centres – I strongly recommend looking for wood recycling centres in your area. Each centre will be different, but to paint you a picture, let me tell you about my local one. It's in a big old warehouse, and most of the workers are young volunteers looking for woodwork experience or retirees wanting to share their knowledge. Shelving stretches from wall to wall, filled with stacks of salvaged wooden boards from the local area. The rest of the space is filled with an ever-changing stock of old counter tops, chairs, barrels, crates... whatever they can save from landfill. Prices are extremely reasonable – much cheaper than anywhere else. The woodworking enthusiasts who run the place are more than happy to talk through your ideas and offer their advice.

Repurposing – you don't need to start from scratch; you can break down old wooden items to use the material. Check out local thrift stores and get creative! Equally, you'll be surprised how many people have wood they want to get rid of – I've had a neighbour offer me wood from a set of drawers he'd broken down; I've asked people having construction work done if I can take the wood from their skip; I've even used an old chopping board to make a lamp. Wood is everywhere.

Faults to look out for

No wood is perfect, but there are some specific flaws you should try to avoid. Start by checking for obvious defects like splits, cracks, missing chunks, large unsightly knots... things like that.

You also want the board to be as straight and flat as possible. You can check this by eye: with one end on the ground, bring the other end to eye level. Look down the surface to see if there's any noticeable misshaping or twisting.

To sum up

- The type of wood you use is up to you, unless the item needs to be food safe, in which case use hardwood.
- Buy wood based on the width and thickness you need, then cut the length as desired.
- Use furniture board when you need extra wide wood, or join narrower pieces together.
- Where possible, check wood for defects and warping before purchasing – or buy extra!

Hand Tools Versus Power Tools

One of the first decisions you'll make in woodworking is what tools to get, and with that decision you'll need to choose between hand tools and power tools. There are pros and cons to both. Which tools are best for you is down to your preferences and situation.

If you're planning to woodwork while your baby sleeps in the room next door, then hand tools may be best for you. If you don't have a lot of free time but want to complete builds quickly, then power tools may be the better option. Most woodworkers have a mix of both depending on what their priorities are. I'm primarily a power-tool user – precision and accuracy are not my strong points, so I like to rely on power tools for their precision. That being said, when I first started out I relied on hand tools because they're more affordable. Also I was pretty terrified of power tools. The fear of power tools holds many people back from starting woodworking, so I hope shedding more light on these tools will help alleviate that fear. I will, however, include hand tool options as well so you can learn about both.

Tools can be expensive to buy new. But buying new isn't the only option. Don't be afraid to keep an eye out for second-hand tools to build your collection. You may also have local stores where you can rent tools, or a makerspace that allows you to use what they have. There are plenty of ways to make woodworking more affordable, and you definitely don't need a huge selection of tools. The beautiful thing about woodworking is that the same thing can be achieved using different techniques with various tools, so the best tool is the one you already have. And if you don't already have it, the next best tool is the one you can afford.

Tools	Pros	Cons
Hand tools	More affordable, less dust projected into the air than power tools, smaller so easier to store, don't make much noise	Take more time, require more physical exertion, require more practice for precision
Power tools	Can complete tasks quickly, less physical exertion needed, offer great precision	More expensive, produce a lot of dust in the air, noisy

Dust management

One of the first things a beginner will notice when starting woodworking is the dust. Whether you're cutting or sanding wood, using hand tools or power tools, you will create dust. If you're working outside, dust isn't going to be a big issue for you, but if, like me, you work indoors, dust is something you will have to contend with. Some people think woodworking indoors isn't even an option due to the dust, but I'm here to tell you, from my trusty attic workshop, that dust can be managed.

A lot of power tools have dust ports with a dust bag connected that will catch some of the dust, but it definitely won't catch it all. To manage a better chunk of the dust, you can hook a workshop vacuum up to the dust port in place of the bag. A workshop vacuum, more commonly called a shop vac, is just like a regular vacuum but it's a bit more durable and has more suction power to manage dust and debris. A lot of people are surprised at how dust-free my workshop is. They expect me to have a complex solution, but I rely mostly on my shop vac.

Hooking the vac up to my power tools while in use captures a significant portion of the dust produced, but it still doesn't get all of it. So here's my big secret for how I keep my workshop so dust free. Are you ready? I vacuum. A lot. Like a lot a lot. Once I've finished cutting the wood, I vacuum the entire workshop before I move on to sanding. Once I'm done sanding, I again vacuum the entire workshop before I move to assembling. It takes up a lot of time, but when your only available working space is indoors, it's a simple solution. And don't forget, a mask isn't just for when you're using power tools, you should also wear it when you're cleaning. Don't let that pesky dust into your lungs.

If you want to upgrade your dust management, there are systems out there to use in addition to a shop vac, like an air filtration system. While you can buy these new, there's also a lot of really helpful DIY solutions out there, so search online to see what will be best for you.

Cutting Wood

In order to woodwork, you need to be able to achieve three things: cut wood, sand wood and join wood. It really is that simple. Once you have the tools to accomplish these three basic steps, you can make an endless amount of woodworking projects!

The first thing to do in any woodworking project is to cut wood. There are so many different tools and ways to cut wood it can feel overwhelming, and power tools are particularly intimidating. I was so scared of saws when I first started and, honestly, I'm still very cautious with new tools. If you feel the fear, instead of letting it hold you back, harness it: it will help you stay vigilant, careful and safe.

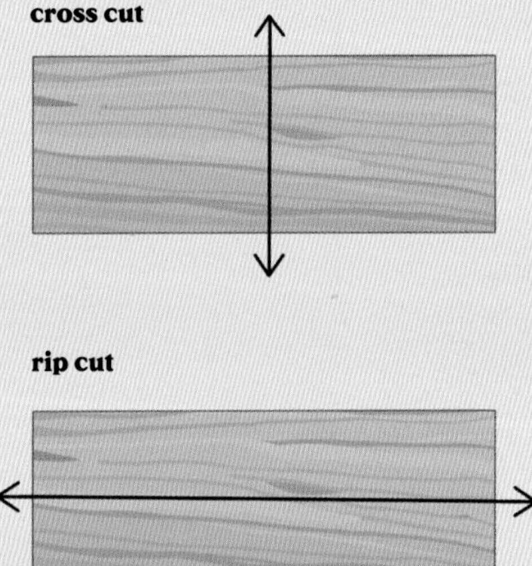

Types of cuts

The two main types of cuts on wood are cross cuts and rip cuts. Cross cuts are cut across the grain; rip cuts are cut along the grain.

We also have two types of angled cut: mitre cuts and bevel cuts. Mitre cuts are made diagonally across the face of the wood. Bevel cuts are angled into the edge of the wood.

Types of saws

Let's talk about some of the power tools and hand tools used to cut wood, and see what they do.

Power tools

Circular saw – this is a handheld, portable saw, and it's probably the most popular type of power saw. It can cut straight and angled cuts by being pushed into the wood by the user. You can also get mini circular saws which are a great alternative if you want something smaller.

Jigsaw – this power saw is primarily used to cut curves and shapes in wood, however it can be used to make straight cuts, and many models also have an angle adjustment for angled cuts.

Mitre saw – a mitre saw is a fixed saw where the user pulls the blade down onto the wood to cut it. This is designed for precision cuts, both straight and angled, and gets its name from mitre joints, which require precise angles.

Table saw – this saw has a blade that emerges from a table and the user pushes the wood into it to make cuts. It's great for making all types of cuts. However, it's worth noting that making cross cuts and angled cuts usually requires extra equipment.

circular saw: can cut rip, cross, mitre and bevel cuts

jigsaw: can cut cross, mitre and bevel cuts and curves

mitre saw: can cut cross, mitre and bevel cuts

table saw: can cut rip, cross, mitre and bevel cuts

Hand tools

Universal hand saw – this is likely what you'd draw if I asked you to draw a handsaw. It's a general purpose saw for making basic cuts in wood, but this isn't the greatest saw for precision cuts.

Back saw – This saw has a solid spine which keeps the blade from flexing and is good for precision cuts. Coupled with a mitre box, a back saw can make straight cuts as well as angled cuts (more on this later).

Coping saw – This is a type of bow saw with a thin blade attached at either end of a U-shaped frame. This saw is able to cut both straight and curved shapes into wood, much the same as a jigsaw.

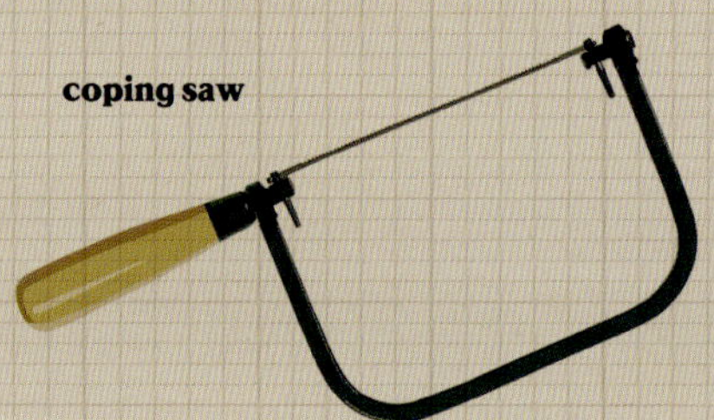

coping saw

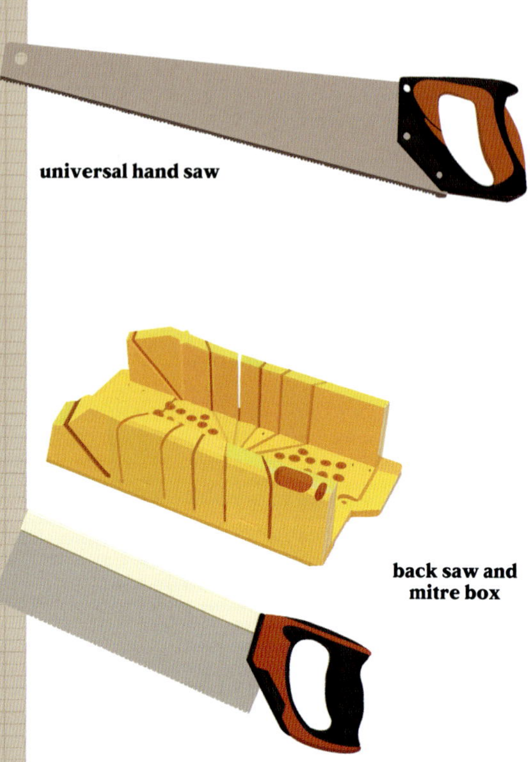

universal hand saw

back saw and mitre box

What saw do you need?

The type of saw you need depends on what you want to make. Most of the saws I've listed can handle straight and angled cuts, so you won't need all of them. Each has its pros and cons:

Back saw and mitre box – will allow you to make most cuts without the need for power tools, but as with all hand tools a box saw requires more time and physical exertion.

Circular saw – unrestricted by width and can be used to make both rip cuts and cross cuts, but it relies on the user setting up fences and guides to make straight and angled cuts.

Jigsaw – can achieve almost every cut and is a great option if budget and space is a challenge, but as the blade has some flex to it, it may not be as accurate as other options.

Mitre saw – makes precision cuts incredibly easy to produce, however it is limited by its cutting width and can only make cross cuts.

Table saw – can achieve most cuts, but requires a lot of space, additional equipment to support some cuts and is a bigger investment.

For power tools, I'd recommend starting out with a circular saw, full size or mini, as it will meet most of your needs. With hand tools, all you need to get started is a back saw and a mitre box. We're going to look at the back saw, circular saw and mitre saw in more detail next.

Kerf

But first, let's take a moment to talk about kerf. The term "kerf" describes the thickness or width of the cut a blade makes in a piece of wood. If a blade is 3mm (⅛in) thick, then it'll remove 3mm (⅛in) of wood when it cuts into it. This is the kerf.

Kerf is important because we need to account for it when making cuts, no matter which tool we're using. For most projects, you mark a pencil guideline on your wood to indicate where to make a cut. If you were to place the blade directly onto the guideline to cut, the kerf will likely be wider than the pencil mark – this will result in the workpiece being slightly shorter than planned. To avoid this, mark where you want to cut, but position the blade slightly to the outside of the pencil line, on the waste side, to make the cut. This will ensure the length of the workpiece is accurate.

Kind of like a new haircut, it's better to cut too long than too short. You can always take another sliver off, but you can't add it back on. You know that saying "measure twice, cut once"? Well it's also okay to cut a few times until it's right.

not accounting for kerf

accounting for kerf

Back saw and mitre box

A mitre box is usually plastic or wooden, with an open top and various slots on the side walls. These slots are what guide the back saw when making straight or angled cuts.

Straight guide slots – the straight slots guide the saw to make a straight cut.

Angled guide slots – the angled slots guide the saw to make mitre and bevel cuts.

Workpiece clamp – these slotting clamps hold the wood in place while you make the cut.

To use the mitre box, secure the box to a worktop using clamps or screws so it doesn't scoot around while you make the cut. Place the wood into the box and use the slotting clamps to hold the wood in place. Now insert the saw into the relevant slot and pull the saw forwards and backwards, always staying within the slot, to complete the cut.

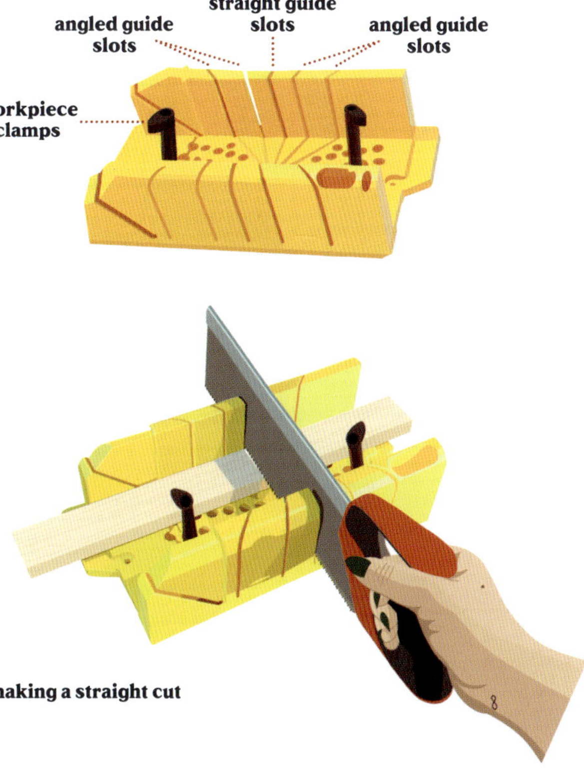

making a straight cut

Circular saw

Let's take a closer look at the circular saw.

Base plate – this is the part that rests on top of the wood while cutting.

Bevel adjustment – this adjusts the angle of the blade for making bevel cuts. It should be set to "0" for straight cuts.

Blade guard – this sits around the blade. As you push the saw into the wood to make a cut, the blade guard moves away to reveal the blade.

Depth adjustment – this allows you to alter the depth of the blade (how far under the base plate it reaches) according to the thickness of your wood. Adjust the depth so it's approx, but no more than, 5mm (¼in) greater than the thickness of your wood.

Handle – the circular saw should be operated with two hands, one on each handle.

Trigger switch – this is the power button that spins the blade.

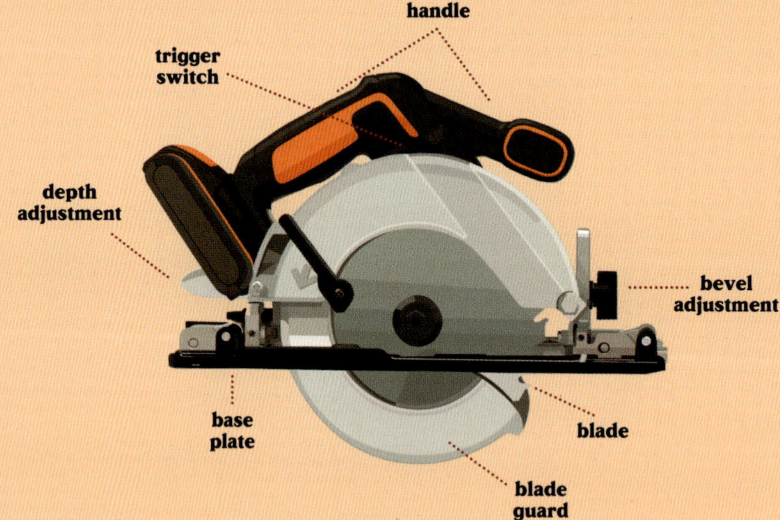

Setting up the wood

Before we cut anything, we need to set up the wood. First, mark the required cut line on the wood with a pencil. Now rest the wood on a flat surface so the full piece of wood is supported. I like to use my worktop, but as the blade of the saw will extend beneath the wood a little during the cut, I place a sheet of sacrificial MDF underneath the wood – this way, the blade cuts into the MDF and not the worktop. The cuts will be shallow, so you can reuse the MDF for future cutting. Clamp the wood securely in place so it won't move during the cut.

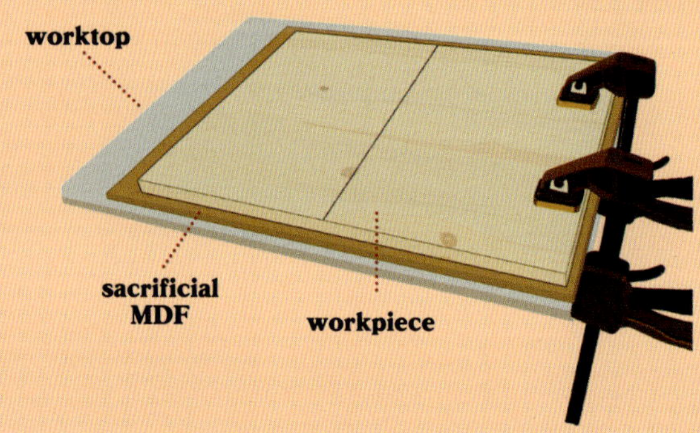

Setting up the saw

Before making any adjustments, make sure the saw is switched off and disconnected from power. First, set the bevel adjustment to 0 for a straight cut – check the manual for your saw; there's usually a small handle or lever to loosen the base plate, which you can then tilt to align with the desired number on the bevel scale. Tighten the handle to lock it into place.

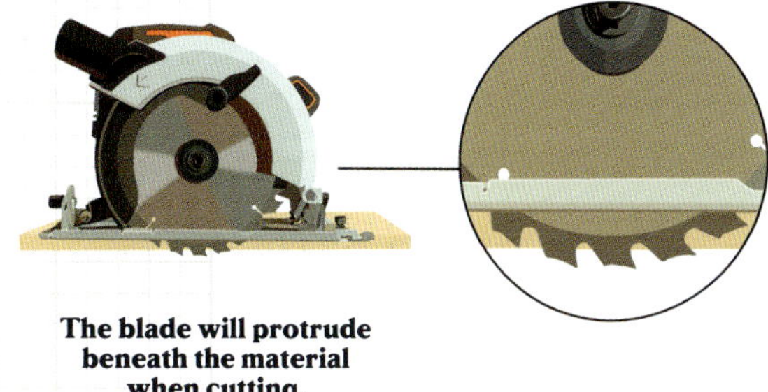

The blade will protrude beneath the material when cutting.

Next, set the depth of the blade – remember this should be greater than the thickness of your wood to ensure it cuts all the way through, but by no more than 5mm (¼in). Check the user manual for your saw – there's usually a handle that loosens the depth mechanism. Manually adjust the depth and tighten the handle to lock it into place. Use the sliding number scale on the saw to align it to the correct depth, or rest the base plate on the edge of the wood and adjust the depth visually (you'll need to pull the blade guard away to see the blade). Just a reminder to switch off and disconnect the saw before any adjustments.

Cutting

A. On the front of the base plate, you'll see a small notch marked with a line and a "0". When making straight cuts, keep this line on the base plate aligned with the pencilled cut line on the wood. Your base plate may also have another line labelled "45" for making bevel cuts, which we'll talk about later in the book.

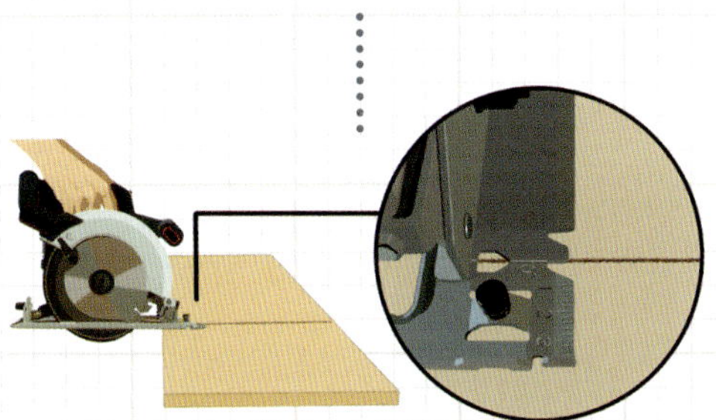

a. Align the base plate guide line with the pencil cut line.

B. Plug in the saw, but keep it switched off. Rest the front of the base plate on the wood, lining up the base plate line with the cut line. It's important that the blade isn't touching the wood yet, as it needs to reach full speed before making contact.

b. Rest the base plate on the wood without the blade making contact.

C. Power on the saw and give it a few seconds for the blade to get up to full speed. Ease it forwards into the wood – the blade guard will move itself out of the way – and make the full cut, keeping the cut lines aligned and the base plate flat on the surface of the wood throughout. Keep both hands on the saw to maintain control.

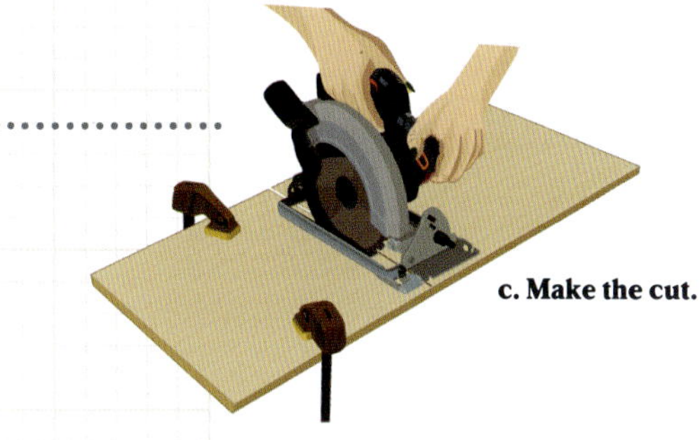

c. Make the cut.

Cutting with a guide

You can use a straight guide to help you keep the saw aligned to the cut line. Simply clamp a straight piece of material onto the wood and glide the base plate against it as you make the cut. First we need to figure out where the guide needs to be positioned.

A. With the saw disconnected, rest the front of the base plate on the wood, aligning the pencil cut line on the wood with the 0 guide line on the base plate. Using a pencil, mark the edge of the base plate.

Remove the saw and extend the pencil line across the full width of the wood.

B. Grab whatever straight edge you're using for the guide and clamp it onto the wood, lining it up with the new pencil line.

C. Now, during the cut, you can run the edge of the base plate against the guide. This will keep the saw straight and the blade aligned with the cut line.

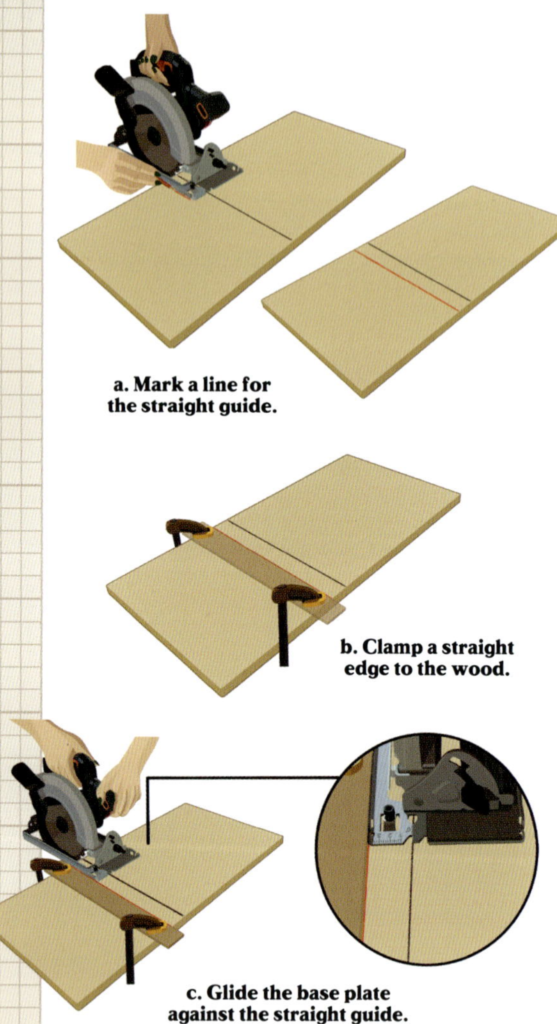

a. Mark a line for the straight guide.

b. Clamp a straight edge to the wood.

c. Glide the base plate against the straight guide.

Kickback

"Kickback" occurs when the blade gets pinched in the wood, causing the tool, or the wood, to jerk backwards, towards the user. Never stand directly behind the saw while cutting; stand to the side of it (whichever side is most comfortable), so you're not directly in its path if kickback happens.

To reduce the chance of kickback, consider how you set up the wood. Kickback happens when the wood begins to sag during the cut, so I like to fully support the wood on a flat surface. I also clamp the wood on just one side of the cut line, so the waste side can move away freely once the cut is complete. Alternatively, you can set up with the waste side hanging over the edge of the worktop, so it can fall to the floor once cut – I don't recommend this for particularly wide boards though, as the weight of the waste side hanging down during the cut can actually cause kickback. You can also use two surfaces to support the wood on either side of the cut line, but ensure the support is efficiently placed so the wood doesn't sag inwards during the cut.

Remember to adjust the blade depth adjustment correctly (no more than 5mm (¼in) greater than the thickness of the wood). The more blade there is exposed at the bottom of the saw, the more chance there will be of kickback.

I want to reiterate here that mini circular saws exist. Tools are not designed with everyone in mind, so handles can feel a little too big for women or anyone who falls outside of the average measurement. You may also find tools like circular saws a little too heavy or bulky. While I've been lucky enough, after many years, to find a full size circular saw that better meets my stature, I still love using my mini circular saw. It has all the same features as a full size saw, and although it has a smaller cutting depth, this is still more than enough for my projects.

mini circular saw

Let's talk tear out

Tear out is the name for when wooden fibres push out like little splinters during a cut in the wood.

Whether you see this on the underside or topside of the wood is dependent on the tool and blade rotation. Let's take a circular saw as an example, which cuts on an upwards rotation so you'd usually see tear out on the topside. Wood is made up of lots of little fibres (I like to imagine this as a bunch of toothpicks). As the blade rotates upwards, each fibre it comes into contact with is supported by the fibres above it so, with nowhere to go, the blade cuts through them cleanly – that is, until we get to the very top of the wood. The fibres here have no fibres above to support them, so when the blade comes up, these fibres push out, causing the little splinters. On a mitre saw, which rotates downwards, you usually see tear out on the underside and backside of the wood.

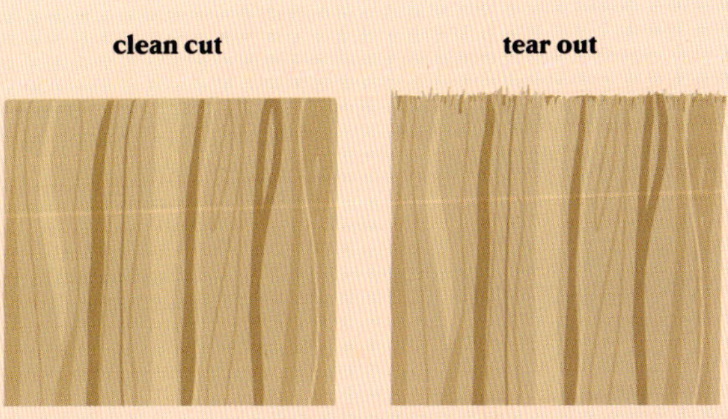

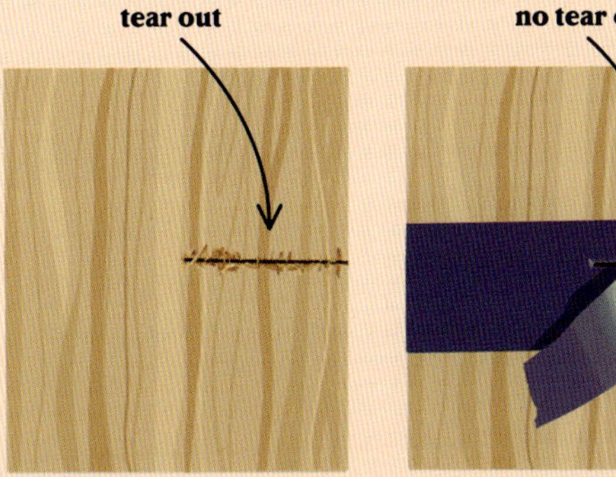

How to reduce tear out

To reduce tear out, we need to give a helping hand to the unsupported fibres so they can be cut cleanly instead of being pushed out. There's lots of ways to do this, but the simplest technique – and the one I use the most – is using painter's tape. Before making the cut, place the tape on the cut line where the tear out usually occurs. This will support the fibres and hold them neatly in place.

Mitre saw

Now let's look at the mitre saw.

Bevel adjustment – this tilts the blade to the left or right for making angled bevel cuts. Set this to 0 degrees for straight cuts.

Blade guard – this sits around the blade and moves itself out of the way to reveal the blade as you bring the saw down to make the cut.

Clamp – most mitre saws come with some sort of clamping system to hold the wood in place while you cut.

Fence – the wood sits against the fence while you make the cut.

Handle – this is the handle you use to bring the blade down onto the wood.

Mitre scale – this pivots the blade to the left or right for making angled mitre cuts. Set it to 0 degrees for straight cuts.

Slide rails – if you have a sliding mitre saw, these rails allow the blade to slide forwards and backwards for cutting wider material. If you have a non-sliding mitre saw, the blade is fixed and there are no rails.

Trigger switch – this is the power button that spins the blade.

Setting up the saw

Before making a cut, we need to make sure the saw is set up and ready. As always, ensure it's turned off and disconnected from power to make any adjustments. Each saw is slightly different, so check the user manual for your model, but the bevel adjustment is usually a handle near the back of the saw that can be twisted to loosen the mechanism. The saw can then be tilted to the side for bevel cuts, or set upright for straight cuts. There's a bevel scale to assist with the adjustment; align it to 0 for a straight cut and tighten the handle to lock it into place.

Next comes the mitre adjustment. There's usually a handle or lever near the front of the saw that can be loosened to pivot the saw to the appropriate number on the mitre scale. For straight cuts, align the mitre scale to 0 and tighten the handle to lock it into place.

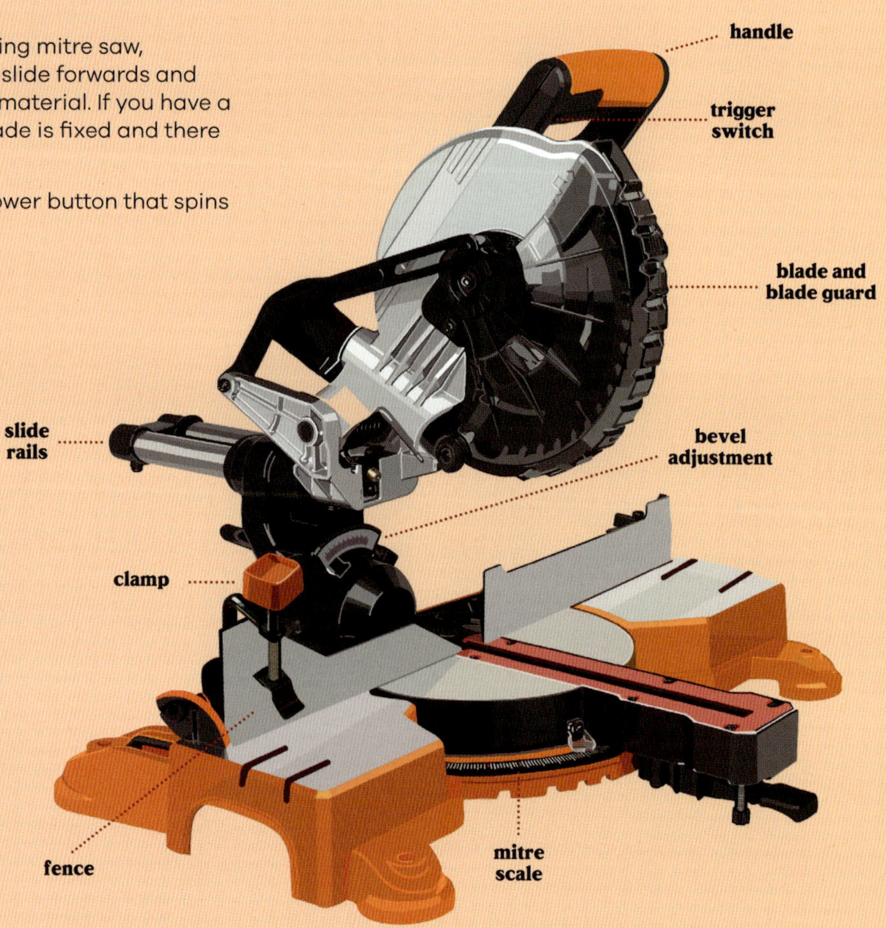

Cutting

Now the saw is set up, it's time to get the wood ready for the cut. Place the wood against the fence, lining up your desired cut line with the blade. The wood must be held in place on one side of the cut line, against the fence, while you make the cut – you can use the clamping system built into the mitre saw or your own clamps (a). You'll see a lot of woodworkers holding the wood in place with their hand – this is safe to do as long as the wood is long enough that your hand is well away from the blade.

Once the wood is secured, hold the trigger switch to start the blade, allowing a few seconds for it to get up to full speed. As you bring the blade down, the blade guard will move out of the way. Bring the blade down as far as it will go to make the cut (b).

a. Clamp the wood securely against the fence.

b. Bring the blade all the way down.

Making multiple cuts

You'll likely come across many projects, including some in this book, that require multiple pieces of wood to be cut to the same length. You can, of course, measure and mark the cut line on each piece of wood, but if you're looking for something a little quicker and more accurate, set up a stop block. A stop block is not one specific thing, rather it's a term for any fixed reference point used when making cuts. A simple example of this would be clamping a scrap block of wood to the fence of a mitre saw and then butting the workpiece against it to make a cut. Now you can cut multiple pieces of wood, one after the other, butting each against the stop block, resulting in an unlimited amount of wood cut to the exact same length. The distance between the blade and the stop block is the length the workpiece will be cut to.

Using a stop block.

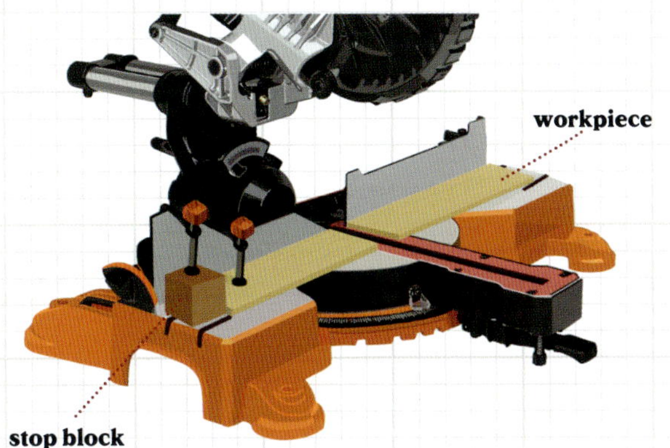

To sum up

- Cut on the waste side of the cut line to account for kerf.
- Use painter's tape to reduce tear out.
- Kickback occurs when the blade is pinched in the wood.
- Always read and follow the manufacturer's instructions for your specific tool.

Sanding Wood

It's unlikely that you'll ever encounter a wood project that doesn't require sanding. It's my least favourite part of woodworking, but it has a big impact on the quality of the finished piece. I found sanding to be one of the least intimidating woodworking tasks when I started out, and the easiest to learn.

What is sanding?

Sanding is the process of removing layers of wood to create a smooth surface. The coarseness of sandpaper is measured in grits; the lower the grit, the coarser the sandpaper, so 80 grit is very coarse while 220 grit is very smooth. You may find some sandpaper sheets designed for hand sanding are simply labelled coarse, medium and fine.

The common grits you'll see in sandpaper in order of coarseness are:

40 - 60 - 80 - 100 - 120 - 150 - 180 - 220 - 240 - 320

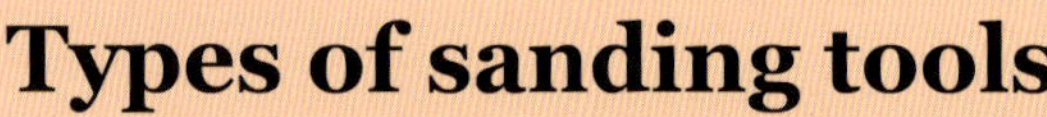

Types of sanding tools

There are a lot of sanding tools out there, so let's cover some of the most popular ones:

Hand tools

Sandpaper and block – this is the most basic way to sand. Using sandpaper alone is hard on your hands and doesn't give an even finish. Simply wrapping the sandpaper around a block of wood allows a better grip and ensures the sandpaper contacts the wood evenly.

sandpaper and block

hand sander

Hand sander (also known as a sand handle) – this basically works the same as the block of wood, but with a handle. You clamp the sandpaper onto the flat base and use the handle to grip.

detail hand sander

Detail hand sander – there's a variety of differently sized and shaped hand sanders for detailed work, when you're hand sanding small, difficult areas.

Power tools

Random orbit sander – as the name suggests, this sander oscillates the sandpaper in small random orbits, which prevents it from leaving the obvious sanding patterns in the wood that you can get from other sanders. The sandpaper attaches to the sander with hook and loop, so it's very easy to attach and remove.

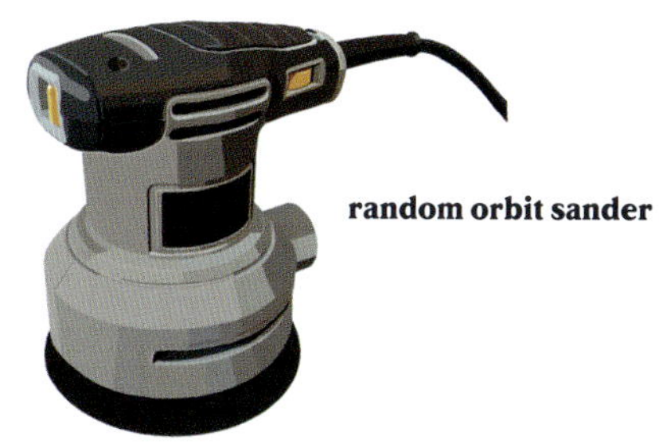

random orbit sander

belt sander

Belt sander – this has a belt of sandpaper that's rotated around the sander, much like the belt on a treadmill. These sanders are good for large wood removal or stripping tough finishes, but aren't as good at fine sanding or for smaller areas.

Detail sander – available in various sizes, detail sanders usually have a specially shaped pad to attach triangular sandpaper to via hook and loop. The shape means these sanders are good for corners and other hard-to-sand areas.

detail sander

The random orbit sander

I'd suggest that for general DIY and woodwork, a random orbit sander is all you need, so let's have a closer look at it.

Handle/palm grip – this is where to hold the sander when it's in operation.

Power switch – this will turn the sander on.

Sanding pad – this is where the sandpaper will attach to the sander via hook and loop.

Variable speed setting – this setting dictates how fast the sander spins. Generally I sand everything at the highest setting, but if you feel like the sander is running away from you, or it's taking too much off, you can adjust the speed to a lower setting until it feels comfortable.

How to sand

Let's cover how to sand your workpiece, whichever sander you choose. Always start at a lower (coarser) grit and work your way to a higher (smoother) grit, moving up through each grit number. The coarser grit will help remove imperfections, but it won't leave the wood feeling perfectly smooth, because the sandpaper itself creates micro scratches in the wood. Each time you move up a grit, you're removing the scratches made by the previous grit. Grits from 180 onwards leave such small scratches they're undetectable – this is when your wood feels smooth and you're done sanding.

Sand with the grain, so that the micro scratches left in the wood will lie in the direction of the grain and will be undetectable; scratches across the grain are more obvious. If you're using a random orbit sander, the sanding pad spins in random orbits so will sometimes sand against the grain. However, you won't have any issues as it does a great job of removing scratches.

Whether you're sanding by hand or with a power tool, place the sandpaper flat on the wood surface and move back and forth along the grain. There's no need to use excessive pressure – let the sandpaper do the work. Move in long motions, keeping light, even pressure at all times. If you're using a power sander, keep it moving. Staying in one spot will remove more wood there and create a dip. Be careful not to dip your sandpaper over the edges of the wood, otherwise you'll round off the sharp lines.

Clean dust from the wood each time you change sandpaper by wiping it down with a dry dust cloth, otherwise you risk trapping dust between the wood and the sander, which can create deeper scratches. When you're done sanding all sides of the wood, the edges and corners should still feel sharp. These should be finished by hand – known as "breaking the edge", which is usually done after assembly. Grab a fine sandpaper, say 220 grit, and gently swipe it once or twice over the full length of each edge. Do the same for each corner. This will keep the clean lines, but soften the edges so they're not sharp and won't be prone to splintering.

For sanding particularly small pieces of wood, tape some sandpaper onto a flat surface and slide the wood back and forth over it by hand.

Where to begin and end

If you're trying to remove an existing finish from wood, such as paint, or if the wood is particularly rough, I'd suggest starting at 80 grit.

If your wood is fairly smooth already, like pre-planed wood from a hardware store, I'd suggest starting at 120 grit.

The majority of woodworking projects can stop at 180 grit. This leaves a surface that's smooth to the touch. Sanding with a grit of 220 and higher can risk making the wood surface too smooth for stains or finishes to penetrate. Some types of finishes and techniques allow for a higher grit finish though, so be sure to check the instructions on any products you plan to use.

So, sanding a rough piece of wood will look like this:

Start with 80 grit, then 100 grit, then 120 grit, then 150 grit, then 180 grit.

And sanding wood that's already fairly smooth:

Start with 120 grit, then 150 grit, then 180 grit.

When to up your grit

I work on an "I can just feel it in my bones" philosophy of when to move to the next grit. But if your bones aren't accustomed to sanding, my advice is get yourself a pencil and lightly draw a squiggle across the wood. Now sand. Once all the pencil marks are gone, that's when you're ready to move to the next grit.

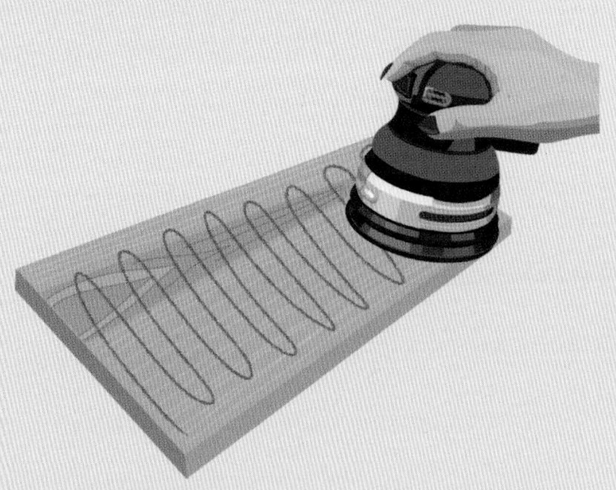

TIP

Sandpaper wears out, and you should change it as soon as this happens, not just when you move to a new grit. How often will depend on each project, but if you're working on a particularly big project, I recommend stopping regularly to feel the sandpaper with your fingers (power off if you're using an electric sander!). If the sandpaper feels very different compared to a fresh piece, then change it. Otherwise, it will be less efficient at its job, and you'll be sanding a lot longer than you need to be.

Before or after assembly?

You might wonder whether you should sand the wood before or after you join the pieces. The answer is definitely before, then maybe after, too. It's a good idea to sand each piece before assembly as once the pieces are assembled, there may be areas that are hard to reach. Once the pieces are assembled, you might have glue squeeze out (which we're going to talk about in the next section), or even pieces that aren't quite flush, so sanding after assembly can neaten everything up.

To sum up

- Start at a low (course) grit and work up to a high (smooth) grit.
- Start at 80 grit for removing existing finish or sanding rough material.
- Start at 120 grit for sanding smooth material.
- Sand up to 180 grit.

Joining Wood

Joints can be secured with wood glue, hardware, or both. There are numerous ways to attach wood; some are pretty simple and some are more complex. We'll be using butt joints and mitre joints for the projects in this book. Fancy joinery isn't a requirement for woodworking, but it's a fun avenue to explore if it interests you. Let's talk about the most common joints.

Types of joints

Butt joint – this joint consists of the end grain of one piece of wood being butted up against the face of another piece of wood. These are my favourite joints because they're really easy, and because I like saying butt.

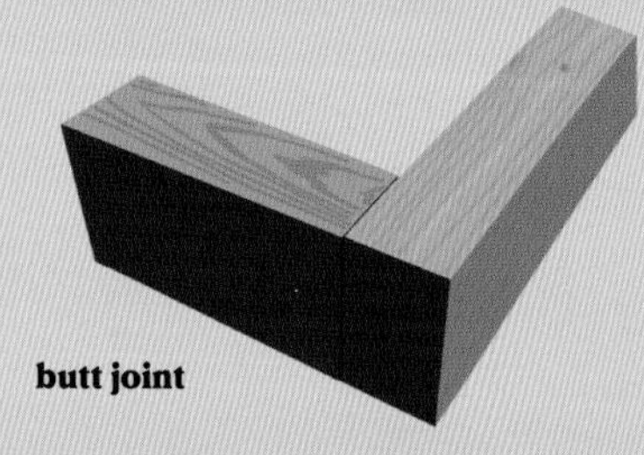
butt joint

Mitred joint – this is when two mitred ends are joined together. You'll see this joint used for picture frames. This is an end grain to end grain joint.

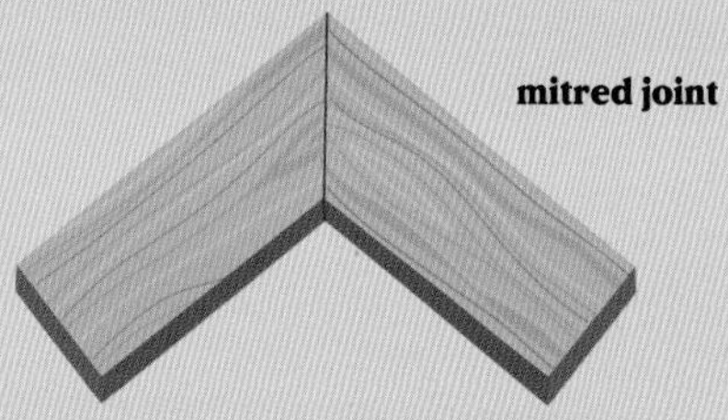
mitred joint

Half lap joint – this joint requires half the thickness of each piece of wood to be removed. The two pieces can then nestle together, providing a strong face-to-face joint.

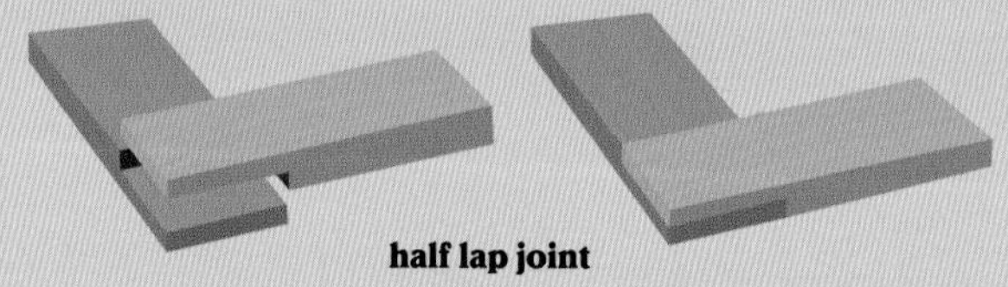
half lap joint

Dovetail joints – considered one of the strongest and most aesthetically pleasing joints in woodworking, dovetail joints consist of tails and pins, cut out in the wood in a trapezoidal shape, that slot together. This joint does not require any additional hardware to reinforce it, because once glued, it's one of the strongest joints around. It does, however, require a decent level of precision.

dovetail joints

About wood glue

Wood glue is strong. Like, really strong. From very early on in my woodworking journey I would hear, "wood glue is stronger than the wood itself". What that means is, if you had a well-glued joint and you tried to break it, the wood would snap before the glue joint did. I specify a "well-glued joint", because glued joints can be weak for a number of reasons, say if a joint has a very small surface area. Joints involving end grain can be a little weak, too, because end grain is like a bunch of straws that suck up the glue into the wood, meaning less glue is left on the actual joint. These joints can be reinforced with additional hardware, if needed – there are several ways to do this. The methods I use most often are screws, pocket holes and dowels, and we'll focus on each of these in detail in later chapters. Face-to-face joints are the strongest and usually don't need any extra reinforcement.

How to use wood glue

Squeeze a line of glue across the area of wood you want to join, and spread it out evenly. You can get little plastic glue spreaders, or you can use your fingers. Now place the joint together. The joint needs to be held firmly in place for 30–60 minutes while the glue sets, and the usual way to do this is with clamps. When that time is up, leave the joint for approx 24 hours for the glue to cure fully.

Spread glue along one of the sides to be joined, then clamp together.

Managing squeeze out

When you clamp wood together, you'll see some glue squeezes out of the joint. This is called "squeeze out" (clever name!). Squeeze out is always going to happen, but we need to manage it so we don't leave glue on the wood surface. There are a few ways to do this: you can wipe it off immediately with a damp cloth, or do what I do and wait for the squeeze out to dry a little, until it's tacky and then scrape it off with an old chisel. Of course, I regularly forget and allow it to dry fully, in which case it requires some serious sanding.

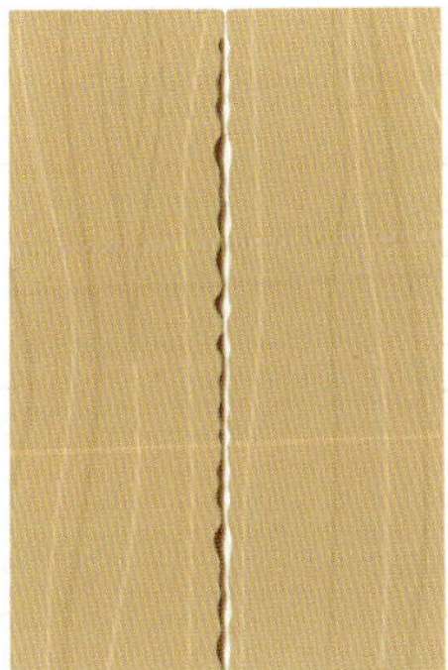

Wood glue is messy

If you're not careful, wood glue can get all over the place, and the problem with this is that wood stain doesn't like wood glue. Any glue on the wood surface will prevent stain from penetrating the wood, which will leave you with a splotchy finish. So, be sure to clean up glue from any of the visible surfaces of your project, and follow up with a final sand before staining, so you're certain the surface is clear of glue. Sometimes the glue isn't visible to the eye. A good way to test if it has been successfully removed is to wet the area with water. The water will penetrate the wood, darkening its colour, but it won't be able to penetrate anywhere there is glue, so it'll quickly reveal any residue left on the surface that still needs to be removed.

Clamps

Clamps come in all sorts of shapes and sizes to suit your purpose. You'll need to clamp wood together for any glued joint so the glue can properly bond. You'll also find clamps helpful to hold joints together while driving in screws. I'd like to add that while clamps are a must-have in most workshops, there are alternative ways to clamp wood. All we're trying to do is hold the wood joints firmly in place until they're bonded.

Types of clamp

C clamp – named due to the shape, this clamp has a fixed frame, with a screwing mechanism to tighten it.

F clamp – also named due to the shape (very creative, I know), this clamp has a sliding jaw that moves up and down the bar and is tightened into place with a screw mechanism.

Quick-action clamp – imagine an F clamp, but instead of having to slide the jaw and then screw or unscrew to tighten it, there's a trigger you pump to tighten and a quick-release lever you pull to loosen. I use these clamps for most of my projects.

Spring clamp – this clamp has a simple spring mechanism. You use pressure to open the clamp and then release it to close the clamp (much like a bulldog clip or claw clip).

Band clamp (strap clamp) – this clamp is different from all the above as it consists of a loop of fabric or metal that can be tightened around the workpiece. These are good for strapping all four pieces of a frame together, for example, or for clamping circular shapes.

Other ways to clamp

I said earlier that there are other ways to clamp wood without actual clamps. I use my clamps in almost every project, but even with a sufficient stock, in some situations I find that some alternatives work just as well or even better.

Tape – if you need to clamp small pieces together, you can simply use painter's tape. Wrap it tightly around the pieces to clamp them, then peel the tape away once the glue is dry.

painter's tape

weight

Weight – If a downwards force is needed to clamp pieces together, then using something heavy is a simple solution. You can use weights, piles of books, a suitcase... the possibilities are endless.

String – this is a great solution for clamping circular shapes. Just tie some string tightly around the workpiece to hold everything in place.

string

To sum up

- Glued joints should be clamped together for at least 30–60 minutes.
- Squeeze out should be removed with a damp cloth immediately or scraped off when tacky.
- Any glue left on the surface of the wood will prevent stain from penetrating.

Stains and Finishes

'Finish' is a general term for any coating applied to the wood, and no project is complete without some sort of finish. Actually, I take that back. You can leave any project completely raw if that's what you want, but without at least a clear coat, the wood won't be protected from moisture, dirt, or scratches.

How you choose to finish your wood is entirely up to you, depending on the look you're after. If you've never worked with stains and finishes before, try out a few different types to get a feel for what you like. I tried a variety of stains before I settled on the brand I use now, and I love it so much I've never been tempted to use anything else.

Most stains are not protective, so once the stain is dry, the wood will need to be finished with a clear top coat to add some protection. You don't have to stain your wood, of course. If you want to keep its natural colour, go straight to the clear protective top coat.

Wood stain and dye

Wood stain is a semi-transparent, coloured liquid that's applied to wood to change its colour. Natural wood tones are the most popular, but you can find stains in almost any colour – you can even make your own!

But wait, what then is wood dye, and how is it different? The terms may be used interchangeably, but there is a difference. Wood stain is similar to a very thin paint; while there is some absorption into the wood fibres, it also leaves a thin film on the surface. This means that the more coats you apply, the more opaque it becomes, and it can eventually obscure the wood grain. Luckily you don't usually need many coats, so it's rare you'll run into this problem. Wood dye, on the other hand, is similar to fabric dye. It absorbs fully into the fibres, changing the colour of the wood without leaving a film on the surface. You can apply multiple coats of wood dye to deepen the colour without obscuring the grain. Which product you use depends on which one you prefer to work with – stain is most popular, but I prefer dye. Moving forward, I'll refer to all colour-changing products as stains, but now you know there is a difference.

Stains and dyes come in a variety of colours.

Types of wood stain

Oil based – Probably the most popular choice, oil stain penetrates the wood deeply and has a slower drying time than other stains, which helps to get a more even finish. The stain can be applied with brushes or rags – these will need to be cleaned with mineral spirits.

Water based – this works the same as oil stain but uses water as the carrier for the colour pigment. It's a good, environmentally-friendly option, and it makes for easy clean up because brushes can be washed with soap and water.

Gel stain – this stain is more like a jelly than a liquid, which can be easier to apply as it won't drip or run. Gel stain doesn't penetrate the wood as deeply and tends to sit on top of the surface.

Make your own – you can water down any acrylic paint to use as a stain. It needs to be a fairly watery consistency, but you'll get different results in vibrancy depending on the water-to-paint ratio.

Applying stain

It's important to note that wood needs to be completely raw for a stain to penetrate. If the wood has paint or finish already on it, it will need to be sanded back to raw before staining. Make sure any areas you want to stain are free of wood glue, too.

I like to use a foam brush to apply stain, but you can also use a painter's brush or a rag. The most important thing is to work swiftly – you don't need to rush, but you need to keep a wet edge so that you're not overlapping dry stain with your next stroke. Apply the stain in a long stroke along the grain from one end of the wood to the other, then move across and apply your next long stroke. Repeat until the whole piece is covered.

Some stains require the excess to be wiped away after application – be sure to read the instructions given for your products. Once the stain is dry, you can apply a second coat to achieve a darker colour.

Types of top coat

A top coat helps to seal the colour and keep it looking fresh, but it also adds a layer of protection to the wood to stop it fading, and protects against scratches and moisture.

These clear finishes come in a variety of options, split into two categories: surface finishes, which sit on top of the wood, and penetrating finishes, which, as the name suggests, penetrate the wood.

Surface

Varnish – this is the finish I use, available as water or oil based. If you have applied stain, the general rule is to use the same base (water or oil) for both. Varnish requires several coats to properly protect the wood and is available in matte, satin and gloss finishes. It has a longer drying time than other top coats, but provides the best UV protection.

Polyurethane – this is probably one of the most popular finishes because of its durability. It's available as both water based and oil based and usually requires fewer coats than varnish as it is thicker. It comes in matte, satin and gloss options.

Lacquer – lacquer is also available as water based or oil based and comes in matte, satin and gloss finishes. It has a much quicker drying time than both varnish and polyurethane.

Wood/furniture wax – This provides a nice, soft sheen to wood and is probably the best finish for keeping the natural colour of unstained wood. Wax provides little protection, and it wears off over time so needs to be reapplied. Those who like the soft look of a wax finish but want to use it on a high-traffic item can finish the wood with a more protective top coat first, then apply wax on top.

You'll notice that lacquer, polyurethane and varnish sound mostly the same. That's because they all do the same job but, with different chemical make-up, they have different properties. For example, varnish is best for UV protection, polyurethane is great for durability in fewer coats than the others, and lacquer has a much quicker drying time than all of them. It all depends on what works for you and what your priorities are.

Penetrating

Penetrating finishes, usually oils, are most commonly used on unstained wood. They deepen the colour of natural wood and highlight the grain pattern. You can apply oil with a rag or brush.

Danish oil – this oil requires several coats to build up a protective layer, and you need to leave several hours between coats. Once the final coat is dry, buff it with a clean cloth for extra sheen. Danish oil has a satin finish and is best for interior use.

Teak oil – similar to Danish oil, teak oil will need several coats, with a decent waiting time between each. Unlike Danish oil though, teak oil has a more matte finish and is suitable for exterior use.

Mineral oil – while mineral oil doesn't have strong protective qualities like Danish or teak, it is food safe so will be your go-to option for chopping boards and wooden cooking utensils.

penetrating oil

TIP

Many top coats come in spray cans, too, which can be handy for small projects with lots of fiddly angles and corners.

Applying clear coats

A clear coat is applied in much the same way as stain, working swiftly with a brush or rag in long strokes along the grain, keeping a wet edge. Don't overwork the first coat by going back and forth over the same area, as this can lift the stain and leave a splotchy finish. Once the first coat is dry, the colour will be sealed in place and you can take a little more time over additional coats.

For an extra smooth result when using surface finishes, before the final coat, run some extra fine sandpaper, like 320 grit, over the surface very gently. A few light swipes will do – we don't want to scratch the finish, we simply want to smooth out any micro bumps that may have developed in the previous coats. Wipe the surface down with a dry cloth to remove any dust, then apply your final coat for a beautifully smooth finish.

Important safety note

There is a fire risk when it comes to oil-based stains and finishes. Oil-based products produce heat as they dry and cure, and while that's not much of a concern for the wood itself, it is a concern for your applicators. Rags or applicators that are left bunched up in a pile can become too hot and spontaneously combust. Any applicators used to apply oil products should be cleaned straight away or spread out to dry in a well-ventilated area before being disposed of. There is no fire risk with water-based products.

Absorption

Water popping, or raising the grain – As we've seen, applying several clear coats and sanding before the final coat gives a glass-smooth finish. But here's another technique that is fun to experiment with. When water is introduced to raw wood, it is absorbed by the cells and expands them. When the wood dries, those cells remain open, leaving a rougher surface. So what does all of that mean? Let's say your workpiece has been sanded to 180 grit so its nice and smooth, but then you add a water-based finish. This will cause the grain to rise, leaving the wood feeling rougher than before. To avoid this, after its final sand and before staining, wet the wood with a damp cloth or spray bottle to raise the grain. Once dry, sand again with 180 grit. Now when you apply the finish, the grain won't rise as much as before so you'll retain a smooth finish.

Wood conditioner – Soft wood in particular can absorb stain at different rates across the same piece of wood, causing some areas to be darker than others. If you're not a fan of this look, you can apply wood conditioner – also known as pre-stain – before staining your workpiece. The wood conditioner is absorbed into the wood and stops the stain from penetrating too deeply, giving a more even and less blotchy finish. Honestly, I quite like the unevenness of stain most of the time. I think it adds character and I aim to embrace the imperfections – in wood and in life! But some pieces look better with a more even finish. Wood conditioner isn't a necessity –experiment and play, and see what you prefer.

Manufactured wood

Most manufactured woods won't stain quite as well as solid wood, so you may be left with an uneven looking finish. Plywood has the best results, but I avoid staining MDF or chipboard. I tend to use manufactured wood in places that won't be visible in the final project or if I'm planning to paint it.

When to apply the stain?

Should you apply your wood stain after or before assembling the workpiece? This is a good question with no definite answer. Let's look at the pros and cons of both.

Staining after assembly means you can sand the workpiece where required. If you need to remove any excess glue from joints, you can do so without ruining the finish, and if you have any misaligned joints, you can sand them flush. BUT if you haven't removed excess glue properly and begin staining, you may have to sand it all back and start again. Also, there might be tight corners and awkward angles that make staining after assembly a bit fiddly, resulting in an uneven application.

Staining before assembly removes any risk of glue being on the wood surface, and if you experience any issues with application it will be contained to a single piece of wood. You also don't have to contend with any awkward corners or angles. BUT wood glue cannot properly penetrate and bond wood that has a stain or finish applied – you'd have to tape off any areas that will require glue to ensure stain doesn't penetrate them. This is doable but takes a bit of practice. Also, it won't be possible to fix any misaligned joints with a quick sand after assembly without removing the stain.

Whenever possible, I stain before assembly, but every project is different and I base my decision on the needs of each one. For the projects in this book, we'll assemble first and stain after – I think that's the most sensible way to approach woodworking from a beginner's standpoint. Feel free to experiment with staining beforehand, but remember to tape off the areas that will need glue.

Having said all of that, I have a confession... If you watch any of my videos online, you'll see some examples where I stain the whole piece before assembly, and I don't tape off areas that are to be glued later. Remember how I said stain leaves a film on the surface, but dye doesn't? So in my defence, I use dye, so there's no barrier to prevent glue from bonding. The bond won't be as strong as it is on raw wood, so I only do this for smaller items where the joints won't need to bear weight. I'm not here to teach you my bad habits, though, so if we could just keep this confession between ourselves, that'd be great.

TIP

As we know, sanding to too high a grit can cause problems when it comes to applying stain. Once you go past 220 grit, you start closing the pores in the wood, so the stain can't penetrate it very well. There's always an exception to the rule though, and here it's the end grain of wood. The end grain is like a bunch of straws that drink up moisture. This soaks more stain in, making the colour of the end grain appear darker than on the face of the board. To counteract this, sand the end grain with a higher grit than the face. So if you sand the face up to 180 grit, sand the end grain up to 220 grit to close the pores a little more and help the colour look more even all around.

To sum up

- Wood needs to be completely raw before applying stain.
- Sanding wood higher than 180 grit may prevent stain from penetrating.
- Ensure that you keep a wet edge when applying stains and finishes.
- Wood glue cannot bond on stained wood.
- Due to fire risk, any applicators used to apply an oil-based finish should be cleaned immediately or spread out in a well-ventilated area to dry.

That may have felt like a lot of information, but don't stress! It all breaks down to cut, sand, join. For cutting, get yourself a saw that suits your needs and budget. For sanding, sandpaper sheets or a random orbit sander is all you need. For joining, focus on basic joints using wood glue or screws (we'll look at this in the next chapter). Yes, you'll make mistakes along the way. That's okay – I still make a lot of mistakes. A lot. But most can be worked with, or – if all else fails – call it a prototype and move on.

So, let's make something!

PROJECT

The Slat Stool

This is an easy project that only requires wood glue for assembly. It features face-to-face joints, the strongest joints of all, so the design creates a sturdy and reliable stool. There is quite a lot of wood to cut for a first project, but there are only three different lengths so it could be a good chance to practice using a stop block (see Cutting Wood: Making Multiple Cuts).

Tools:

- Saw
- Sander

Supplies:

- Wood glue
- Painter's tape
- Weights (or clamps)
- Stain (optional)
- Clear coat (optional)

Cutting list:

- x14: 40 x 4.4 x 1.8cm (15¾ x 1¾ x ¾in)
- x16: 35.6 x 4.4 x 1.8cm (14 x 1¾ x ¾in)
- x8: 35 x 4.4 x 1.8cm (13¾ x 1¾ x ¾in)

Cut the wood to the cutting list and sand each piece up to 180 grit.

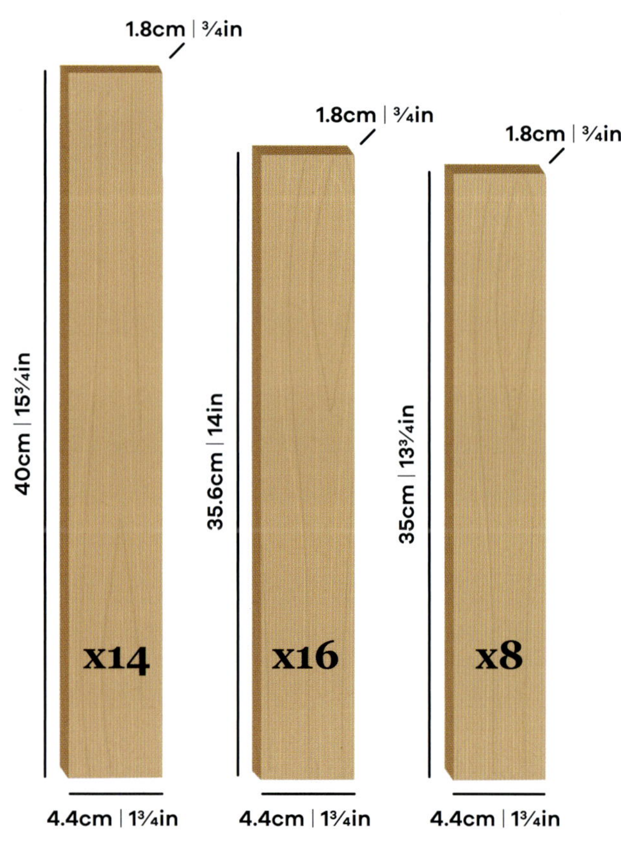

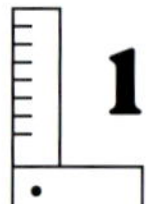

1

Find a wall or other flat vertical surface to push up against to help keep the pieces aligned. Protect your surface from glue by taping a piece of cardboard or a plastic sheet to it.

Lay one 35cm (13¾in) seat piece flat on its face. Grab two of the 35.6cm (14in) shorter leg pieces and butt them up to either end of the seat piece. Add a little tape to hold them in place, then flip the whole thing over so the taped side is now face down. Push the seat piece against the wall.

TIP

The 35cm (13¾in) pieces will make the seat. The 35.6cm (14in) pieces and 40cm (15 ¾in) pieces will make the legs. You can use any dimension of wood for this project – the only change you'll need to make to the cutting list is the length of the shorter legs, which should be the length of the longer legs minus the width of the wood.

2

Now add wood glue over the upward-facing surface of the leg pieces, all the way up to and including the edges of the seat piece as shown (we don't need to apply glue all along the seat piece).

3

Place a 40cm (15¾in) longer leg piece onto each glued area, pushing up against the wall to make sure the pieces align at the top and using your fingers to ensure the pieces are aligned at the sides. Use a damp cloth to remove any squeezed-out glue – it's important to do this as you go with this project.

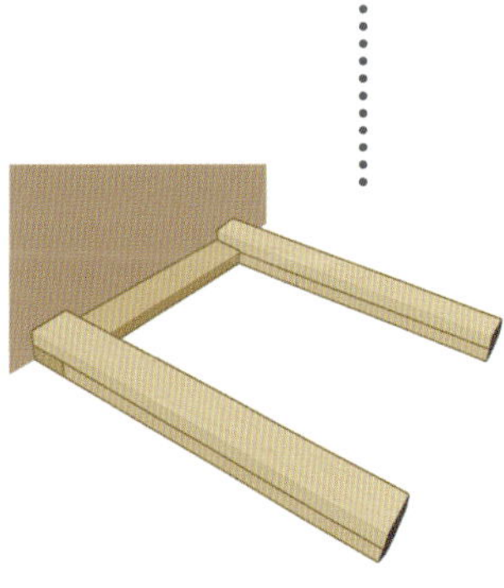

4

Add glue to the upward-facing surface of the longer legs. Place a seat piece and then two shorter leg pieces in place, just like step 1, pushing them against the wall to ensure they align at the top and using your fingers to align the sides.

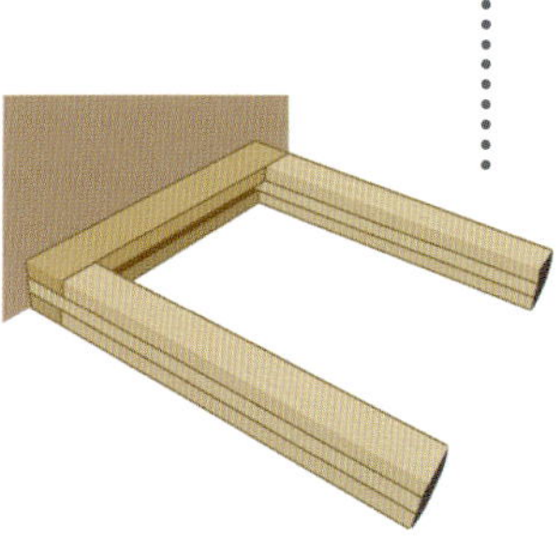

5

Repeat Steps 2 to 4 until all pieces are in place, sandwiched together with glue. Please don't stress if you notice some of the pieces aren't quite the same length – we'll deal with that a bit later on.

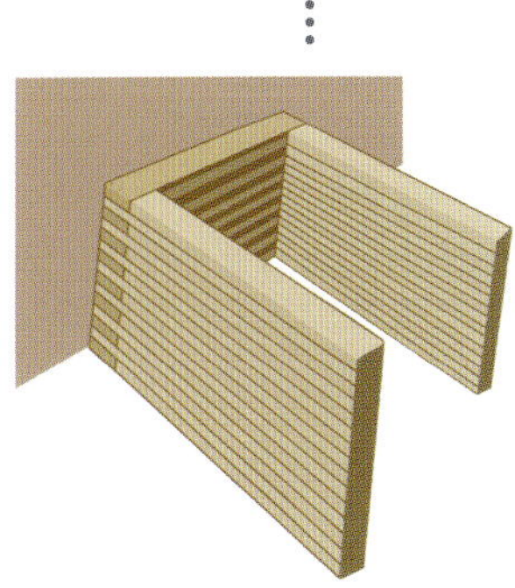

TIP

If you find the wood shifts on the wet glue as you add more layers, don't fret. Glue up one layer, then go do something else for five minutes to allow the glue to get tacky. Then come back and build up the next layer. Repeat. Alternatively, a little trick is to hold two sheets of low grit sandpaper (40 or 60 grit) above the glue and rub them together – small specks of the abrasive will come loose and sprinkle onto the glue – you only want a few specks. Now when you place your next piece of wood on top, the specks will create friction and prevent any slipping.

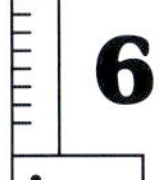

6

Place something heavy on each leg to clamp the pieces down while the glue dries. You can use anything heavy like stacks of books or the weight of your parents' expectations.

Once the glue is dry, give the whole piece a quick sand. If any of the pieces aren't quite the same length, or the sides aren't quite aligned, sand until the excess is removed.

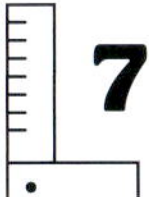

7

The final thing to do is add your desired finish – stain it, paint it or leave it raw. I stained my stool with a light pine colour and sealed it with wax. And that's it, you did it! You woodworked!

SWITCH IT UP

The great thing about this build is you can easily adjust the size to make all sorts of things. Make it wider for a long bench or smaller for a stepping stool.

PROJECT

The Sofa Arm

This flexible sofa arm will fit any size sofa. It will give you a flat surface for your drink and protect your sofa fabric from drips. You could also make a few to use as placemats, or make smaller ones for coasters.

Tools:

- Saw
- Sander

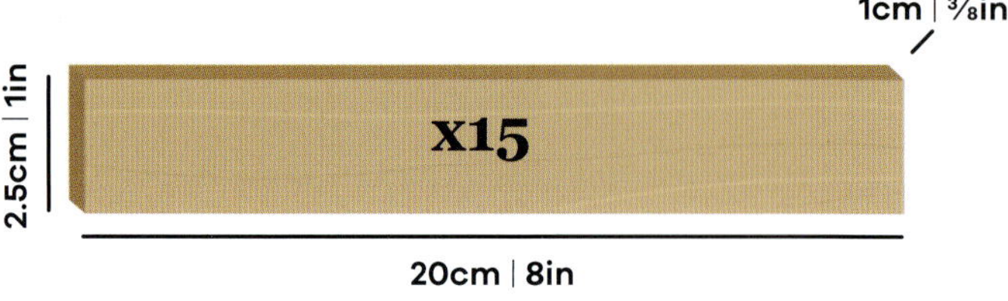

Supplies:

- Hessian (burlap) – slightly larger than 38 x 20cm (15 x 8in)
- Wood glue
- Scissors or craft knife
- Clamps (or tape)
- Stain (optional)
- Clear coat (optional)

Cutting list:

- x15: 20 x 2.5 x 1cm (8 x 1 x ⅜in)

Cut the wood to the cutting list and sand each piece up to 180 grit.

You can use any dimension of wood for this project – I think it looks best under 1cm (⅜in) thick.

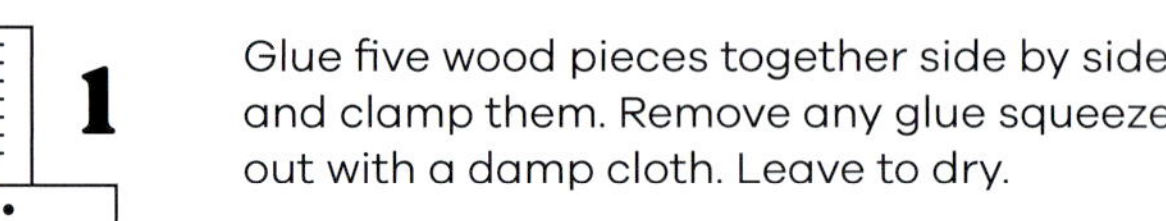

1 Glue five wood pieces together side by side and clamp them. Remove any glue squeeze out with a damp cloth. Leave to dry.

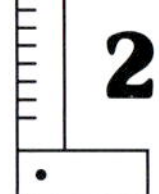

2 For this project, we'll stain and clear coat all the pieces before assembly to avoid the pieces sticking together, but leave one face of the wood completely raw because this is the side we'll glue to the hessian (burlap). So stain one face side as well as the sides and ends of all the pieces, including the five-piece panel from step 1, then add your chosen clear coat.

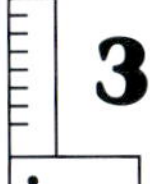

3

Once dry, lay the wood pieces down side by side, with the glued panel in the centre and all raw unstained sides facing up. Clamp some scrap wood to the worktop to keep the pieces snugly in place.

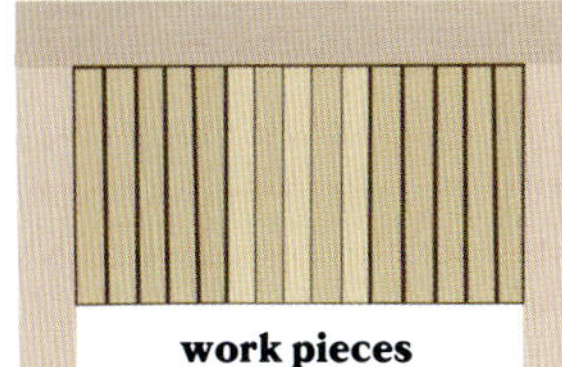

4

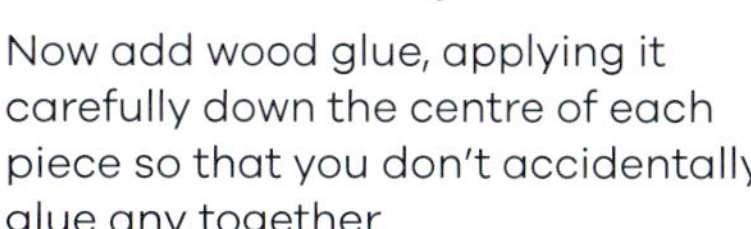

Now add wood glue, applying it carefully down the centre of each piece so that you don't accidentally glue any together.

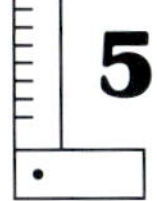

5

Next, lay the hessian (burlap), over the glued surfaces. Add some weight on top (a stack of books or paint cans will do) – I recommend placing a plastic bag between the fabric and the weights, in case any glue seeps through. Leave to dry.

6

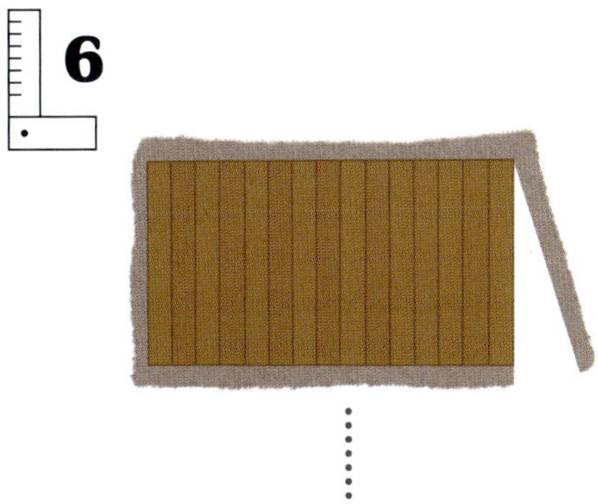

Once dry, trim the excess fabric away using scissors or a craft knife. If the fabric starts to fray, seal the edges with glue. You might find the odd bit of glue has stuck some of the wood pieces together – a little pressure should separate them easily. Now you have a flexible sofa arm!

About the Drill

A drill is used to make holes in wood as well as to drive in screws. Seems simple, right? However, due to the different types of drills, the different drill bits and the various settings, drills can end up feeling overwhelming. But trust me, it's easy.

Types of drills

There are a few different types of drills, so lets cover the basics:

- **Combi drill** – can be used to drill holes in both soft and hard materials, as well as driving in screws.
- **Drill driver** – used for drilling holes in soft materials like wood and plastic, as well as driving in screws.
- **Hammer drill** – used for drilling holes in hard materials like bricks and masonry.
- **Impact driver** – used for driving in screws. These are not used for drilling holes.

Personally, I use a combi drill because it can do most things. Some people prefer to have separate drills for each requirement, but for the sake of clarity and budget, let's focus on combi drills.

Bits

In order to drill a hole, you'll need a drill bit. This is the part that's rotated by the drill and cuts into the wood. The drill bit is tightened into the chuck of the drill and the trigger switch spins the drill bit. There are different drill bits for different materials, so ensure you get ones suitable for wood. To drive a screw into wood you'll need a screwdriver bit, which we'll cover later.

Combi drill settings

Let's talk about the various settings on a drill and what they're for.

Chuck – the chuck consists of three metal jaws that are tightened onto a drill bit.

Clutch setting – the clutch setting can be twisted around to select a variety of things. First, you'll see a drill bit icon, this setting is for when you're drilling holes into wood. The hammer icon can be used when drilling holes into brick and masonry. The rest of the settings are numbers and these relate to the amount of torque, which is what we'll use when driving in screws. Torque is the amount of force the drill will deliver. You use a higher torque for larger screws or driving into hard wood and a lower torque for small screws or driving into soft wood. Due to the variety of screw sizes and wood types, there's no rulebook on what torque to use for each project – it's best to start with a lower torque and adjust it as you go. If the torque is too low, the drill will stop spinning. If the torque is too high the drill bit can slip off the screw head.

Forwards and reverse switch – this changes the rotation of the drill between clockwise and anticlockwise, or, more simply, forwards and backwards. When you're driving a screw into wood you'll want the forwards setting, when you're removing a screw from wood you'll want the backwards setting. The same goes for when you're drilling a hole.

Speed setting – the speed setting allows two speed options. Setting 1 is the lower speed, ideal for driving in screws, and setting 2 is high speed, ideal for drilling holes.

Trigger switch – this is the power button; pressing and holding the trigger starts the drill rotation. The speed of the rotation is dictated by how much you press in on the trigger. Pressing gently results in a slow speed, pressing all the way results in a high speed.

How to drill

Loosen the chuck by twisting it anticlockwise to open the jaws. Place the drill bit into the jaws and twist the chuck clockwise to tighten it. Ensure the drill bit is centred and all three jaws make contact with it. Set your clutch setting to the drill bit icon.

Use clamps or a clamping alternative to hold the wood steady and secure while drilling. If you're drilling a hole all the way through a workpiece, put some scrap wood underneath so you don't drill into your worktop. Place the tip of the drill bit onto the wood, hold down the trigger and use a medium, even pressure to push the bit into the wood. Always keep the drill bit perpendicular with the wood throughout drilling so you get a straight hole. Once done, switch the direction control into reverse and gently press the trigger as you bring the bit out of the wood. Be aware that drill bits get hot so when you're done drilling, allow the drill bit to cool down before removing it from the drill.

But why do we need to drill holes into wood? It's because if we want to use screws, we need to create pilot holes first.

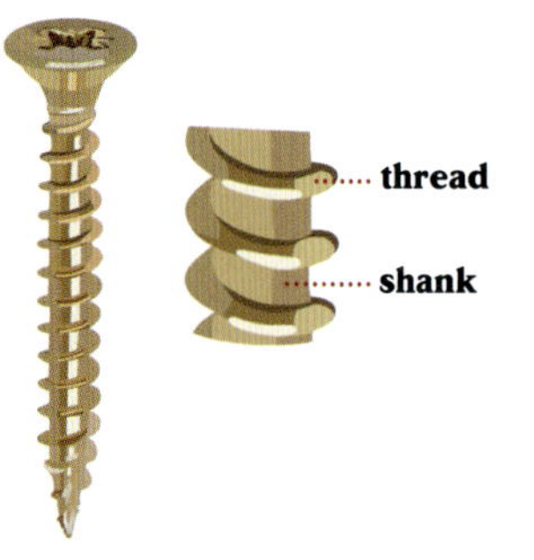

Pilot holes

Driving a screw directly into wood without a pilot hole causes stress on the wood and will lead to splitting. Making a pilot hole first creates space for the screw to enter, thus reducing stress on the wood, and helps guide the screw where it needs to go.

So what size should you drill a pilot hole? Use a drill bit the same diameter as the screw's shank, minus the threads.

A hole that's too big won't allow for the threads to grip into the wood, which is what creates the holding power. A hole too small will cause too much stress on the wood and lead to splitting. The easiest way to pick the right size drill bit is to hold your drill bit in front of the screw; you don't want to see any of the shank, but you do want to see the threads poking out.

too small

too big

just right

Next, you want to make sure you drill a hole the same depth as your screw's length. To check the depth, hold the screw alongside the drill bit – where the screw ends is the depth you want. To mark the depth, you can simply use a piece of painter's tape on the drill bit, and you stop drilling once the tape meets the wood's surface.

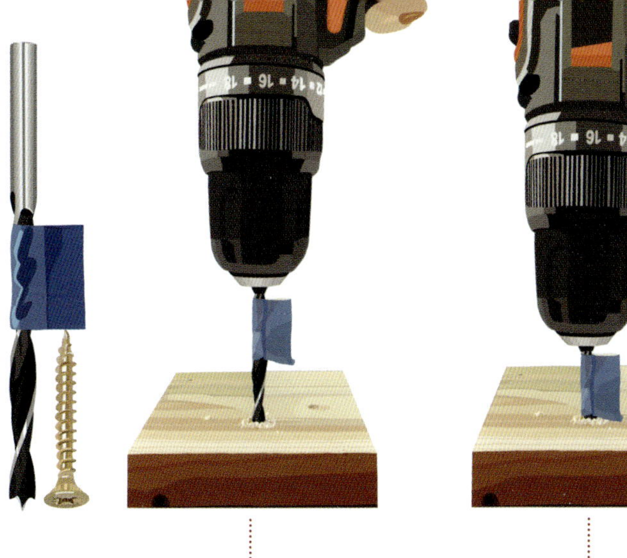

TIP

I like to mark where the hole needs to go by drawing a cross with a pencil onto the wood. Where the two lines intersect is where the hole is drilled. Drawing a cross can help with accuracy when you need to place the hole at a specific measurement. Once you've drilled the pilot hole, clean up the sawdust produced before moving on to driving in the screw.

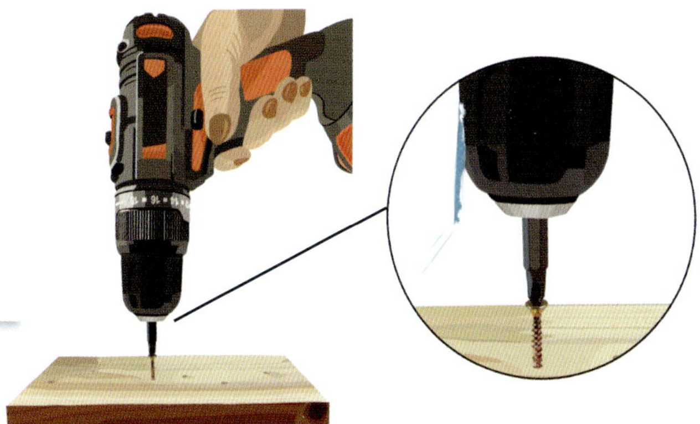

Driving in screws

When it comes to screws, you'll change your drill bit for a screwdriver bit and change your clutch setting to torque. The screwdriver bit is installed the same way as the drill bit; loosen the chuck, insert the screwdriver bit and tighten the chuck. Start at a lower torque and if the drill stops, adjust the torque setting higher.

The screwdriver bit should fit snugly into the screw. You'll be able to feel if it's the wrong size: a bit that's too small will slip around in the screw head, and one that's too big won't sit in the screw fully. Both will cause the screwdriver bit to slip in the screw head when driving. Once you have the right bit inserted into the drill and the wood securely clamped in place, you can place the screw in the pilot hole and drive in the screw.

Types of screws

There are lots of different screws designed for different materials, so for woodworking you'll want to use wood screws (they're not made of wood, just made for wood!). The most common screws are the slotted head screw, which requires a flat-tip screwdriver bit, and the Phillips head screw, which requires a Phillips screwdriver bit.

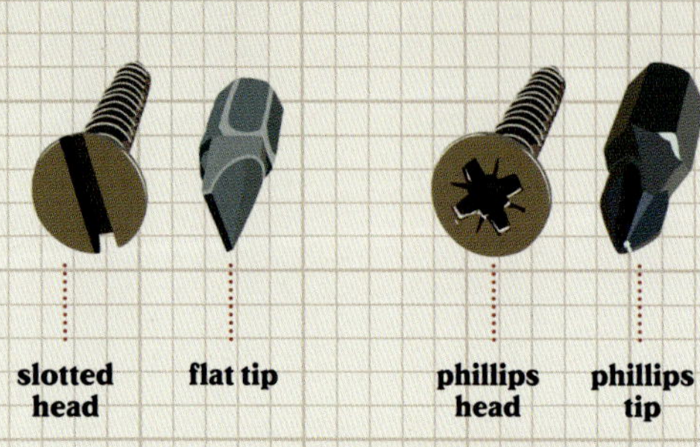

There are also different shapes of screw heads, the two main being countersunk (or flat head) screws and rounded head screws. A countersunk screw sits flush with the wood surface so it's not as visible, but you do need to countersink the pilot hole first (instructions coming up next). A rounded head screw sits on top of the wood surface.

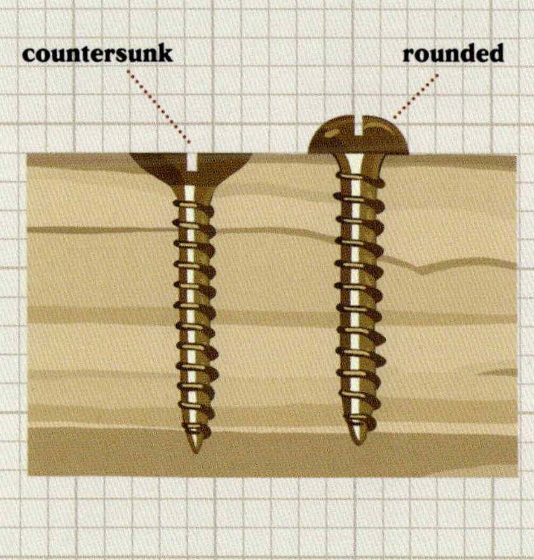

TIP

When it comes to screw size, the general rule is to have one-third of the screw sitting in the top piece of wood and two-thirds in the bottom piece you're joining it to, without the screw poking out the underside of the material. Hold the screw up to your workpiece to check the size. The gauge or diameter is the thickness of the screw, and there's no hard rule for this. The most commonly used gauge is #8 which is around 4mm (1/8in). The thicker the wood, the thicker the screw should be.

Countersink bit

If you're using a countersunk screw, you'll see the head is flat on top and tapered towards the shank (as opposed to rounded heads that have a round top and flat bottom). This is so the screw can sit flush in the wood, but in order for that to happen you need to countersink the pilot hole. This just means drilling out a conical shape along with the pilot hole, so the screw head can sit snug in the hole.

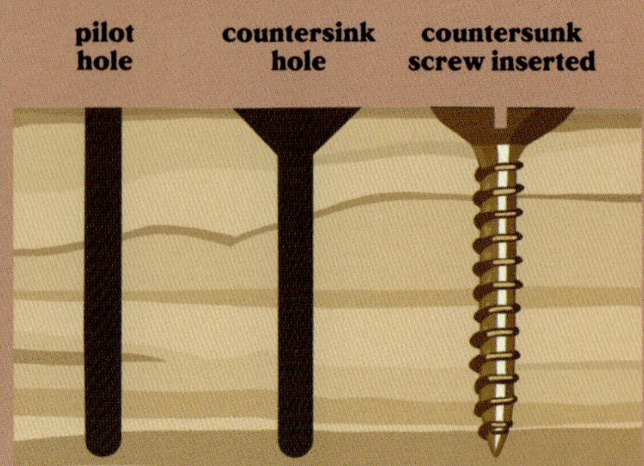

You can get countersink bits that attach to the drill bit so you can drill the pilot hole and create the countersink at the same time. Or you can get a standalone countersink bit, which means you drill the pilot hole as usual with your drill bit, then switch the bit out for the countersink bit and drill the countersink hole. How deep you drill with the countersink bit will dictate how large the countersink hole is. You want the countersink hole to match the size of the screw head you'll be using, so stop and check the hole against the screw head – if it's not quite big enough then drill a little more.

If you use a countersunk screw without drilling a countersink hole, the screw won't sit flush in the wood. As the tapered part of the head makes contact with the wood and compresses into it, it may cause the wood to split.

I highly recommend getting a countersink bit from the start. Once you start building things, you'll quickly realise the majority of your projects are best served using countersunk screws. There's very few instances in which I'm happy for the screw head to stand proud from the surface. We'll be using countersunk screws in the majority of the projects in this book.

Other bits

Standard bits are good for drilling small holes, but there are other options if you need larger holes. I use standard bits up to 10mm (3⁄8in) in diameter; after that, I find it best to use one of the following:

- **Forstner bit** – this creates a neat, flat-bottomed hole and is used when you need a precise hole that doesn't cut all the way through the wood.
- **Hole saw** – this is actually a small saw that cuts out a perfect hole all the way through the wood.
- **Spade bit** – this can carve out larger holes, both partially through the wood and all the way through, but the finish can be a bit rough.

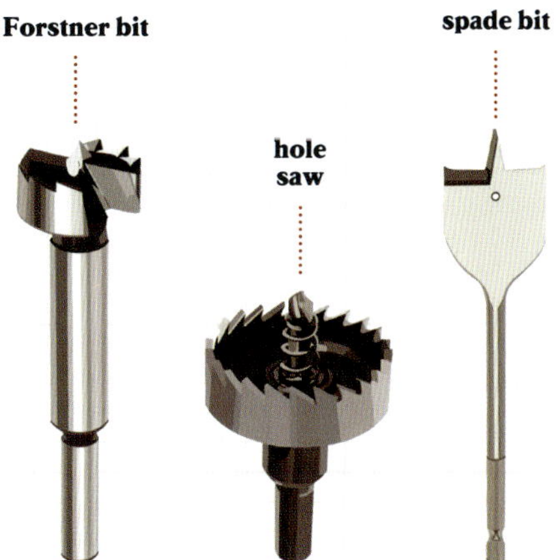

To sum up

- **Drilling a hole**: use a wood drill bit; set the clutch to the drill bit icon.
- **Driving a screw**: drill a pilot hole; use a screwdriver bit to drive the screw; set the clutch to the numbered torque setting, starting with a low torque and adjusting if necessary.
- **Screws**: screw length should be one-third in the top piece and two-thirds in the bottom piece.

Now you understand the settings and uses of a drill, you'll see drilling is a pretty simple process. And while there are a variety of drills out there, most DIY and woodworking enthusiasts will find a combi drill will meet their needs.

The Mini Shelf

This is a really simple build that uses just a handful of screws. It's also incredibly versatile. You can change the dimensions to create a shelf of any height or any width, or even add additional shelves.

Tools:

- Saw
- Sander
- Drill
- Clamps (or tape)

Supplies:

- Screws
- Stain (optional)
- Clear coat (optional)

Cutting list:

- x2: 55 x 12 x 2cm (21⅝ x 4¾ x ¾in)
- x2: 24 x 12 x 2cm (9½ x 4¾ x ¾in)

Cut the wood to the cutting list and sand each piece up to 180 grit.

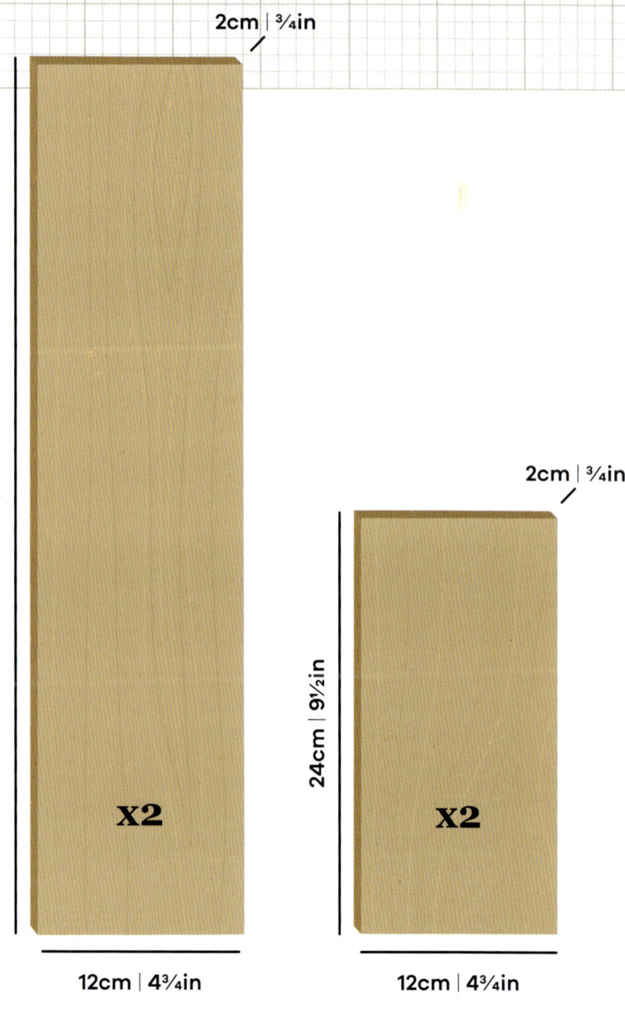

TIP

You can actually use any dimension of wood for this project. As long as all 4 pieces are cut from the same width of wood, you don't need to make any changes to the cutting list (unless you want to of course!).

1

To help align the shelving during assembly, first place the two longer pieces together, face to face, ensuring the ends are aligned. Measuring from one end, make a mark at 33cm (13in) and draw a pencil line across both pieces.

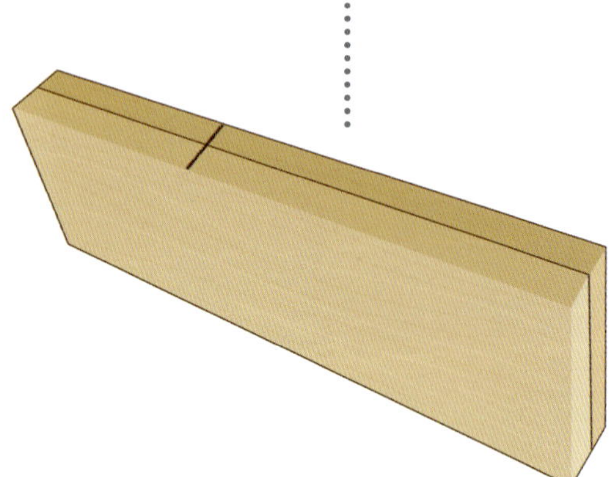

2

Now it's time for assembly. With the two long pieces on their sides, place one shorter piece between them, aligning it along the bottom. Place the second shorter piece so the bottom of it aligns with the two pencil lines. Use a few clamps to hold everything in place.

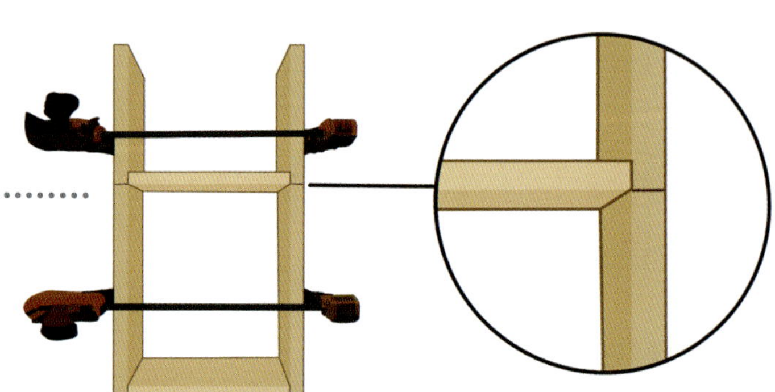

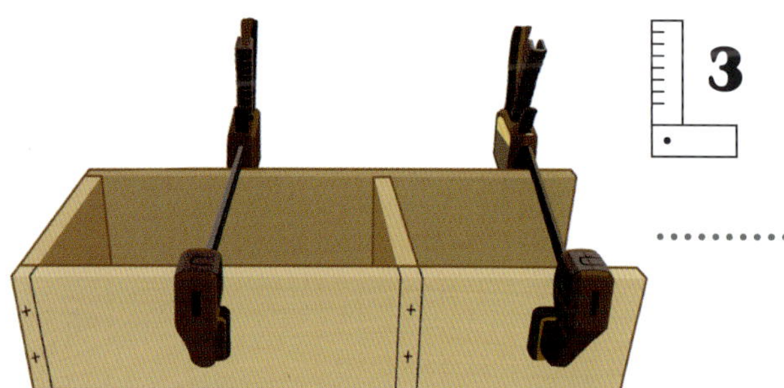

3

Now we're ready to start screwing it together. First, create the pilot holes. We want to make sure the screws go through the side piece and directly into the middle of the shelf pieces. If you feel unsure doing this by eye, you can use a ruler to draw a line down the outside, representing each edge of the shelf pieces. This will ensure your pilot hole will be made in the centre of the shelves. Mark a cross approx 3cm (1⅛in) from each edge.

Drill the pilot holes on the centre of the crosses and countersink the holes. Then drive a screw into each hole. These are butt joints.

And with that, the assembly is done. Remove any leftover pencil marks with an eraser or sandpaper and then complete the piece in your desired finish. I stained mine in a dark oak colour and sealed it with wax.

SWITCH IT UP

You can adjust the final size of this project to suit your needs. Make a wider one to create a bookshelf, or add some extra shelves to make it into a spice rack.

PROJECT

The Candle Holder

The use of a drill isn't limited to just driving screws. By making larger holes in wood, it can be used for all sorts of things, like making this candle holder.

Tools:

- Saw
- Sander
- Drill
- 21mm (⅞in) Forstner drill bit

Supplies:

- x5: 21mm (⅞in) candle cups
- Stain (optional)
- Clear coat (optional)

Cutting list:

- x1: 30 x 7 x 4cm (12 x 2¾ x 1⅝in)

Sand your chosen wood up to 180 grit.

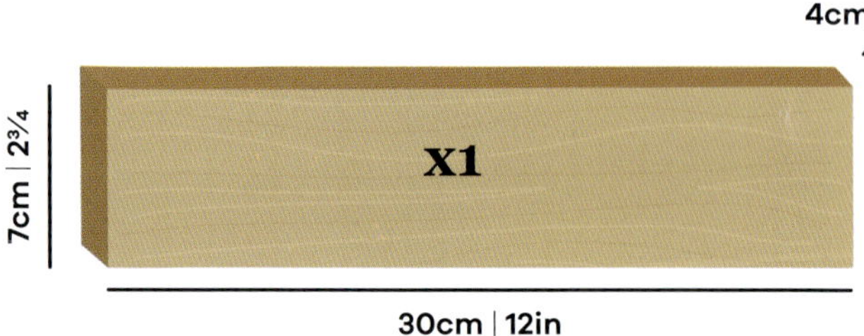

TIP

I used a chunk of sapele wood leftover from a previous project. You can use any wood of any size, as long as it's thicker than the depth of the candle cups, which is about 2cm (¾in).

1 First, mark where to drill the holes. This 30cm (12in) piece of wood will fit five candles. Start by marking a hole in the centre, which is at 15cm (6in). Add two more holes at either side, spacing them 5cm (2in) apart.

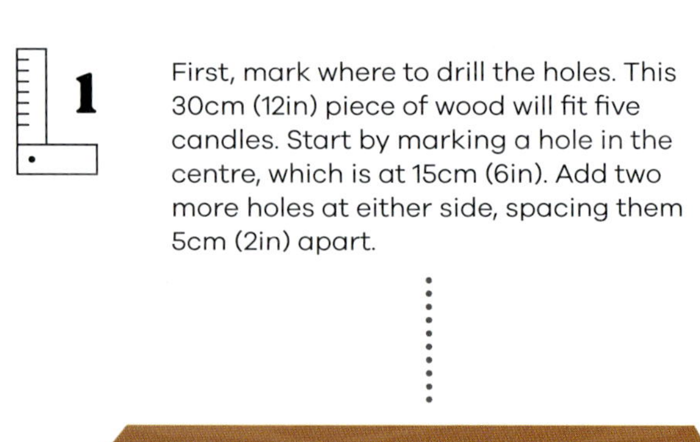

2

Next, use a 21mm (⅞in) Forstner bit to drill a hole on each marked spot, to a depth of approx 2cm (¾in). Stop every now and then to pop a candle cup in to test the depth (the tape trick for marking depth that we looked at in *How to Drill* is a bit harder to use with a Forstner bit); if it's not yet deep enough, drill a little more.

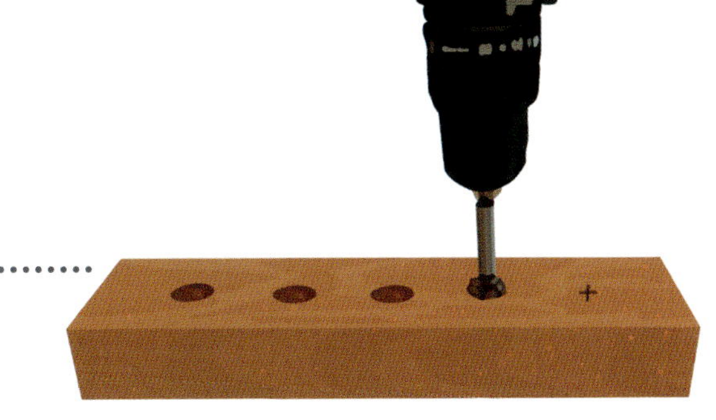

3

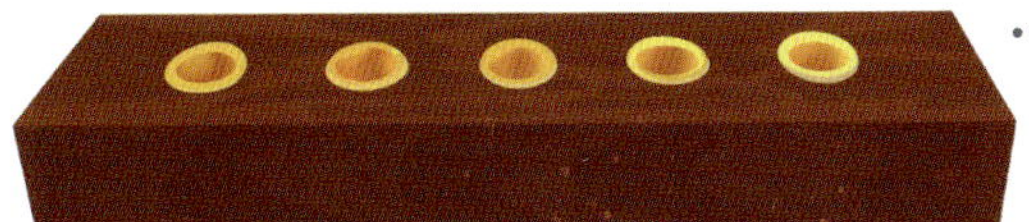

Once all the holes are drilled to depth, you can move on to finishing the wood. As I was lucky enough to have this stunning sapele, I skipped the stain and instead finished it with some oil to bring out the grain pattern. Now pop the candle cups into their new home, and you have a finished candle holder.

The Accessories

Drills, saws and sanders may be the stars of the show in a workshop, but the supporting cast is vital, too. There's an abundance of tools and accessories out there to support woodworking projects. Let's take a look at some that I consider to be essential for any workshop.

Tape measure

This might be kind of an obvious one, but woodworking requires us to measure things. Whether you use a ruler or a tape measure, being able to measure wood length and wood placement is pretty important. A tape measure is a long flexible ruler that extends and retracts, which makes it a great space saver, and it can measure a much longer distance than a standard ruler.

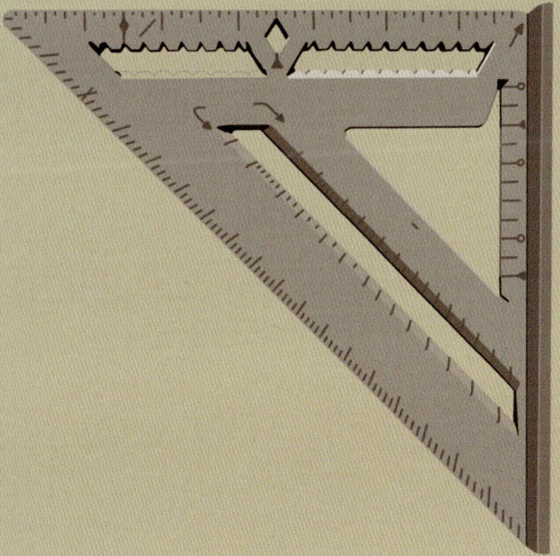

Speed square

I know it's called a speed square, but this is actually a triangle. A speed square consists of two 45 degree corners and one 90 degree corner. It has multiple uses, but one of the most common is using it to draw a straight line. There's a lip on one of the straight sides to set against the edge of the wood, then a line can be drawn down the other straight side of the speed square, ensuring the line is perfectly square with the wood's edge. The same can be done for marking a 45 degree line, using the long diagonal side of the speed square. There's various annotations on the square to assist with scribing different measurements, and it can even be pivoted to mark different angles.

Clamps

We've talked about clamps and how important they are already, but it's worth repeating. Clamps can be used to hold joints together as you wait for glue to dry or while a screw is being inserted, as well as holding workpieces steady against the worktop for cutting and drilling. I have multiple quick-action clamps in various sizes, which I use in almost every project.

Spirit level

A spirit level is used to check if a surface is level. There's a small vial of liquid with a bubble inside it. It's the position of the bubble that's important. Place the spirit level flat on the surface; if the bubble rests perfectly between the two marked lines, the surface is level. If the bubble rests on one side of either of the lines, then it's not level. The side where the bubble rests indicates the direction in which the surface is slanting. A spirit level can be used throughout the making of a project to check the wood is square, and ensures you're not about to serve dinner on a lopsided table.

Lint-free cloths

A lint-free cloth is designed not to shed fibres during use. This makes it the perfect cloth to use when wiping down wood, because it'll remove any sawdust from the surface without leaving pesky fabric fibres that could eventually get caught up in the stain and finish. No need to wet the cloth, use it dry to clear away any dust and debris.

Chisel

If you're planning on hand cutting more complex joints like dovetails, then you'll need a variety of chisels in various sizes. But even if you're not making this kind of joinery, a chisel can still come in handy. Whether it's cutting away small pieces of wood for minor adjustments or scraping off dried glue, it's handy to have at least one in the toolbox.

About Wall Fixtures

A lot of the projects I make are designed to be hung on a wall, including shelves, coat hooks and mirrors. This leads to a common question: how? There are lots of ways this can be done, so here are a few options.

Sawtooth hanger

These are a good option for lightweight items, and you'll likely have seen them on picture frames. Sawtooths are usually attached with screws, with the teeth at the bottom. The teeth then hang onto a nail, screw, or hook in the wall. Due to the profile of sawtooths, the hung item will not sit flush against the wall.

Installation

To install a sawtooth hanger, place it on the back of the workpiece and mark the two fixing holes with a pencil. Remove the hardware and drill pilot holes on the marks. Return the sawtooth into position, lining up the holes, and drive in screws to attach it. For small, lightweight items use a single hanger. For larger pieces, use at least two hangers to distribute the weight.

Mark the fixing holes.

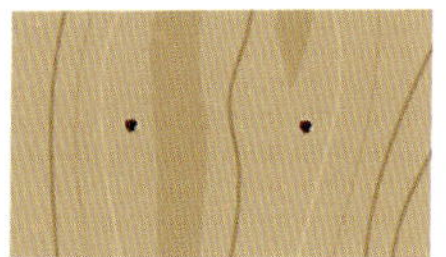

Drill pilot holes.

Attach with screws.

Keyhole hanger

This metal plate has a keyhole shaped cutout, with a narrow slot at the top and a circle at the bottom. A keyhole hanger is installed flush in the wood and then hung onto a screw in the wall. The circle cutout is designed to be larger than the screw head, and the slot narrower. When hanging the item, place the circle cutout over the screw in the wall, then slide the item down so the screw head sits firmly in the narrow slot. The item will hang flush to the wall. Use a single keyhole hanger for small items, and at least two for larger items.

Insert a screw head into the circle cutout.

Slide the hanger down.

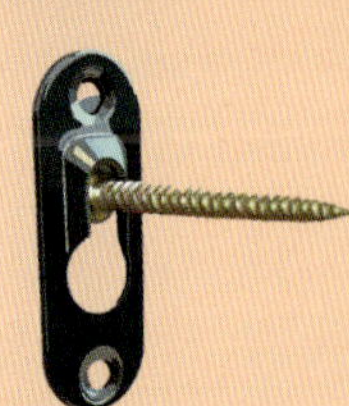

Keyhole hangers are most commonly oblong, however there are circular ones, too. Some have a flat profile, while others have a protruding face. They all do the same thing and are installed in the same way.

Installation

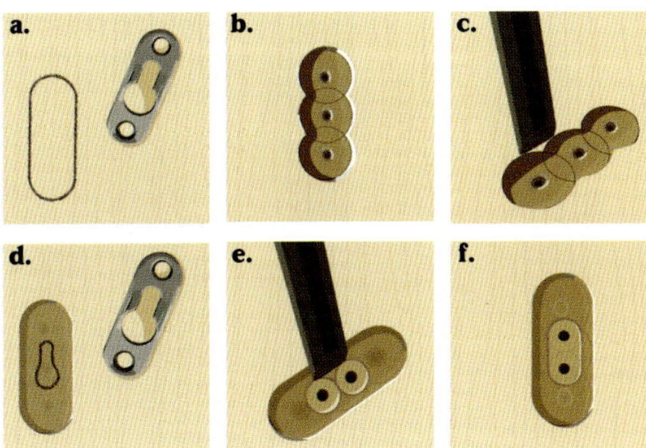

To install a keyhole hanger, first make a hole for the hanger to fit into. Place the hanger on the back of the workpiece and draw around it (a). Drill a few holes along the outlined shape, deep enough for the hanger to sit flush in. Use a drill bit with the same diameter as the width of the shape (b).

The small excesses of wood left between each hole are called ears – remove these with a chisel (c). For a circular keyhole hanger, use a Forstner bit to drill a single hole.

Next we need to make a hole for the inner keyhole shape. Place the hanger in the hole and draw around the inner shape (d). Using a smaller bit, drill along the shape as before and remove the ears (e). The hole needs to be deep enough for a screw head to sit in. Once done (f), you're ready to install the keyhole hanger as follows:

Mark the fixing holes, drill the pilot holes, then attach with screws.

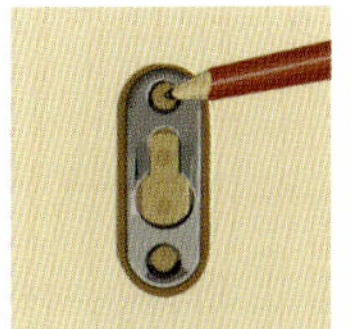

Mark the fixing holes.

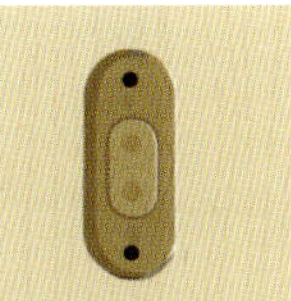

Drill pilot holes.

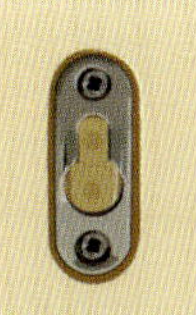

Attach with screws.

Screws

Some items can be screwed directly to the wall, instead of hanging them. Drill a pilot hole all the way through the item, and countersink it. Prep the wall with a hole and wall plug (rawlplug/anchor). Hold up the workpiece and drive a screw through the pilot hole and into the wall hole.

What about the wall?

How to drill into a wall depends on the type of wall. Check what type of drill bit and screws are needed for your particular walls – don't use woodworking drill bits! Most walls will need a wall plug inserted into the hole to increase holding power. When the screw is driven in, the wall plug expands to grip the sides of the hole. Always check for wires or pipes behind the wall before drilling – you can use a handheld detector for this, which is held against the wall and beeps if it senses anything.

To sum up

- **Sawtooths:** mark the fixing holes, drill the pilot holes, attach with screws. The teeth should be at the bottom.
- **Keyholes:** drill the outer and inner shapes into the wood to install flush, remove any ears with a chisel. The keyhole slot should be at the top.
- **Screws:** drill a pilot hole and countersink the workpiece.
- **Wall:** check for wires and pipes before drilling into a wall. Use a wall plug in the hole.

Being able to confidently hang things on the wall will up your home décor game. Of course, for us renters, there's always damage-free adhesive strips if you can't put holes in the wall. Now let's make some things to hang on the wall!

PROJECT

The Block Shelf

There's a lot of different ways to make and install shelving, and for this block shelf we're going to use the simplest option, which is screwing directly into the wall. The additional blocks add some visual interest and can be customised to whatever style you like.

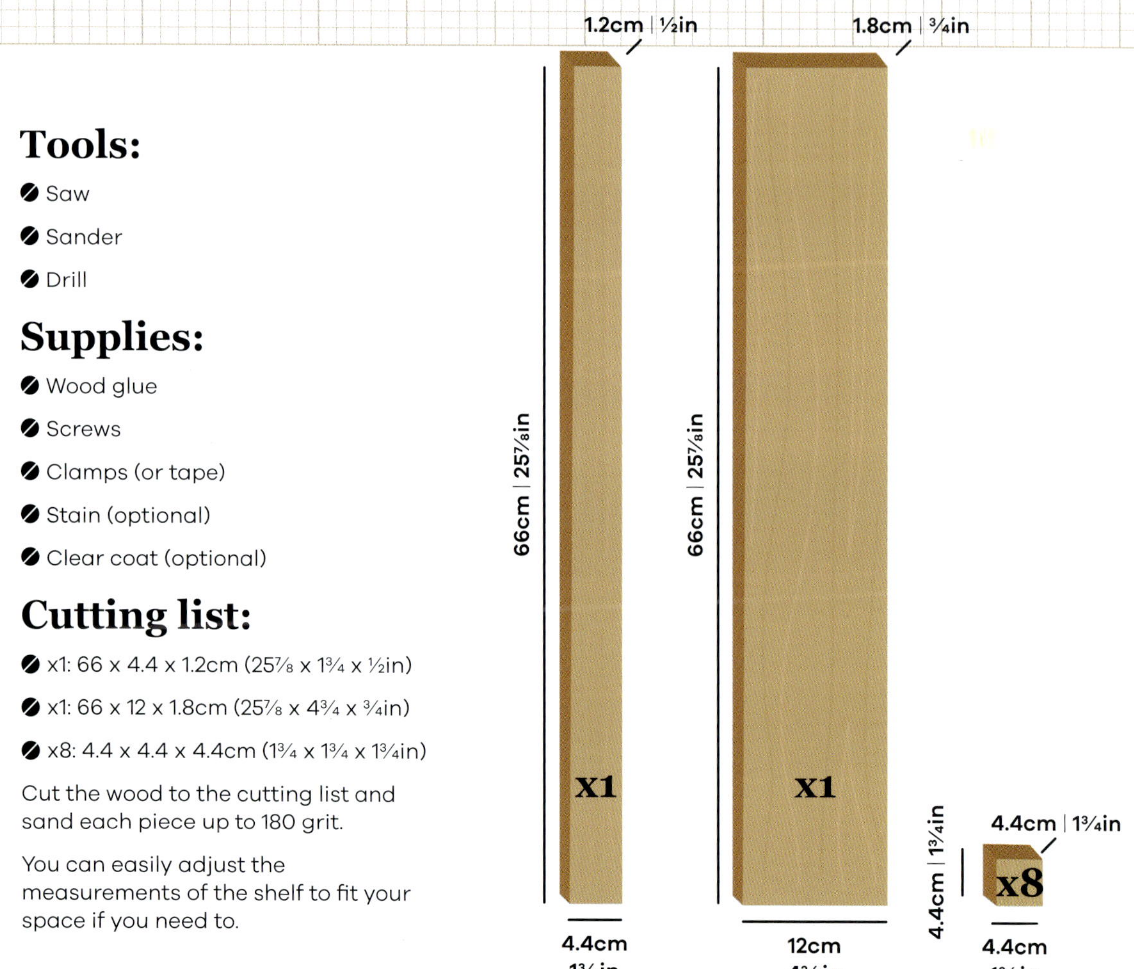

Tools:

- Saw
- Sander
- Drill

Supplies:

- Wood glue
- Screws
- Clamps (or tape)
- Stain (optional)
- Clear coat (optional)

Cutting list:

- x1: 66 x 4.4 x 1.2cm (25⅞ x 1¾ x ½in)
- x1: 66 x 12 x 1.8cm (25⅞ x 4¾ x ¾in)
- x8: 4.4 x 4.4 x 4.4cm (1¾ x 1¾ x 1¾in)

Cut the wood to the cutting list and sand each piece up to 180 grit.

You can easily adjust the measurements of the shelf to fit your space if you need to.

MACBETH

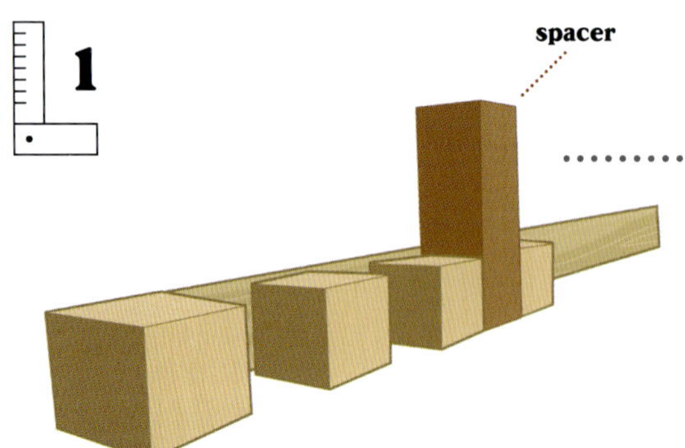

To make the block base, glue the 4.4 x 4.4cm (1¾ x 1¾in) square blocks onto the face of the 66 x 4.4cm (25⅞ x 1¾in) piece of wood. Start by gluing the first block flush with the edge. If you have any of the 4.4 x 4.4cm (1¾ x 1¾in) wood leftover from cutting the blocks, use it as a spacer while you glue each block down. Using this spacing should mean all eight blocks fit perfectly on the 66cm (25⅞) piece end to end.

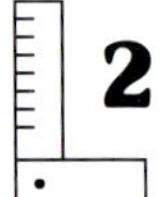

Once they're all in place, use a scrap piece of wood, or anything that's long and flat, and place it along the front of the blocks, then add clamps onto each end. This will ensure all the blocks are held in place while the glue dries. If you don't have clamps, try laying the wood on its back so the blocks are facing upwards. Lay a long piece of wood over the top and place something heavy on it.

3

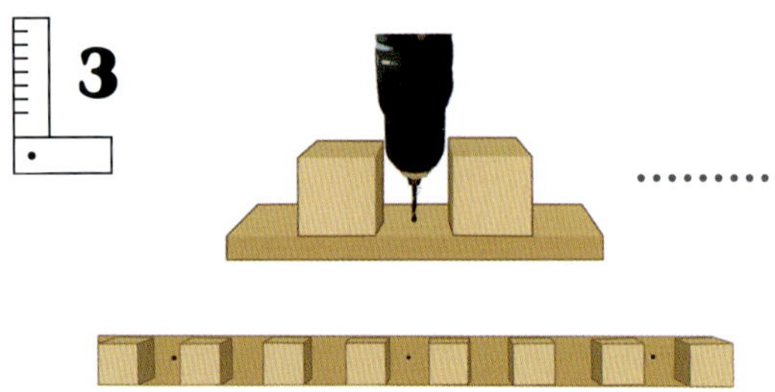

Once the glue is dry, it's time to drill the pilot holes that we'll use to attach the project to the wall once it's complete. Working in between the blocks, drill and countersink one pilot hole in the very centre of the block base and another on each end.

Before attaching the shelf to the block base, add your chosen stain and finish to all the pieces. I stained mine in a dark shade and finished it with a few coats of varnish.

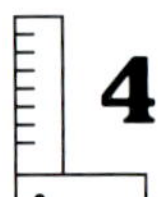

To attach the shelf to the block base, clamp the pieces together and drill pilot holes through the shelf and into the block piece. I did one in the centre and one on each end. Be sure to countersink the holes, then drive in the screws.

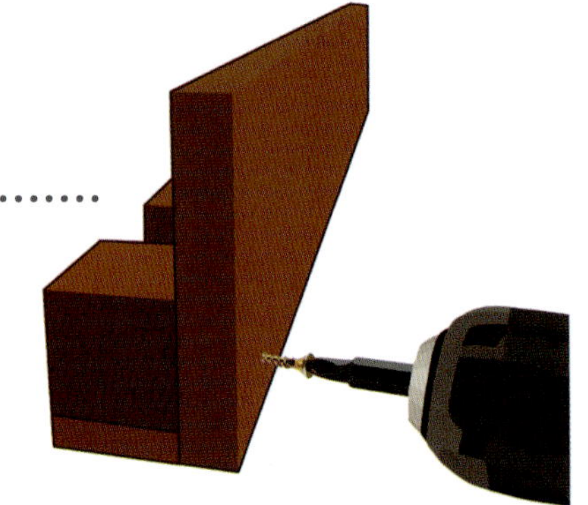

5

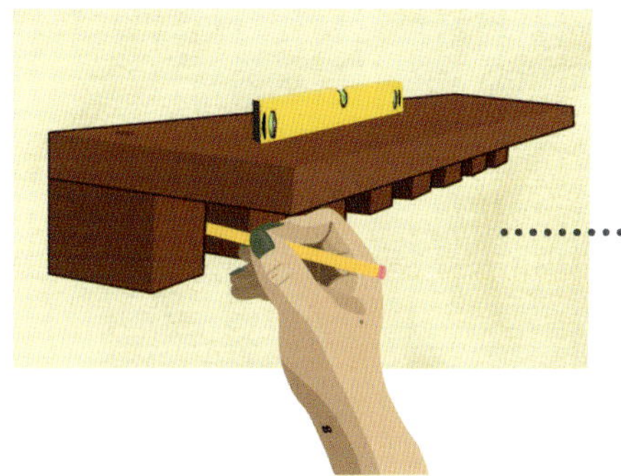

Now the shelf is complete, you're ready to attach it to the wall. First, hold up the shelf where you want to install it. You can rest a spirit level on the shelf to make sure the shelf is straight, then use a pencil to mark through the three pre-drilled holes onto the wall. Now you can put the shelf down and drill the required holes over the marks on the wall. Remember to check for any pipes or wires before drilling, and assess what bit is required for your wall type. You'll likely need to insert wall plugs (anchors) into the holes.

6

Hold the shelf back up, align the holes in the shelf with the holes in the wall, and drive the screws in.

If you don't like visible screw heads, you can get decorative screw caps, or use wood-effect stickers in the same colour as the wood, placing them over the screws. Alternatively, don't be afraid to pull some nail polish out. Painting the screw heads with a nail-polish colour that's similar to the wood colour is a great way to camouflage them.

SWITCH IT UP

As well as adjusting the size of this shelf to fit any space, you can change up the block design to add whatever decorative style you like. You can add thin strips of wood for a slatted effect, or even some decorative moulding.

PROJECT

The Vinyl Shelf

I'm a sucker for a simple, sleek design, and this shelf meets that brief perfectly. Created with just three pieces of wood, it can be made in an afternoon. If records aren't your thing, resize it for books or art instead.

Tools:

- Saw
- Sander
- Drill

Supplies:

- Wood Glue
- Wall hanging hardware x2
- Clamps (or tape)
- Stain (optional)
- Clear coat (optional)

Cutting list:

- x2: 100 x 4.4 x 1.2cm (39¼ x 1¾ x ½in)
- x1: 100 x 1.8 x 1cm (39¼ x ¾ x ⅜in)

Cut the pieces as per the cutting list and sand them up to 180 grit.

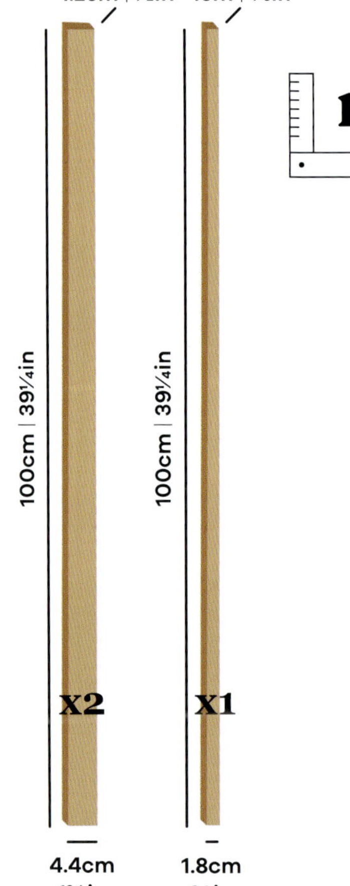

1 The width of this shelf will accommodate three vinyl sleeves; if you amend the width, just ensure all three pieces of wood are cut to the same length.

Spread glue along the face of the smaller piece and attach it to the face of a larger piece, aligning the bottom edges.

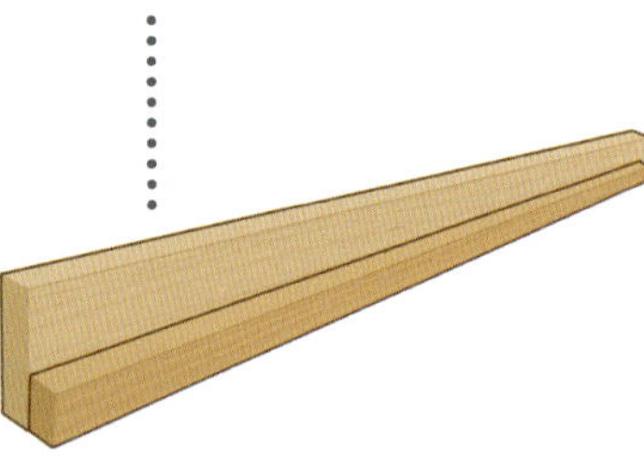

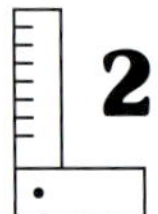

2 Add some glue to the other side of the smaller piece and place the second larger piece against it. Ensure the ends are aligned flush with one another and clamp them together while the glue dries.

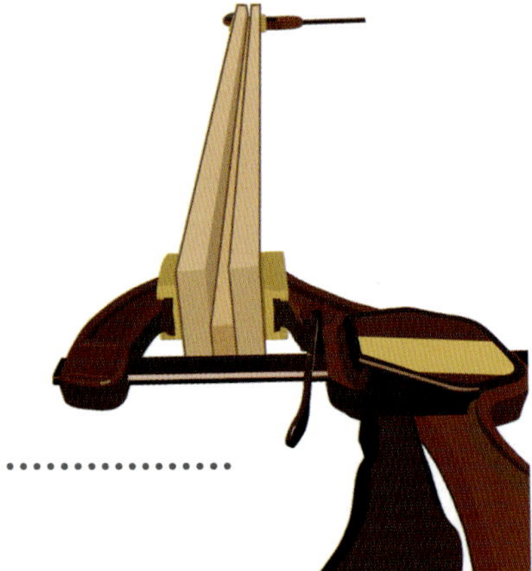

3

Install your chosen wall hanging hardware. I installed two keyhole hangers, one on each end of the shelf. Then finish the shelf in your desired style. I stained mine in a light pine colour and sealed it with a few coats of varnish.

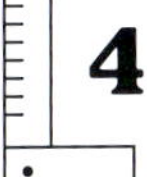

4

Prep the wall with the appropriate holes, wall plugs (anchors) and screws, then hang the vinyl shelf on the wall ready to display your favourite records.

TIP

A little hack for helping align the holes in the wall is to stick a long strip of painter's tape to the back of the shelf and mark both keyhole hanger slots with a pen. Then remove the tape from the vinyl shelf and transfer it to the wall. Now you know exactly where to drill the holes to make sure they're the correct distance apart.

About Paint

I love the warmth of wood tones and the intricacies of wood grain, but it can be fun to throw a pop of colour in there too. I'm a big fan of colour blocking with crisp, clean lines – it's the easiest way to customise a piece, so don't be afraid to go wild with some colour.

Paint types

There's all kinds of paint you can use on wood and each has its pros and cons.

Oil based paint – has great durability, but it has high VOCs (volatile organic compounds), which are basically chemicals that evaporate from the paint into the room, which aren't great for the environment or your lungs. Applicators will need to be cleaned with mineral spirits.

Water based paint – has low VOCs, and applicators can be cleaned easily with soap and water, but it has less durability than oil-based.

Latex paint – affordable and easy to apply, it does have lower durability than oil-based paint but due to its wide accessibility, it's a popular paint to use on wood.

Acrylic paint – similar to water-based paint with a little more durability, however it's usually more expensive.

Chalk paint – has become hugely popular over the last several years due to requiring very little prep work. It doesn't have great durability so usually requires a decent top coat for protection.

I like to use water-based paints and acrylic paints. It's purely down to personal preference, so play around with different types to get a feel for what you like.

Preparation and application

Before starting any painting, you'll need to prep the wood. This means sanding it up to 120 grit and wiping it with a dry cloth to make sure it's free from dust. Sanding too high a grit can make the surface too smooth for the paint to adhere to. Then you'll want to apply primer to help the paint adhere to the wood and provide a good base for a smooth, even finish. Make sure the primer is compatible with the type of paint you plan to use. Then you can begin painting. You'll get a more even result by applying several thin coats rather than one or two thick coats. Every paint has different coverage and requires a different number of coats, so you won't know how many you need until you start painting. It'll usually take two or three coats.

If I'm using both stain and paint on the same project, I stain and clear coat the piece first. I then tape off the area I want to paint and proceed with primer and paint. If you paint directly onto wood that's been stained but hasn't had a top coat, the paint can lift the stain from the wood and cause it to seep through the paint colour, leaving you with a discoloured finish. Depending on which type of paint you're working with, you may want to finish with a clear top coat to provide extra protection.

Painter's tape

There's nothing I enjoy more than a tape peel to reveal a perfectly crisp line. But you may have already experienced the disappointment of finding the paint has bled through the tape, leaving a fuzzy line. To avoid this, we need to ensure the edge of the tape is perfectly sealed. Some painter's tape has a water-activated adhesive that helps seal the edges – just run a damp cloth along the edge to activate the sealer. These tapes are a little more expensive though, so when using cheaper tape, I run my finger along the edge of the tape to make sure it's securely stuck down. To seal it, I apply a matte clear varnish to the edge of the tape – I get the tiniest amount on a brush and run it along the entire tape edge, then wait for the varnish to dry before applying the primer and paint.

I recommend keeping the tape in place while applying however many coats of paint you need, then peel the tape away when the final coat is still wet.

That is my sure-fire method to achieve crisp, clean lines every time.

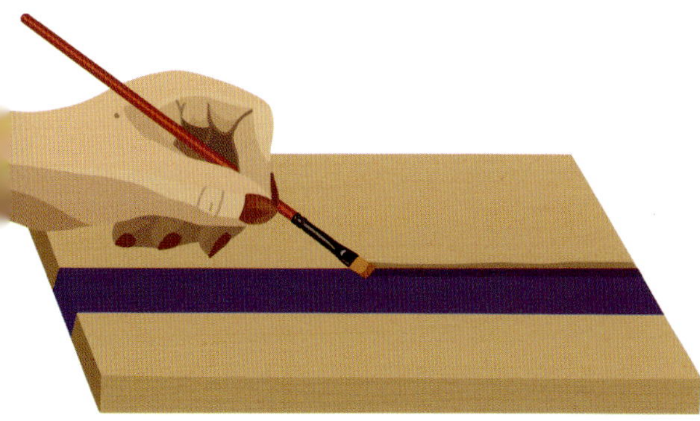

Paint pens

What about when you want to add intricate shapes or lettering? That's when acrylic paint pens come in handy. Accuracy is not my strong point, and my hands are ready to start shaking as soon as I reach for a paint brush. Paint pens feel much more natural to hold and use.

I also like to use the trace and draw method, especially for lettering. I print out the lettering in the size I need and colour the back of the paper with pencil or chalk. Then I tape the paper onto the wood and use a pen to draw around the letters. Now when I remove the paper I've got a perfect transfer of the lettering onto the wood and I can then go in with the paint pens.

To sum up

- Most paint types can be used on wood.
- Prep is key: sand, clean and prime.
- Seal the edges of tape with clear matte varnish to get crisp, clean lines.
- Use acrylic paint pens for lettering and small shapes.

Don't be afraid to go wild with some colour. It's only paint. And the good thing about working with solid wood is you can always sand the paint off if you feel like a change. Whether you like bright and bold, soft and neutral, or deep and autumnal (that's me!), paint can help you bring a little more of yourself into each project.

PROJECT

The Plant Box

I'll be honest, I can't keep plants alive. I've tried, but it never ends well. That doesn't mean my home is devoid of greenery – I just have a lot of fake plants. Whether you're a fake plant owner like me, or you're a green goddess single-handedly keeping our green friends alive, here's a cute plant box to give your favourite houseplant a new home.

Tools:

- Saw
- Sander
- Drill

Supplies:

- Screws
- Wood glue
- Painter's tape (optional)
- Paint (optional)
- Stain (optional)
- Clear coat (optional)

Cutting list:

- x3: 20 x 20 x 1.8cm (7¾ x 7¾ x ¾in)
- x2: 16.5 x 20 x 1.8cm (6½ x 7¾ x ¾in)
- x2: 20.5 x 2 x 2cm (8 x ¾ x ¾in)
- x4: 7.5 x 2 x 2cm (3 x ¾ x ¾in)

Cut the wood to the cutting list and sand each piece up to 180 grit.

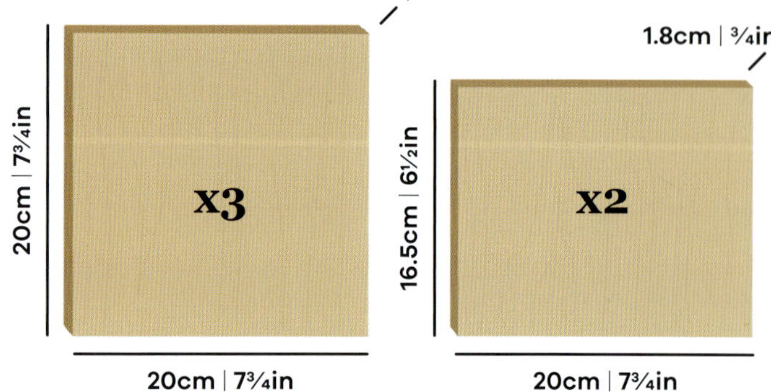

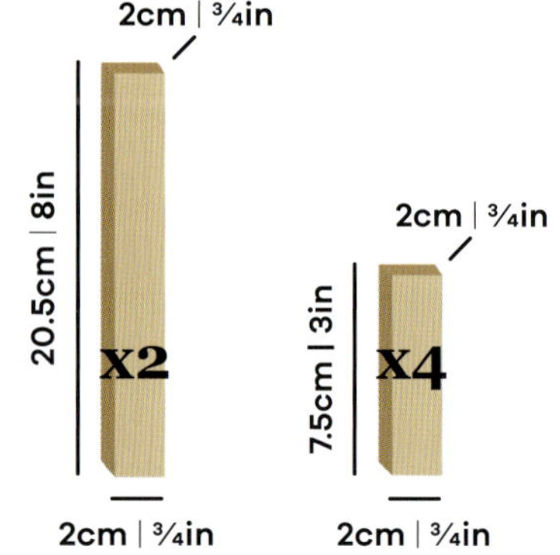

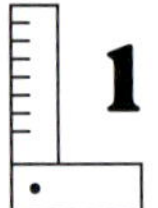

1 Lay a 16.5cm (6½in) piece on your worktop and butt a 20cm (7¾in) piece against the end grain. Hold the wood in place with clamps. This is the first joint we're going to attach with screws. Drill and countersink two pilot holes approx 3cm (1⅛in) from each end, then drive in the screws. Repeat the same with the remaining 16.5cm (6½in) piece and another 20cm (7¾in) piece.

TIP

I'm using furniture board (timber board) for the plant box because the wood needs to be 20cm (7¾in) wide. Furniture boards are made up of narrower boards joined together to make a single wide board. If you can't get your hands on furniture boards, you can buy narrower boards and glue them together side by side to create the width you need.

2 Now we can bring those two joined pieces together and attach them to create a box. Drill and countersink two pilot holes approx 3cm (1⅛in) from each end, then drive in the screws. Repeat on the other side.

3 Lay the final 20cm (7¾in) piece over the top to create the base of the box and attach it into place with two screws on each side. I recommend drilling the holes 5cm (2in) from each end to avoid the risk of running into the screws that are holding the side panels together. That's the box assembly complete.

4 To make the brackets for the plant box to sit on, simply add some wood glue onto the ends of each of the 20.5cm (8in) pieces and place a 7.5cm (3in) piece on each end. Clamp them in place while the glue dries.

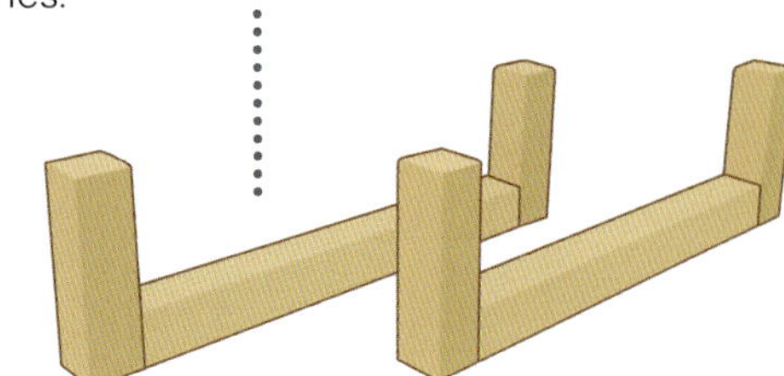

5

Now it's onto the fun bit. Stain and top coat both the box and brackets in your desired finish. I stained mine in a light pine colour and sealed it with a few coats of matte varnish. Because we're going to add some colour blocking to the bottom half of the box, I only stained a little over half of the box, leaving the bottom raw.

6

Once the clear coat is dry, it's time to prepare for painting. Add a line of painter's tape all the way around the box, about halfway down. The easiest way to make sure you get the tape straight all the way around is to make a small pencil mark on each corner, measuring 11cm (4¼in) from the top. Then when applying the tape, ensure it aligns with each pencil mark.

Grab a small paintbrush and some matte varnish, and seal the edges of the tape.

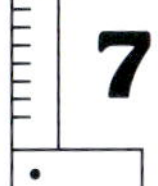

7

Once the varnish is dry, go ahead and apply the primer and paint. Keep the tape on in between coats, then, with the final coat still wet, carefully peel the tape away to reveal a perfectly crisp line. Apply a clear coat to the painted area to protect it from any scratches.

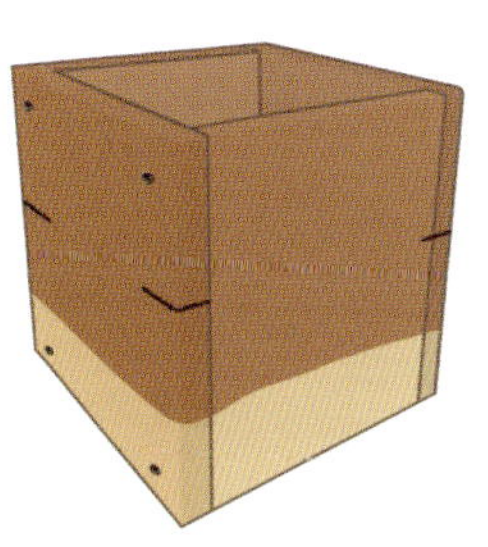

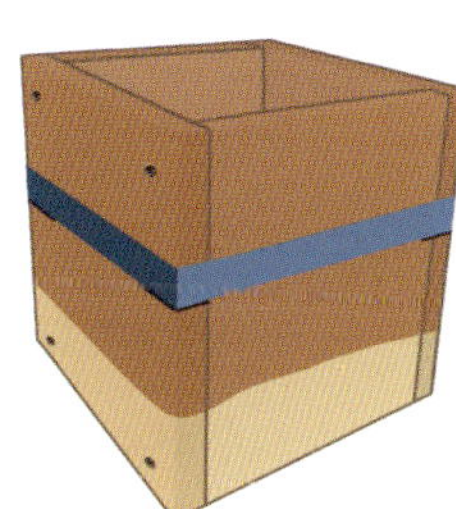

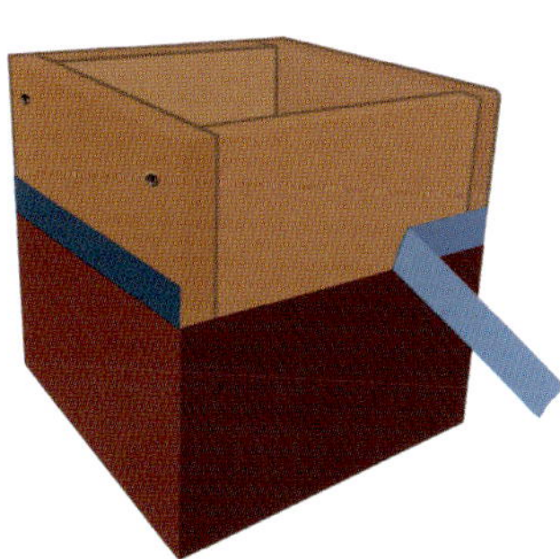

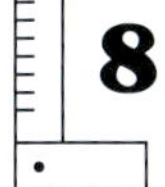

8

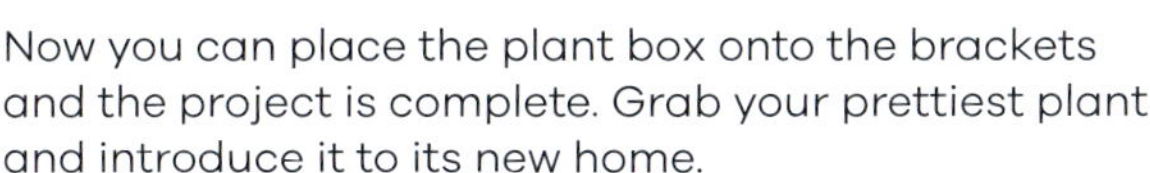

Now you can place the plant box onto the brackets and the project is complete. Grab your prettiest plant and introduce it to its new home.

SWITCH IT UP

This design isn't just for our plant friends. Make a tall, slim one and use it for holding kitchen utensils, or make a short, wide one to store toiletries.

PROJECT

The Game

Woodworking isn't just about making practical or pretty things – it's also about having fun. And what better way to celebrate your new skills than with a game? Whether you call it noughts and crosses, tic-tac-toe or something else, it's a game everyone can play.

Tools:

- Saw
- Sander
- Scissors or craft knife

Supplies:

- Acrylic paint pens
- A handful of coffee stirrer sticks
- Wood glue
- Hessian bag (optional)
- Stain (optional)
- Clear coat (optional)

Cutting list:

- x3: 13 x 4.4 x 1.2cm (5⅛ x 1¾ x ½in)
- x2: 13 x 1 x 1cm (5⅛ x ⅜ x ⅜in)
- x2: 11 x 1 x 1cm (4⅜ x ⅜ x ⅜in)
- x10: 2.5 x 2.5 x 1cm (1 x 1 x ⅜in)

Cut the wood to the cutting list and sand each piece up to 180 grit.

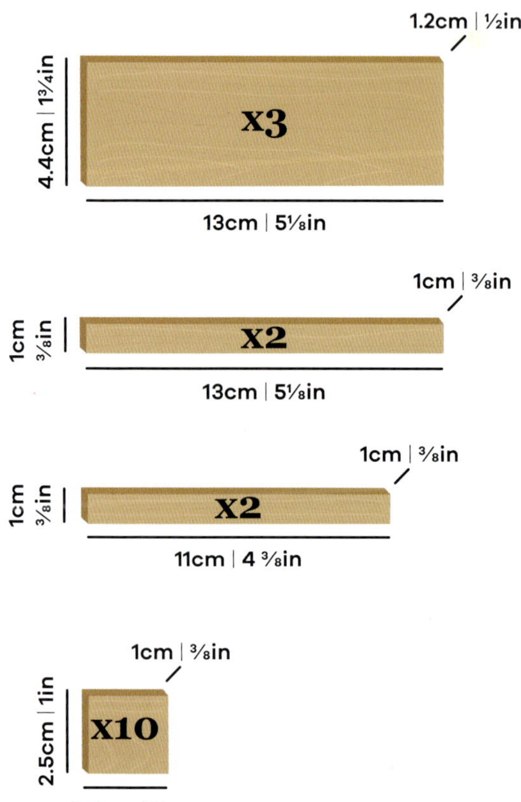

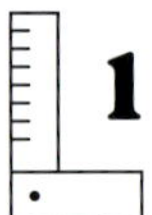

1

Glue the three 13 x 4.4cm (5⅛ x 1¾in) pieces together side by side to create the base of the game board. Clamp together until the glue is dry.

2

Now glue the two 13 x 1cm (5⅛ x ⅜in) pieces and the two 11 x 1cm (4⅜ x ⅜in) pieces on top of the game board to create a border.

3

To make the grid, cut two coffee stirrers to approx 11cm (4⅜in) in length using a craft knife or scissors. I honestly recommend just eyeballing the placement, but if you'd rather be exact, you can measure it. The main board inside the borders will be approx 11cm; divide this into thirds, marking approx 3.7cm (1½in) from each side with a pencil, then glue down the stirrers to create the vertical lines of the grid.

TIP

If you find the coffee stirrers too fiddly, don't stress – you can always forego the sticks and draw the grid with a paint pen instead. If you decide to draw the grid, wait until the final piece has been stained and top coated to do this.

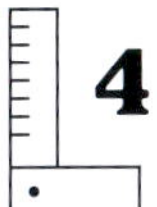

Cut some more coffee stirrers to approx 3.4cm (1⅜in) in length and glue them in between the vertical lines to create the horizontal lines of the grid. Again, just go for it and have faith that you can eyeball a roughly accurate grid, or you can measure the placement as before.

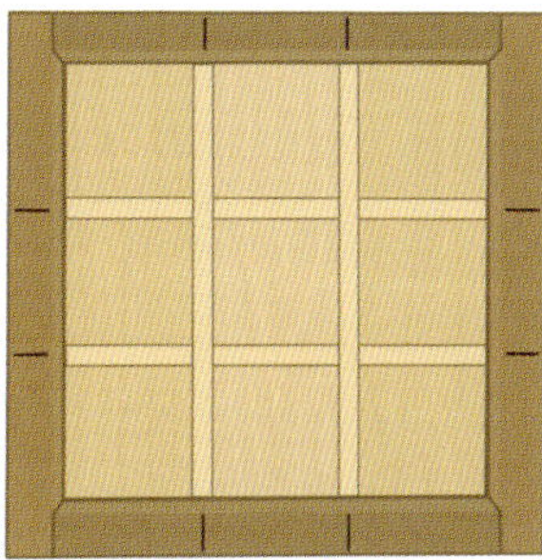

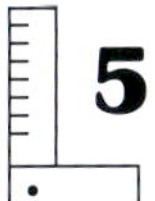

Once the glue is dry, stain and top coat the whole game board, as well as the ten square game pieces.

For the game pieces, I printed out the Xs and Os on regular paper. I then covered the back of the paper in chalk, taped it chalk-side down to the wood and traced around the letter to transfer the outline. Then grab a paint pen and draw on the letters. You may want to apply one more clear coat once the letters are dry, to protect them from any scratches.

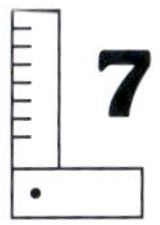

To avoid losing the game pieces, and to make it easier to take the game out and about, I used a small hessian bag to keep them in. And that's it, your game is complete!

SWITCH IT UP

Change up the design however you want. You could personalise the game by using star signs instead of the traditional Xs and Os, or you can play this game on a larger grid, like 5x5, to make it a little more challenging.

CHAPTER 5: THE ANGLES

About Angles

Maths isn't my strong point, so when it came to figuring out angles, I felt a little intimidated. That might sound a bit odd for a woodworker, but I believe you don't have to be great at numbers to woodwork. The reality is that the most common angle you create in woodworking is a 90-degree right angle, which is pretty simple – it's just two pieces of wood, both cut at 45 degrees and joined together. And most tools are designed to make angles simple.

Right angle joints

A mitred right angle is when two pieces of wood are cut diagonally across the face at 45 degrees, then joined together.

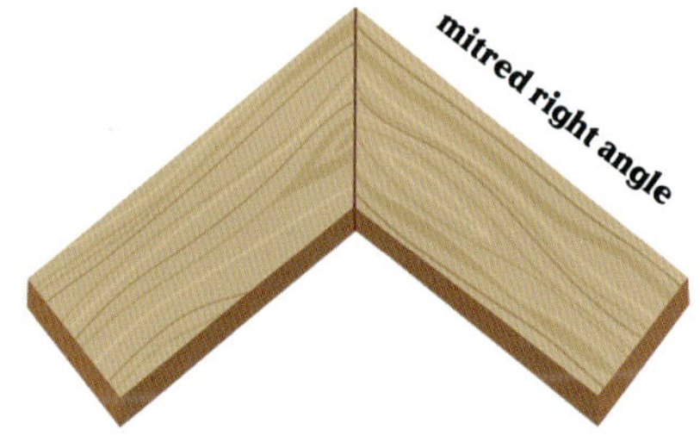

A bevelled right angle is when two pieces of wood are cut at 45 degrees into the edge of the wood, then joined together.

How to cut angles

Back saw and a mitre box

A mitre box has slots cut out to guide a back saw for making accurate cuts (see Cutting Wood: Back saw and mitre box). The angled slots will usually be labelled with the angle degree. Place the saw into the relevant slot and cut. It's as simple as that.

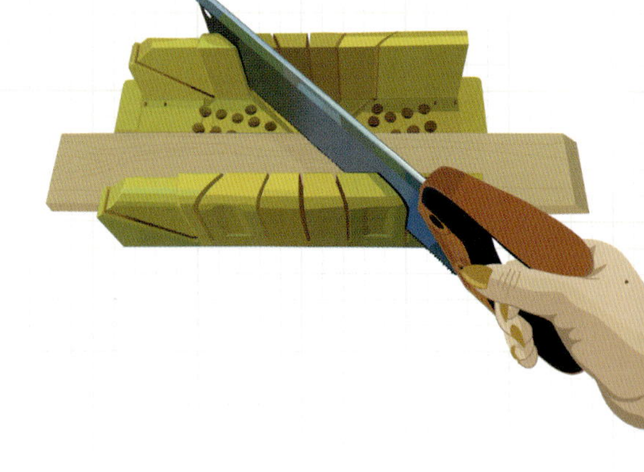

Mitre saw

There's no easier way to cut an angle than with a mitre saw. A mitre saw has angle adjustment scales built in, so you can move the blade for both mitre cuts and bevel cuts to the exact angle you want.

For bevel cuts, the blade is tilted over to the left or right. Each model is different, but there's usually a handle near the back of the saw that can be turned to loosen the adjustment mechanism. The blade can then be manually tilted over to the left or right, aligning with the required angle on the bevel scale. The bevel scale is usually located near the back of the saw, underneath the blade. Once aligned to the required angle, tighten the handle to lock the position. From there, the cut can be made as usual; clamp the wood into place and bring the saw all the way down onto the wood.

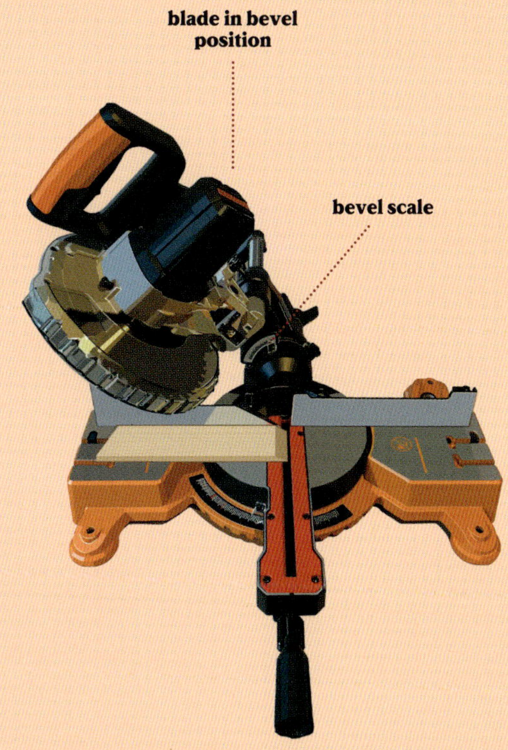

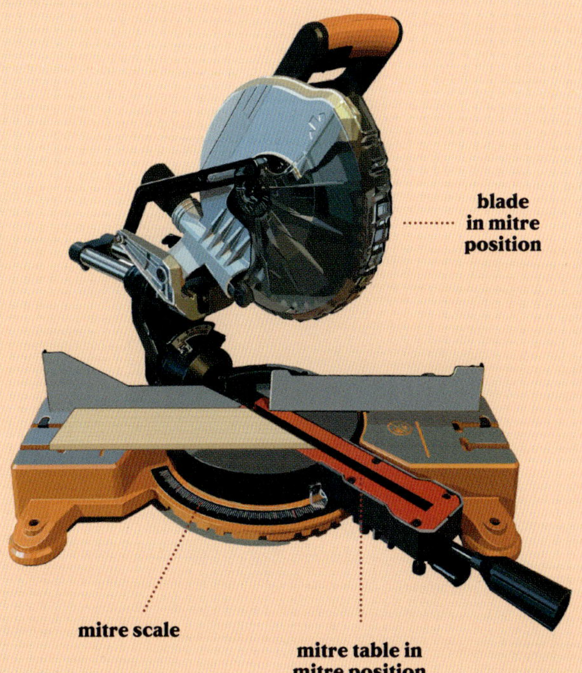

For a mitre cut, the blade remains upright rather than tilting over. Instead, both the blade and the mitre table are rotated around to the left or right. There's usually a handle or lever at the front of the saw that unlocks the mitre adjustment. The blade can then be rotated to line up to the desired angle on the built-in mitre scale and locked into place. Rotating the blade automatically rotates the mitre table, too. The mitre scale is usually at the front of the saw on the mitre table. Once the blade is positioned and locked in, the wood can be secured to the fence and the cut can be made as usual.

Circular saw

With a circular saw, most models have an angle adjustment built in for bevel cuts. Check the user manual for your specific saw. There's usually a handle or lever that unlocks the base plate, which can then be manually tilted to the left or right, aligning the built-in bevel scale to the desired angle. The bevel scale will be located on the body of the saw, usually near the front. The base plate can then be locked into place. Now, when the base plate is flat on the wood's surface, the blade will be angled as per the bevel scale. For bevel cuts, keep the cut line on the wood aligned with the 45 guide line on the front of the base plate.

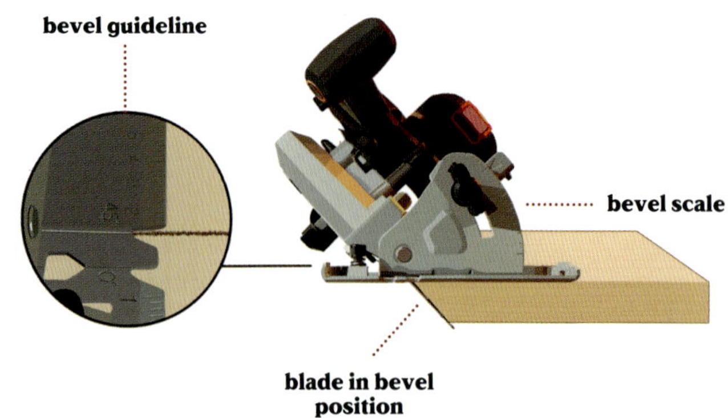

For mitre cuts, because a circular saw is free held, we need to do a little more to get the desired angle. I use a speed square to mark the cut line on the wood at the angle I want (see The Accessories: Speed Square). For a 45 degree angle, simply hold the speed square against the edge of the wood and draw a line along the angled side.

You can then clamp a straight edge guide such as a scrap piece of wood or the speed square itself to the wood to guide the saw against. This method also works for cutting with a jigsaw.

Other angles

The fundamental rule of angles is that if you're attaching two angled pieces of wood together, the finished angle will be the total of those two pieces. So far, I've talked about making 45-degree cuts to create 90-degree right angles, but the same techniques can be used for making any angle. For example, if you have two pieces of wood cut at 25 degrees, once joined they'll make a 50-degree angle.

If you want to cut an angle to fit into a specific spot, for example the corner of a wall, you can use a digital angle finder, which is basically two rulers attached on a hinge. You can open it up and place it in the spot you want to measure, and the digital screen will tell you the exact angle.

How to clamp angles

The usual clamps we use for butt joints can't adjust around an angle. For 90 degree angles, you can get right-angle clamps (corner clamps) to help with this.

Another way I like to clamp angles together, which is an especially great method when the angle isn't 90 degrees, is with painter's tape. Lay out a long strip of tape with the sticky side facing up. Place the wood onto the tape with the tips butted up against one another (a). Add wood glue (b) and then use the tape to bring the angles together (c). Tape firmly in place while the glue dries (d).

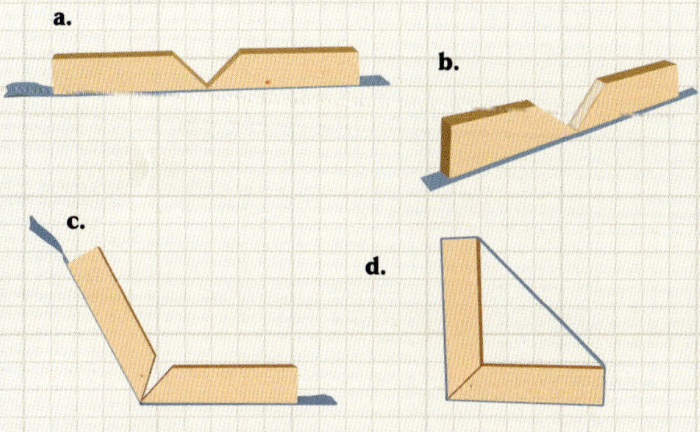

Accuracy

It's not uncommon to end up with imperfect angles. If a tool isn't perfectly tuned or the wood is slightly warped, your cut may be out by a fraction of a degree. Most of the time this won't matter, but if you're making something like a picture frame that requires each corner to be precisely 90 degrees, that small fraction can mean the final piece isn't perfectly square. It can even leave you with tiny gaps in the joints. Precision takes practice – get to know your tool and tune it to get the perfect angle. Just know that there are thousands of videos online with advice on how to improve the accuracy of angled joints, and they only exist because it's not as easy as we wish it was.

Examples of corner clamps.

The same rules apply to angled joints as straight joints. Wood glue alone can be used to secure joints together. If the joint is particularly weak, like when it has a small surface area, additional hardware, like screws, can be used to reinforce the joint. We'll be looking at other joinery methods like pocket holes and dowels in the next chapter, which can be used for both straight and angled joints.

To sum up

- The most common angle you'll need is 90 degrees.
- 90-degree angles are made up of two pieces cut and joined at 45 degrees.
- Use a digital angle finder to measure existing angles.
- Use right-angle clamps or painter's tape to clamp angles together.

Using mitred or bevelled joints instead of butt joints can really elevate the final look of a project. Luckily both hand tools and power tools make cutting angles pretty simple. While it can take a bit of practice to get perfect accuracy, that shouldn't be a reason to hold you back from starting. A slightly imperfect angle is still a good angle to me, and you only get better at something by doing it. So it's time to start cutting some angles.

The Flower Art

I love using dried flowers in my woodworking projects, and this design brings wood, flowers and art together in an unexpected way.

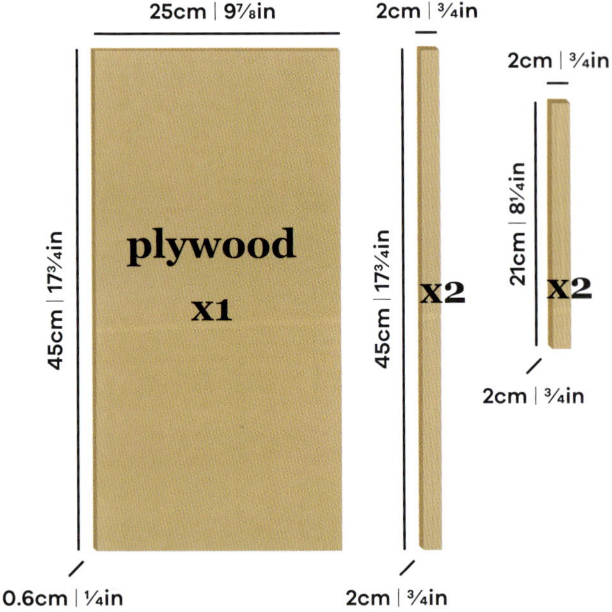

Tools:

- Saw
- Sander
- Drill

Supplies:

- 12mm (½in) drill bit
- x7: 7.5 x 1.2cm (3 x ½in) glass tubes
- x2: hanging hardware
- Wood glue
- Clamps (or weights)
- Stain (optional)
- Clear coat (optional)
- Dried flowers

Cutting list:

- x1: 45 x 25 x 0.6cm (17¾ x 9⅞ x ¼in) plywood
- x2: 45 x 2 x 2cm (17¾ x ¾ x ¾in)
- x2: 21 x 2 x 2cm (8¼ x ¾ x ¾in)
- x7: 1.8 x 1.8 x 0.4cm (¾ x ¾ x ⅛in)

Cut the following with a 45-degree mitre on both ends. Length measurements are based on the longest sides.

- x2: 29 x 1.8 x 0.4cm (11⅜ x ¾ x ⅛in)
- x2: 21 x 1.8 x 0.4cm (8¼ x ¾ x ⅛in)
- x2: 13.5 x 1.8 x 0.4cm (5¼ x ¾ x ⅛in)
- x4: 12.5 x 1.8 x 0.4cm (4⅞ x ¾ x ⅛in)
- x4: 10.5 x 1.8 x 0.4cm (4⅛ x ¾ x ⅛in)
- x2: 5.5 x 1.8 x 0.4cm (2⅛ x ¾ x ⅛in)

Cut the wood to the cutting list and sand each piece to 180 grit.

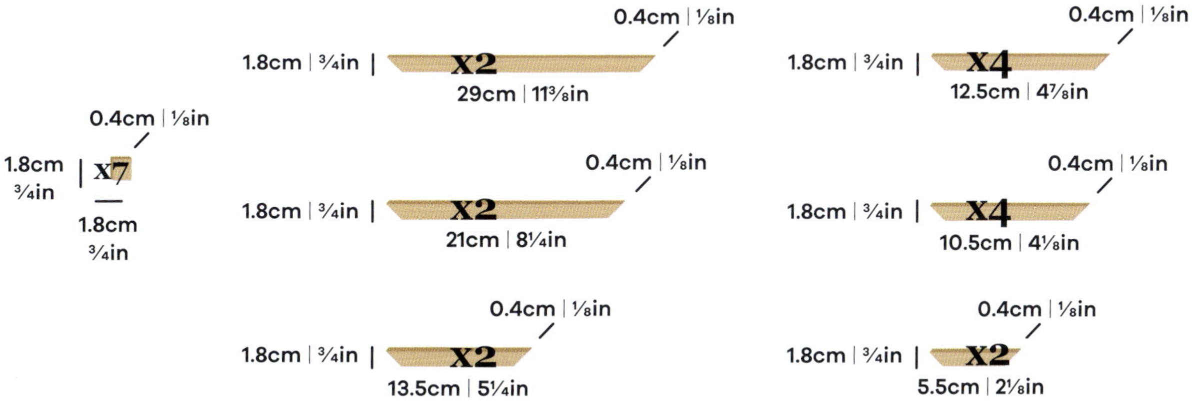
0.4cm | ⅛in
1.8cm | ¾in
x7
1.8cm | ¾in
0.4cm | ⅛in
1.8cm | ¾in
x2
29cm | 11⅜in
0.4cm | ⅛in
1.8cm | ¾in
x2
21cm | 8¼in
0.4cm | ⅛in
1.8cm | ¾in
x2
13.5cm | 5¼in
0.4cm | ⅛in
1.8cm | ¾in
x4
12.5cm | 4⅞in
0.4cm | ⅛in
1.8cm | ¾in
x4
10.5cm | 4⅛in
0.4cm | ⅛in
1.8cm | ¾in
x2
5.5cm | 2⅛in

Before we start assembly, we need to drill seven holes for the glass tubes. Grab a 45 x 2cm (17¾ x ¾in) piece and mark the very middle with pencil for the centre hole.

Then mark the remaining holes, spacing them 5.5cm (2⅛in) apart. Using the 12mm (½in) bit, drill each hole to approx 1cm (⅜in) deep.

Now we can begin assembling. Glue the two 45 x 2cm (17 ¾ x ¾in) pieces and the two 21 x 2cm (8 ¼ x ¾in) pieces on top of the plywood to create the frame. Ensure the piece with the drilled holes is at the bottom. Place something heavy on top to clamp them in place while the glue dries.

Once dry, make a pencil mark in the centre of each border piece to help us visually align the angled pieces when we create the mosaic art next.

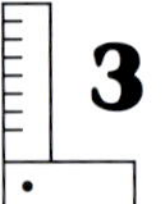

We'll start the mosaic by doing a dry fit before glueing anything down, to make sure all the pieces align neatly. First grab the two 29cm (11⅜in) pieces and place them into position. An end should meet each corner at the bottom, and the top point should align with the centre line marked in pencil on the border.

TIP

If you find during your dry fit that some of your mitred pieces don't quite fit, don't panic – cut a little bit more off each one until it slots into place.

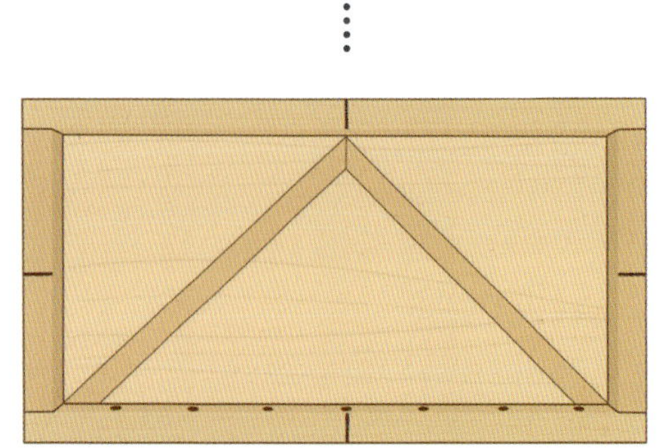

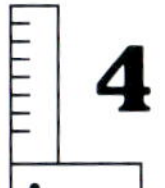

4

Now add the 21cm (8¼in) mitred pieces, visually aligning the top point with the centre mark, and ensuring the bottoms touch the bottom border. Repeat the same process with the 13.5cm (5¼in) pieces and then the 5.5cm (2⅛in) pieces. All of the top points should visually align with the centre mark on the border, and the other ends should all make contact with the bottom border.

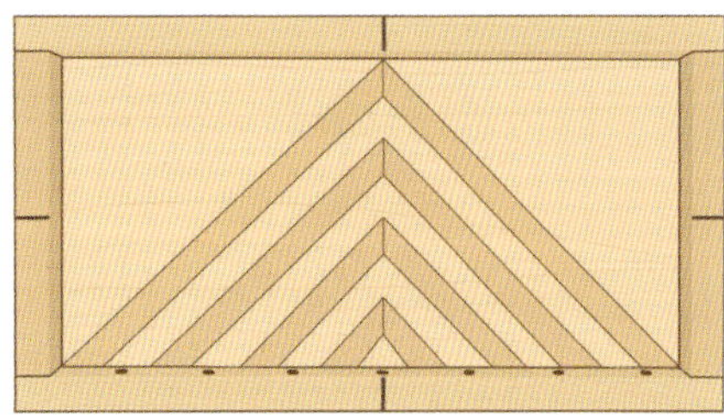

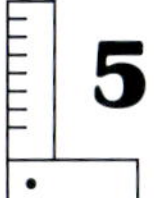

5

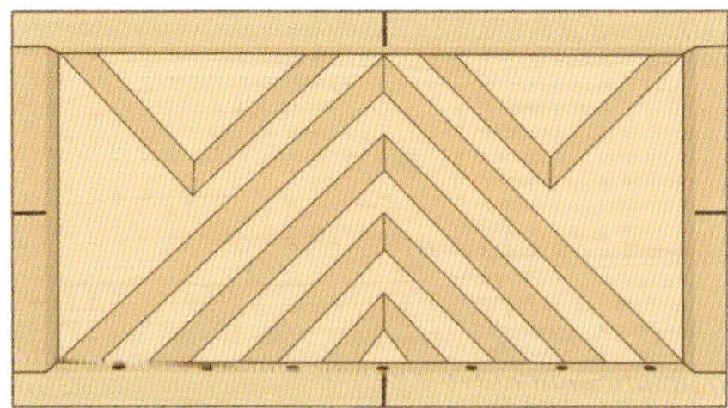

Now for the 12.5cm (4⅞in) pieces. Place these in the top corners. There's no need to align them with any centre marks – the end of one piece should fit snugly into the top corner and the second piece should mirror it, creating a point facing downwards. Do this for both upper corners.

The 10.5cm (4⅛in) pieces fit into the space at the left and right edges, with the points facing inwards and lining up with the centre of the side borders.

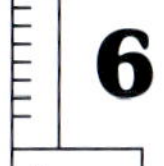

6

Once all the mitred pieces are in position, place the small squares into the point of each triangle, except for the very bottom triangle. Once you're happy everything fits, go ahead and glue each piece down. Place something heavy on top to clamp the pieces down while the glue dries. Once the glue is dry, remove the pencil marks with an eraser or sandpaper.

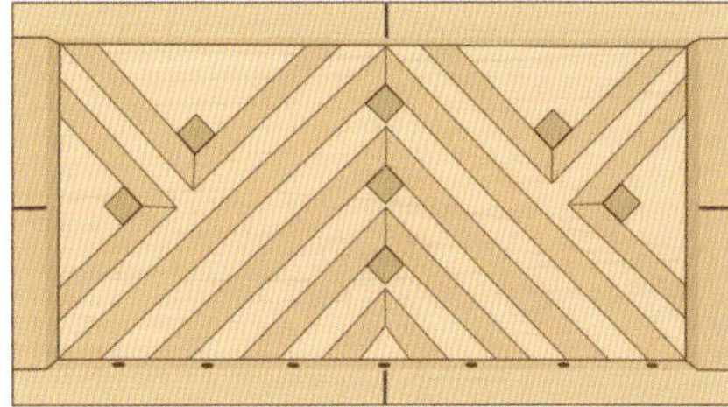

Now add your preferred finish. I stained mine in a medium oak colour and opted for a spray varnish for ease around all the corners. Once dry, I added a little pop of colour to the squares using acrylic paint. Add your choice of hanging hardware to the back – I added two sawtooth hangers, one on each side.

Pop the glass tubes into the holes and fill them with some beautiful dried flowers. And just like that, we made art.

SWITCH IT UP

If you're a plant lover, you could add some water to the glass tubes and use it as a propagation station. Or forgo the tubes altogether and just enjoy your beautiful mosaic.

PROJECT

The Book Wedge

This is one of my favourite designs. Perfect for a book lover, it's essentially a giant bookmark – when you're done reading for the day, pop the book onto the wedge, leaving it open to the page you're on. And when you're done seeing for the day, you can slip your glasses inside!

Tools:

- Saw
- Sander

Supplies:

- Wood glue
- Clamps (or tape)
- Stain (optional)
- Clear coat (optional)
- Paint (optional)

Cutting list:

- x1: 28.5 x 6.9 x 1.8cm (11¼ x 2¾ x ¾in)
- x4: 20.5 x 6.9 x 1.8cm (8 x 2¾ x ¾in)

Cut the wood to the cutting list. The 28.5cm (11¼in) base piece should be cut with a 45-degree bevel on both ends. The four 20.5cm (8in) pieces should be cut with a 45-degree mitre on both ends. The length measurements are based on the longest sides. Sand all the pieces up to 180 grit.

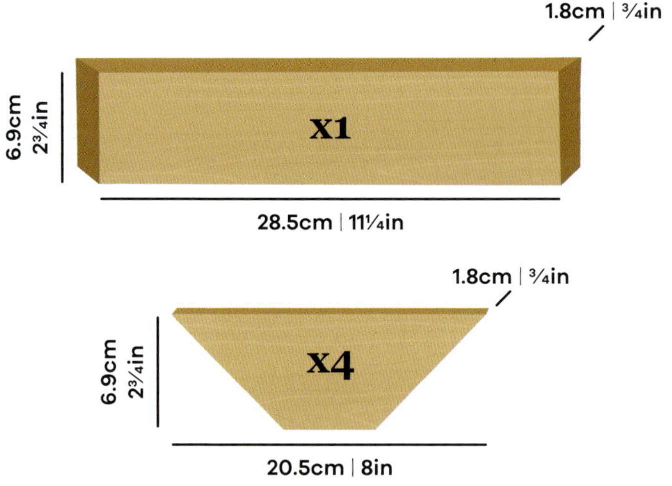

1

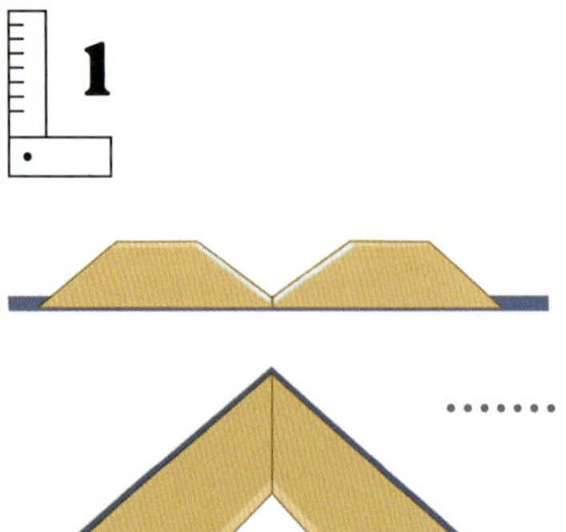

Grab two of the mitred pieces and glue one end of the mitre to the other. You can use corner clamps for this, or you can use the tape trick as shown. Allow the glue to dry.

Repeat with the other two mitred pieces so you end up with two triangles.

2

Once the glue is dry, it's time to attach them to the bevelled base. Run some glue along the inside bottom edges of the mitre triangles.

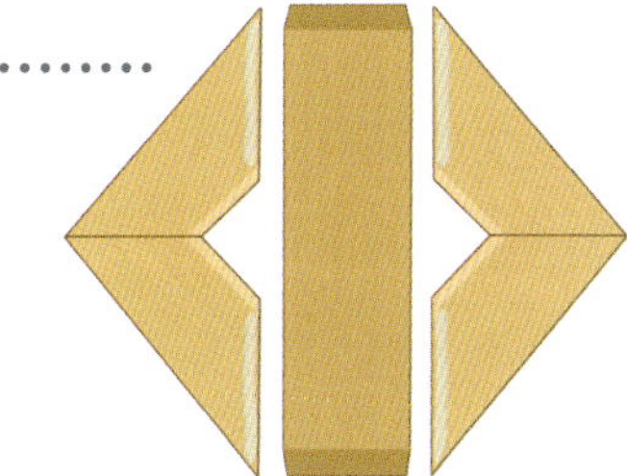

3

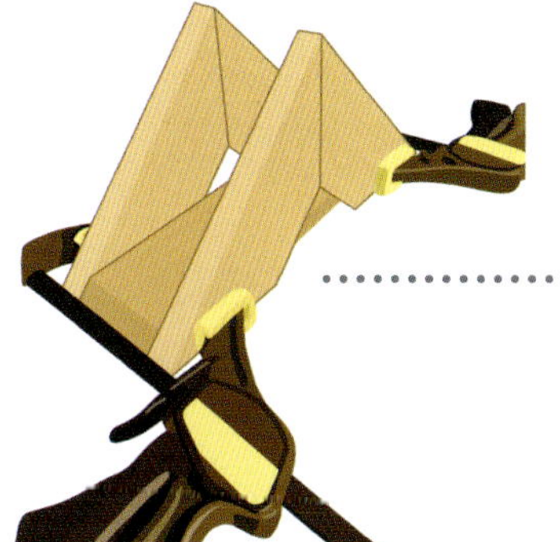

Place a triangle on either side of the bevelled piece and clamp them all together until the glue dries.

Now the assembly is complete, finish the piece however you'd like. I stained mine in a light pine and sealed it with clear varnish before adding some green colour blocking using painter's tape.

SWITCH IT UP

I'm a big believer that books should look lived in, which is why it doesn't concern me to keep the spine open on the wedge. If you're someone who doesn't want your book doing yoga on the daily, you can use the middle space as a book stand instead. Also, my brother had the genius idea of clipping a mini reading lamp onto the wedge for those who like to read in the dark.

The Workshop

I know it can feel like woodworking isn't possible unless you have a garage or studio space to set up a workshop. Having a dedicated space does make it much easier, but you can still woodwork without one. I didn't have a dedicated space when I started out, so I worked on my projects outside on the doorstep and stored my limited tools in a corner of my room when I was done.

When I moved house, I still didn't have a garage space, but I did have a converted attic space. And while an attic may not seem ideal for a workshop, it was like a dream come true to me.

That being said, I'm not the most organised person, so it quickly looked like a dumping ground. I could never find anything, and I constantly felt like I was running out of space as poorly stacked piles of wood and tools encroached further and further across the room. But I have a secret weapon: my sister. She is the super-organised other half of me (and she illustrated this entire book by the way) so she took the reins and transformed my workshop into a functional, organised space, using lots of clever space-saving storage.

So, let me share some of the space saving and organisational options with you. Whether you have an entire garage, or just a small corner in the spare room, hopefully these will help you to make the most of the space you have.

Folding workbench

This is a great option if you have very limited space. I used a folding workbench back in the days of working on my doorstep. On top of providing a surface to work on, many also have various features to help clamp wood or tools safely in place, as well as a size adjustment to extend the work surface area. When not in use, it can be folded flat for easy storage, taking up minimal space.

Workbench on wheels

Now that I'm working in the attic, I have a little more space to play with, but having a moveable work surface allows me to rearrange the space when I need to. I have a simple workbench on castor wheels that I can pull out, then roll away to tuck into the side of the room when not in use. The workbench has two shelves beneath the worktop, so I can store tools and supplies on it, too.

Stackable crates and boxes

I use stackable crates for all my scrap wood, but they can be used for anything. Having storage that's easily stackable means you can make the most of vertical space, rather than taking up precious floor space. Adding castor wheels to the bottom crate can also help with space, as you can roll it away into a cupboard or under a table when not in use.

Pegboard

If you have some wall space, hanging a pegboard is a game changer. I made my own pegboard using a few sheets of MDF, but you can buy pre-made ones, too. Being able to hang tools and supplies on the wall instead of storing them in boxes saves hugely on floor space. It also keeps things organised and makes it much easier to find what you need.

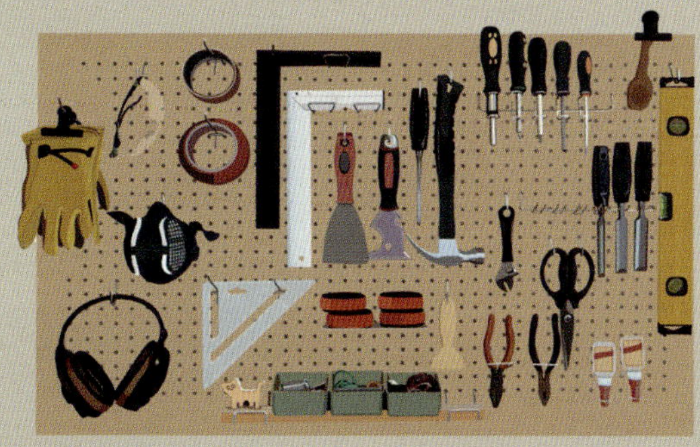

Labels

This is something I totally overlooked until my sister came in to save the day. Labelling storage boxes is a real time saver. Instead of trawling through three or four boxes until I find what I need, I now know what's in each box, which means less time searching and more time making. I also have small stackable boxes for storing sandpaper with each box labelled with the sandpaper grit.

About Invisible Joints

So far we've learnt how to join wood using screws, but this usually leaves visible screw heads on the surface of the wood. That might be fine when the screw heads are out of sight on the back of the piece, but for some builds the screws will be placed somewhere visible. If you find screw heads unsightly, there are other options.

Pocket holes

A pocket hole is drilled at an angle into one piece of wood, from the face of the board down to the end grain. The board is then joined to another piece of wood (the target piece) by driving a screw through the pocket hole and into the target wood.

The top of the oval holes can be filled with pocket hole plugs. Once cut flush, you're left with a smooth surface and no visible screws. You can buy premade pocket hole plugs, or you can use a plug cutter to make your own.

Pocket holes don't always have to be plugged though. Most of the time, because they enable us to join wood via the face of the board, the hole can be made on the unseen side of the joint. If we're making a frame, for instance, instead of driving screws in through the side, leaving the screw heads visible, we can use pocket holes at the back of the frame to join the wood, leaving no visible screws or holes. In this instance, plugging the pocket holes won't be necessary.

Pocket hole jig

The easiest way to create pocket holes is with a pocket hole jig. Each jig will be slightly different so be sure to check the instructions, but the overall usage remains the same. Let's look at a pocket hole jig in more detail.

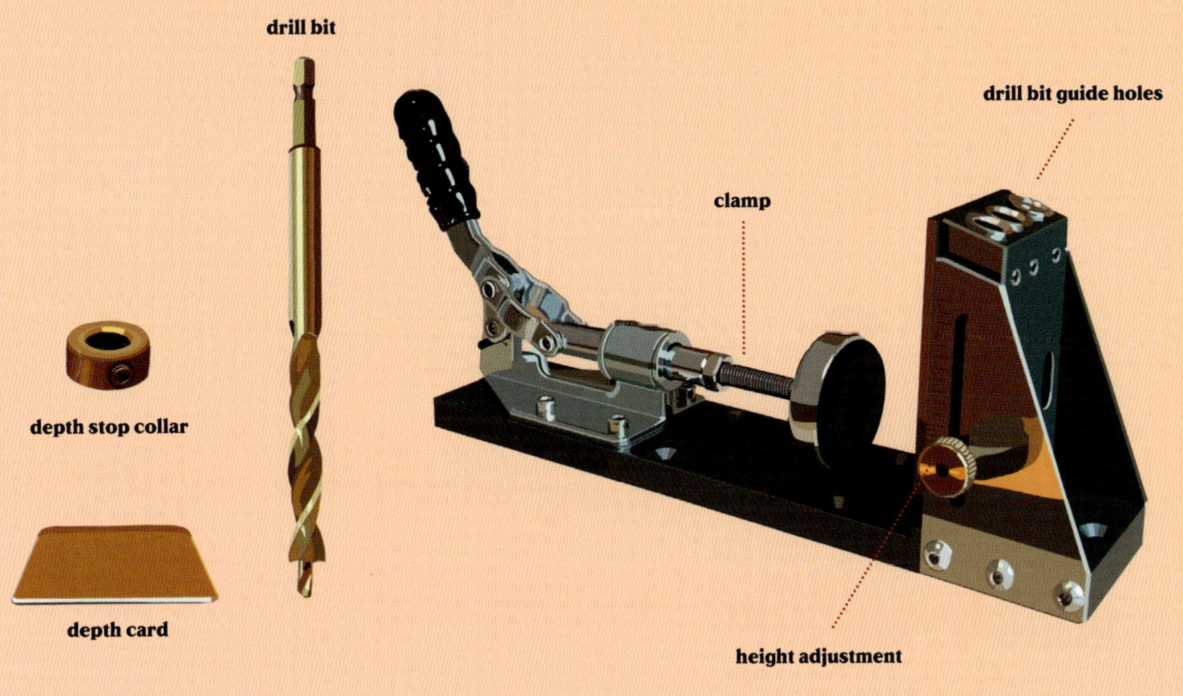

- **Clamp** – the clamp is used to secure the wood in the jig so it doesn't move when drilling the holes.
- **Depth card** – this thin card is used when setting the depth stop collar on the drill bit.
- **Depth stop collar** – this is placed on the drill bit to ensure the hole is drilled to just the right depth. It comes with an Allen key to tighten and loosen the collar.
- **Drill bit** – pocket hole drill bits have a stepped design; the smaller part drills the pilot hole and the larger part drills the required angle.
- **Drill bit guide holes** – these holes guide the angle of the drill bit when drilling the pocket holes.
- **Height adjustment** – this is usually a sliding mechanism with labelled measurements. It adjusts the height of the guide holes based on the thickness of the wood.

Using a pocket hole jig

Before drilling any pocket holes, we need to set up the jig. First set the height adjustment to the thickness of the wood to ensure the drill bit guide holes are at the correct height. Slide the mechanism to line up to the relevant measurement and lock it into place. For example, if the wood is 1.8cm (¾in) thick, slide the mechanism until the arrow aligns with 1.8cm (¾in) on the jig.

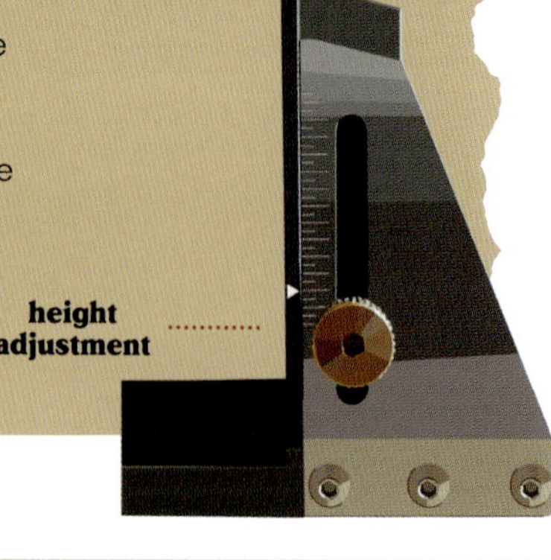

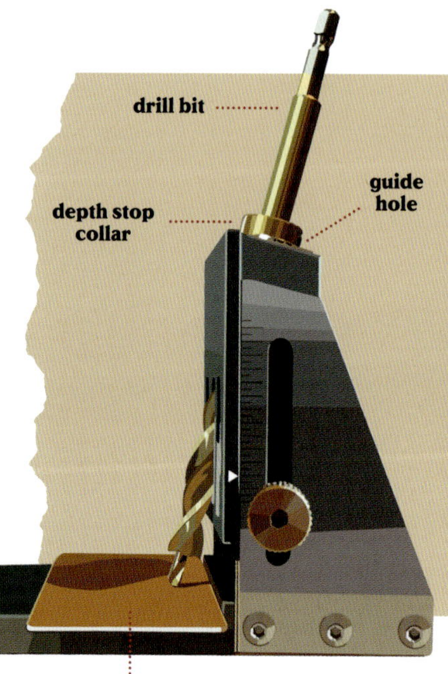

Next we need to attach the depth stop collar to the drill bit so the hole is drilled all the way through the wood, but stops before we reach the bottom of the jig. Place the drill bit into one of the guide holes until it touches the bottom of the jig. Then place the depth card beneath the tip of the bit to lift it up a fraction from the base of the jig. Slip the depth stop collar onto the drill bit from the top and slide it down until it touches the guide hole. Tighten the collar onto the drill bit using the Allen key. Now you can install the drill bit into the drill as usual.

Clamp the wood securely into the jig using the built in clamp. Place the drill bit into the guide hole and drill into the wood until the depth stop collar reaches the guide hole and you're unable to drill any further.

Joining the boards

Now the hole has been drilled, it's time to join the board to the target piece of wood. Clamp the pieces together and drive the screw into the hole.

a.
Add glue to pocket holes.

If the pocket holes will be visible on your piece, it's pretty simple to fill them. After driving in the screw, place some glue in the hole (a) and then insert a pocket hole plug (b). Once the glue has dried, cut away the excess with a hand saw so that it's flush with the wood, and give it a quick sand until smooth (c).

b.
Insert plugs into pocket holes.

c.
Trim and sand the plugs.

Pocket hole screws

Not all screws are made equal, and when it comes to pocket holes, it's best to use pocket hole screws. In fact, using a screw that isn't designed for pocket holes will cause the wood to split. Due to the nature of pocket holes, it's difficult to drill a pilot hole into the target piece at the correct angle. To overcome this , pocket hole screws are designed with self drilling tips that drill the hole as you drive the screw in, negating the need for a pilot hole. What length and diameter pocket hole screw you need will depend on the thickness of the wood. The pocket hole jig will come with a guide advising which size screws to use based on the wood dimensions.

Dowels

Dowels are cylindrical pieces of wood used to reinforce joints. This can be done visibly or invisibly.

For a visible look, the hole is drilled all the way through one board and into the target piece of wood. The dowel is inserted with some glue and then cut flush with the face of the board, leaving a visible circle.

visible dowel

For an invisible look, a hole is drilled partway into both pieces of wood, and one end of the dowel is inserted into each hole with a little glue.

invisible dowel

For the invisible look, there are three key things we need to achieve: ensuring the holes in both pieces of wood line up perfectly, are the correct depth and are drilled perfectly straight.

One way to ensure the holes in both pieces of wood align is to simply measure and mark the placements with a ruler and pencil. As long as the holes are drilled at the same distance from both edges, then the holes in each piece of wood will align. This is a simple method but it does require accuracy. While there's no exact rule on where the placement should be, holes should be at least 1cm (⅜in) away from the end of the wood. If you drill any closer to the end, the wood may split.

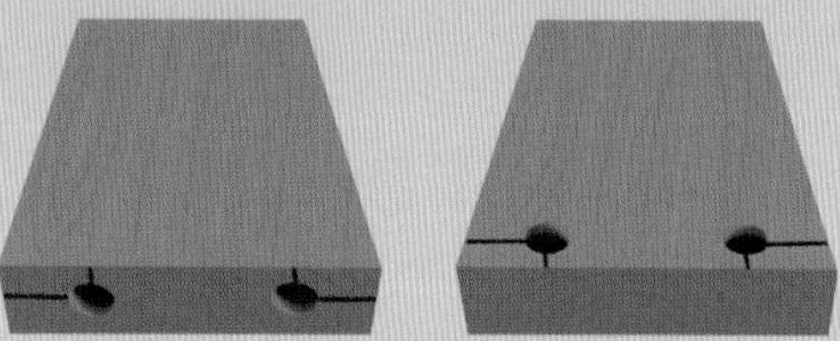

Measure and mark placement with pencil.

Another option is to use dowel marker pins. These are small metal pins with a little spike on the head. They're designed to sit inside a pre-drilled hole and mark the corresponding hole on the joining piece of wood. First drill the holes into one piece of wood, then pop the dowel marker pins inside the holes. Align the second piece of wood where it is to be joined and press down onto the pins. The spikes will dent the second piece of wood, indicating where to drill the corresponding holes.

Alignment with dowel marker pins:

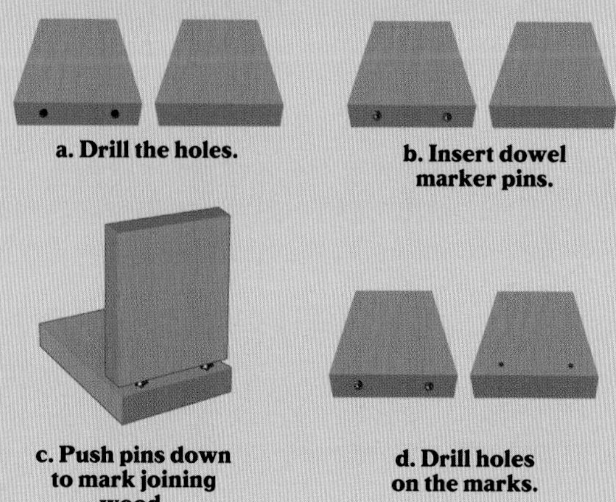

a. Drill the holes.

b. Insert dowel marker pins.

c. Push pins down to mark joining wood.

d. Drill holes on the marks.

Once we've established the correct hole placement, we need to ensure the holes are drilled to the correct dimensions so the dowel will fit. Let's say we're using dowels that are 6mm (¼in) in diameter. The holes need to be 6mm (¼in) wide, so we'll use a 6mm (¼in) drill bit. For the depth, the holes in each piece of wood need to be half the length of the dowel plus an extra 2mm (1/16in) to allow for the wood glue. So if our dowel is 30mm (1⅛in) in length, each hole needs to be approx 17mm (⅝in) deep.

Drilling the same depth hole in each piece of wood isn't always possible. If the wood is only 18mm (¾in) thick, then drilling a 17mm (⅝in) hole into the face of the board will end up breaking through to the other side. To avoid this, you need to leave about 5mm (¼in) of wood intact. So for wood that's 18mm (¾in) thick, the hole should only be around 13mm (½in) deep. The hole going into the end grain of the wood can go a lot deeper as there is no danger of breaking through – we just need both depths to add up to the full length of the dowel, with extra space for glue. In my example, we can drill a 13mm (½in) hole into the face piece and a 21mm (⅞in) hole in the end grain of the other piece. When joined together, the total hole is still 34mm (1¼in), which is the length of the dowel plus an extra 2mm (1/16in) in each hole to account for glue.

The final thing we need to achieve is to ensure the holes are perfectly straight. Dowels rely on accuracy to work. You might discover that you were born with the uncanny ability to drill perfectly straight holes without any additional guidance. If so, yay for you. If not, a cheap and cheerful solution is a drill guide – a small block with pre-drilled holes of various sizes. Place the block on the wood and the drill bit into the relevant sized guide hole. As you drill, it will help to keep the drill bit straight.

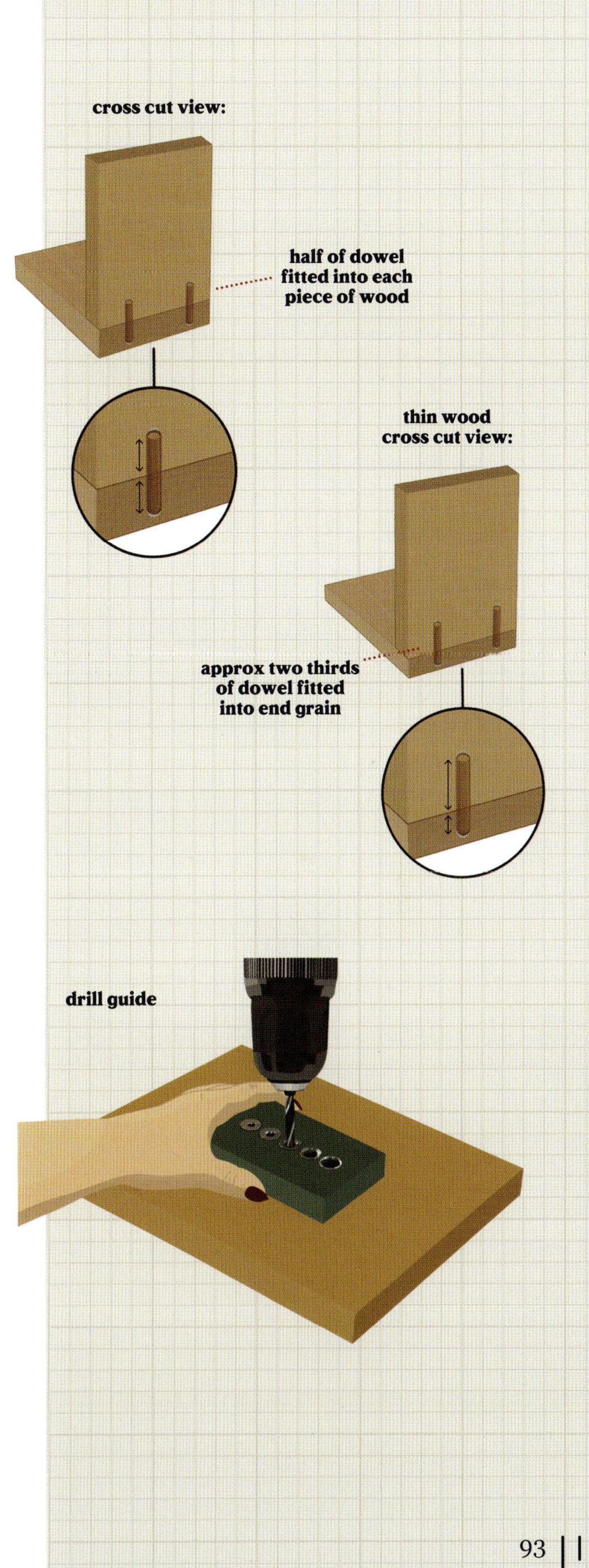

Installing dowels

Now we've covered how to drill the dowel holes, let's look at the final step to install them. First, add some glue into each of the holes. Use something small such as a toothpick to spread the glue inside the holes and ensure they're evenly covered. Now push the dowels into one piece of wood – you may need to tap them lightly with a hammer or mallet to ensure they're all the way in. Some glue will flood out of the holes – this is normal. Wipe the excess away with a damp cloth. Now align the second piece of wood over the dowels and push it down into place. Remove any glue squeeze out with a damp cloth.

TIP

You can use a hammer to tap the second piece of wood down onto the dowels, but I recommend putting a scrap piece of wood on top of the workpiece. This way, any damage the hammer might cause will be confined to the scrap wood.

For a visible dowel look, glue and clamp the joint together first (see The Essentials: Joining wood). Now drill holes through the top piece of wood into the second piece. The holes need to be shallower than the length of the dowels so they can be cut perfectly flush after installation. Add glue into the holes and insert the dowels, using a hammer or mallet to tap them in fully. Wipe off any excess glue that floods out. Once the glue is dry, cut the excess dowels flush with the wood using a hand saw, then sand smooth. You will be left with visible circles in the wood. Using the same species of wood for the dowels as the main project creates a subtle look, but you can also use a different species to create contrast.

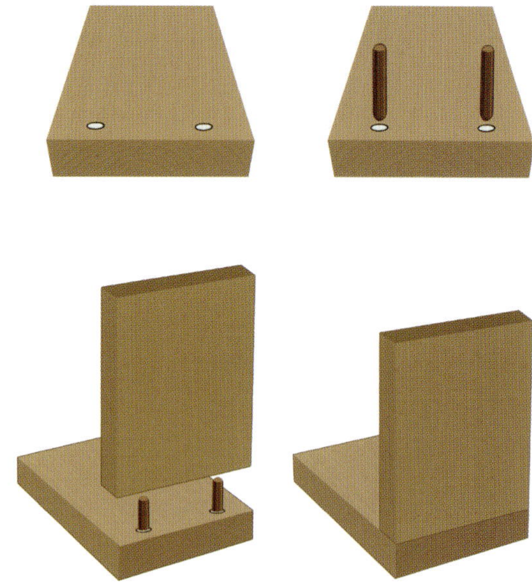

invisible dowel install

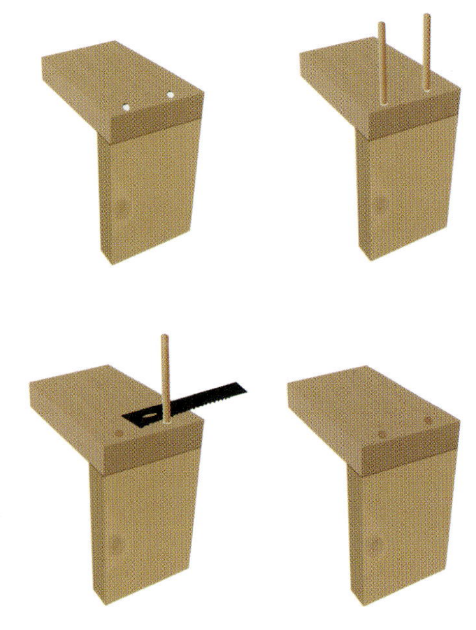

visible dowel install

Dowel jig

A dowel jig is an extra piece of equipment to help improve the accuracy of making dowel holes. There's a whole variety available, each with different features. Some are fairly simple blocks, with guide holes to help keep the drill bit straight during drilling and a ruler guide that can be used to help manually align the placement of the holes. Others are a little more extensive, with built-in mechanisms to set the wood thickness, hole placement and hole depth, helping to align each hole with perfect accuracy.

If you plan to use dowels regularly, a dowel jig is a worthwhile investment. While there are some with hefty price tags out there, there are plenty of affordable ones on the market that still have all the bells and whistles.

What size dowels to use

The diameter of the dowel should be roughly a third of the thickness of the wood. So, if the wood is 18mm (¾in) thick, the dowel should be 6mm (¼in) in diameter. For invisible dowels, the length should be around twice the thickness of the wood. So if the wood is 18mm (¾in) thick, the dowel should be roughly 36mm (1½in) in length. For visible dowels, the length should be three times the thickness of the wood. So for wood that's 18mm (¾in) thick, the dowel should be around 54mm (2¼in) in length. You'll rarely find dowels that match these sizes exactly, so see this more as a guide than a rule.

There's no hard rule on how many dowels to use for a joint. Naturally, the wider the joint the more dowels you should use.

To sum up

- Pocket holes require a pocket hole jig and pocket hole screws.
- For the pocket hole jig, set the wood thickness on the jig and set the depth stop on the drill bit.
- For dowel holes, use a drill bit the same width as the dowel and allow an extra 2mm (1⁄16in) in depth to account for glue.
- For invisible dowels, the diameter of dowels should be around a third of the thickness of the wood; the length should be around twice the thickness of the wood.
- For visible dowels, the diameter should be around a third of the thickness of the wood and the length should be around three times the thickness of the wood.

Invisible joinery isn't a necessity, especially for beginner projects, but it can help elevate the final look of a piece, and it's a fun new skill to learn. The next projects are going to use invisible joints, but they can easily be made without them. I'll share the alternatives in the steps, so if you're not ready to tackle invisible joints just yet, you don't have to miss out on these projects.

The Frame Shelf

This is a design I've come back to again and again. I've used various sizes, methods and decoration over the years, but today we're going to bring it back to its original simplicity. Don't worry if you don't have a pocket hole jig – instead of pocket holes, you can join the frame using flat corner brackets.

Tools:

- Saw
- Sander
- Drill
- Pocket hole jig

Supplies:

- Pocket hole screws
- x2 hanging hardware
- Screws
- Painter's tape
- Clamps
- Stain (optional)
- Clear coat (optional)

Cutting list:

- x2: 50 x 4.4 x 1.8cm (19⅝ x 1¾ x ¾in)
- x1: 34.8 x 4.4 x 1.8cm (13¾ x 1¾ x ¾in)
- x2: 26 x 4.4 x 1.8cm (10¼ x 1¾ x ¾in)

Cut the wood to the cutting list and sand each piece up to 180 grit. You may prefer to cut the 34.8cm (13¾in) piece at the end (see Tip).

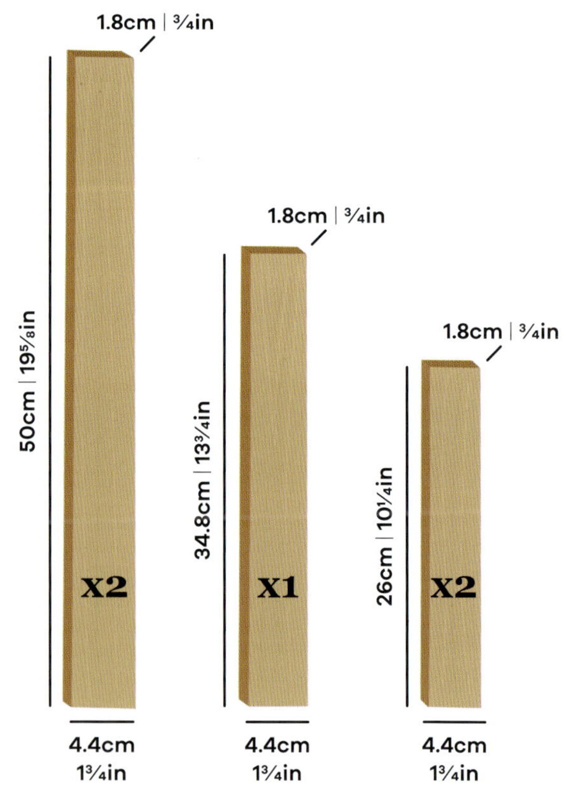

TIP

The 34.8cm (13¾in) piece is for the shelf that will be attached to the frame – this measurement is based on the width of the final frame. I found it easier to wait until the frame was assembled before cutting the shelf piece, because then I could hold the wood against the frame and mark the cut line so it matched the width exactly.

1

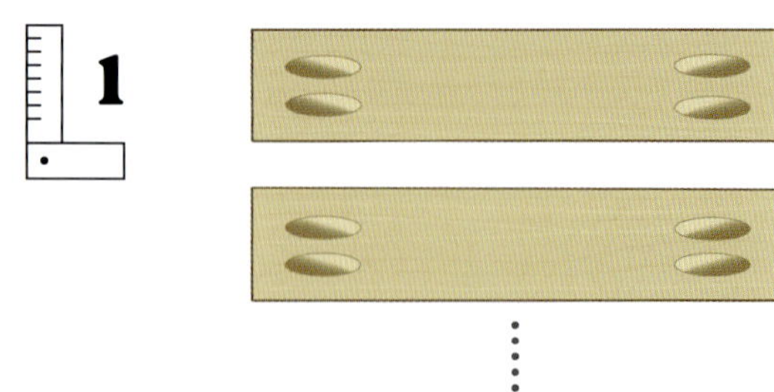

If using a pocket hole jig, set it to the thickness of the wood, then set the depth collar on the drill bit. Drill two pocket holes into each end of the 26cm (10¼in) pieces.

2

Lay the frame pieces in place, with the 26cm (10¼in) pieces butted in between the 50cm (19⅝in) pieces. Add some clamps to hold them in place.

3

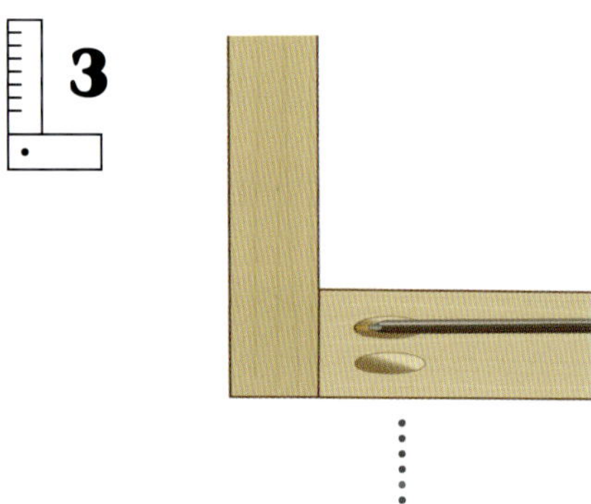

Drive a pocket hole screw into each pocket hole to attach the frame together. If you're using flat corner brackets instead of pocket holes, lay the brackets across the joint and mark the holes required. Drill the pilot holes then drive the screws through the brackets.

4

Before we move on to attaching the shelf, it's easier to attach the hanging hardware now while the frame can lay flat. I installed two keyhole hangers on the back, one on each side.

5

Now we can attach the shelf. From the bottom of the frame, measure 15cm (5⅞in) up on each side and draw a pencil line. This is going to help us align the shelf.

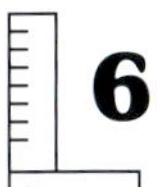

6

Lay the shelf across the frame, ensuring the bottom of it aligns with the pencil lines. Using some painter's tape, secure the shelf firmly to the frame.

7

Now we need to access the back of the frame to screw the shelf into place. To do this, I found it easiest to use some scrap wood piled up for the frame to sit on. This allows the frame to sit flat, face down.

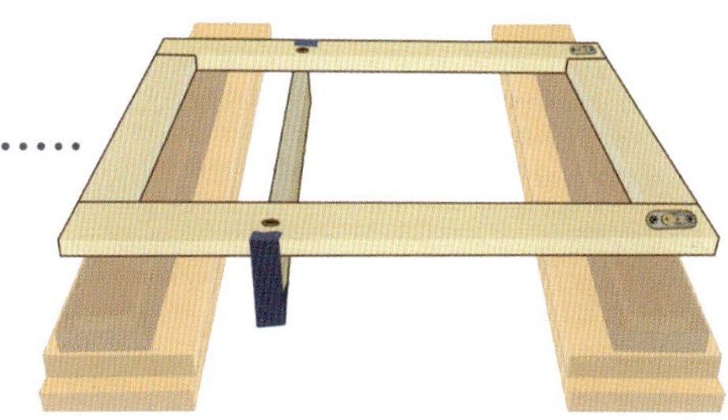

Mark a hole on each side of the frame then drill and countersink the pilot holes. Drive the screws in to attach the shelf. Remove any leftover pencil with an eraser or sandpaper.

Now assembly is complete, you can finish the frame shelf however you like. I stained mine in a medium warm tone and sealed it with a few coats of matte varnish.

SWITCH IT UP

Not only can the dimensions of this frame shelf be adjusted to suit your needs, there's lots of other ways to customise the design, too. Use decorative moulding to add more visual interest to the frame, or colour block the lower half of the frame to bring a pop of colour into your home.

PROJECT

The Brush Holder

If you're reading this book, you must be a creative. If you're a creative, you'll own paintbrushes. With this little project, you can keep your brushes within easy reach. Join the wood pieces with dowels or screws – it'll look cute either way. As well as paintbrushes, you could use it to hold pens, or drill larger holes for kitchen utensils.

Tools:

- Saw
- Sander
- Drill

Supplies:

- 6mm (¼in) drill bit
- x4: 30 x 6mm (1⅛ x ¼in) dowels
- Wood glue
- Clamps (or weights)
- Stain (optional)
- Clear coat (optional)

Cutting list:

- x2: 20 x 4.4 x 1.8cm (7⅞ x 1¾ x ¾in)
- x2: 7 x 2.1 x 2.1cm (2¾ x ⅞ x ⅞in)

Cut the wood to the cutting list and sand each piece up to 180 grit.

1.8cm | ¾in

4.4cm 1¾in

x2

20cm | 7⅞in

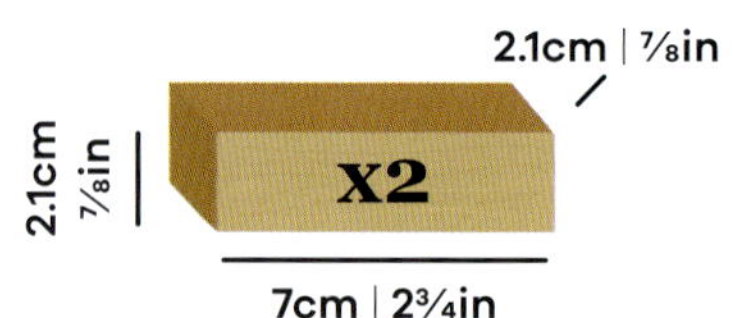

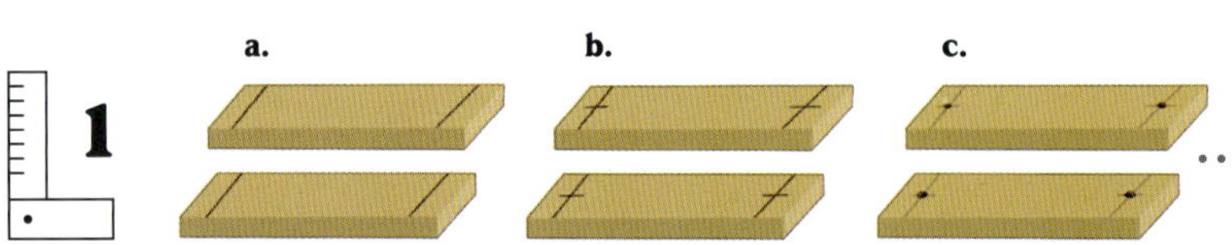

Grab the 20cm (7⅞in) pieces and draw a pencil line 13mm (½in) from each end (a), then mark the centre of each line (b). Drill a dowel hole at each point where the lines intersect (c), using a 6mm (¼in) bit to a depth of 1.2cm (½in).

2

Grab the 7cm (2 ¾in) pieces. On each end grain, draw an 'x' from corner to corner. With a 6mm (¼in) bit, drill a dowel hole in the centre of each x, to a depth of 2.2cm (⅞in).

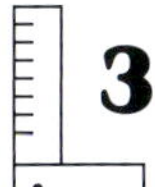

3

Next we drill the holes for the brushes. Grab one of the 20cm (7 ⅞in) pieces. On the side without the dowel holes, mark the centre for the middle hole. Then mark three holes on either side, spaced 2cm (¾in) apart. Using a 6mm (¼in) bit, or the best size for your brushes, drill each hole all the way through.

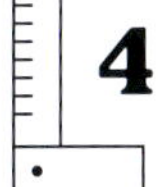

4

It's time to assemble. Grab the other 20cm (7⅞in) piece, add glue to the dowel holes and push in the dowels. Grab the 7cm (2¾in) pieces and add some glue to the holes at one end, then push one onto each dowel.

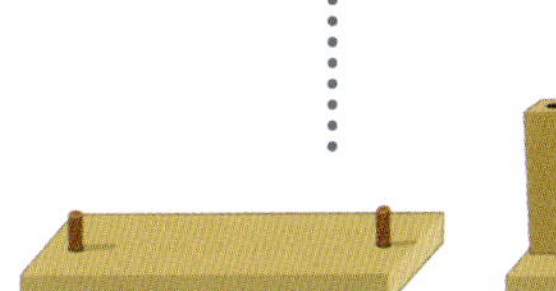

5

Add glue to the top holes of the 7cm (2¾in) pieces and insert the dowels. Glue the dowel holes on the remaining 20cm (7 ⅞in) piece and push it down onto the dowels. Clamp the joints together for the glue to dry.

Now finish the holder however you want. I stained mine in a medium pine and finished it with a few coats of varnish.

About the Jigsaw

A jigsaw isn't a must-have to start your woodworking journey, but it's a fun addition to your tools when you're looking to build your collection. A jigsaw allows us to create curved cuts, which opens up a whole new range of possibilities within our projects.

What is a jigsaw

A jigsaw is a power saw with a long thin blade that moves in an up and down motion. Unlike the mitre saw and circular saw, which can only cut in a straight line, a jigsaw can be used to cut all sorts of shapes and curves. While a jigsaw can tackle most lines, be aware that it will struggle with extremely tight curves. Let's take a closer look.

- **Base plate** – this is the part that will rest on the wood whilst cutting.
- **Bevel adjustment** – this adjusts the angle of the base plate to allow for bevel cuts.
- **Blade** – the blade will cut the wood.
- **Blade clamp** – this holds the blade in place.
- **Speed adjustment** – this sets the maximum speed of the blade.
- **Trigger switch** – how much you press on the trigger will dictate how fast the blade moves.

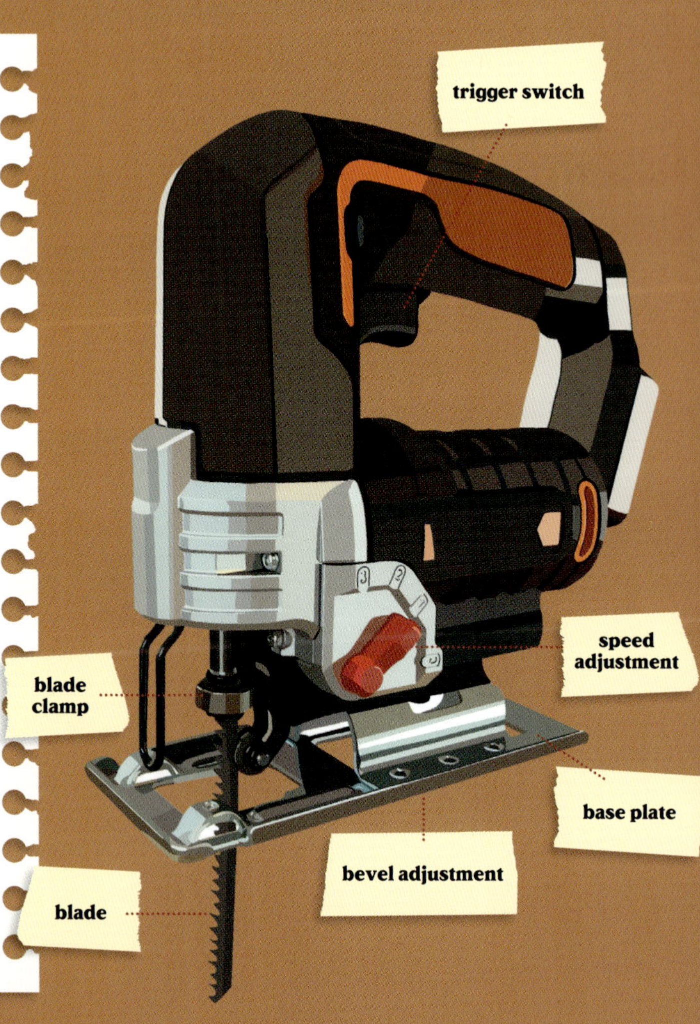

Using a jigsaw

Before we cut anything, we need to draw our cut line and set the wood up ready for cutting. The jigsaw blade is quite long and will protrude out of the bottom of the material, so ensure your setup allows for blade length and make sure there isn't anything underneath the workpiece that the blade might run into – this includes clamps, wires and, most importantly, your precious self. I like to set mine up across two work surfaces with a space in between where I'll line up the cut line. Ensure the wood is clamped on one side to keep it in place while you cut.

set up for cutting

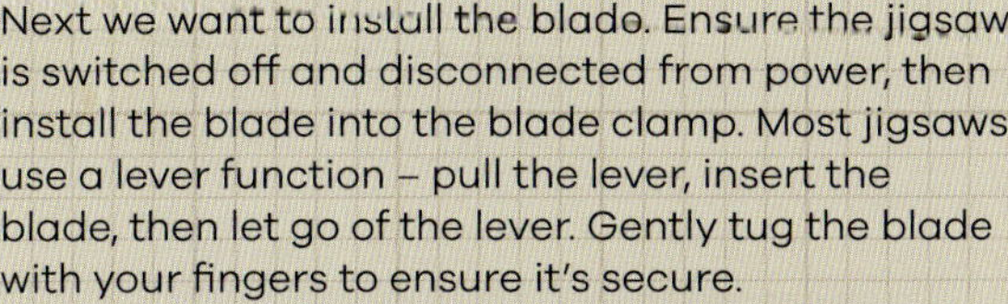

Next we want to install the blade. Ensure the jigsaw is switched off and disconnected from power, then install the blade into the blade clamp. Most jigsaws use a lever function – pull the lever, insert the blade, then let go of the lever. Gently tug the blade with your fingers to ensure it's secure.

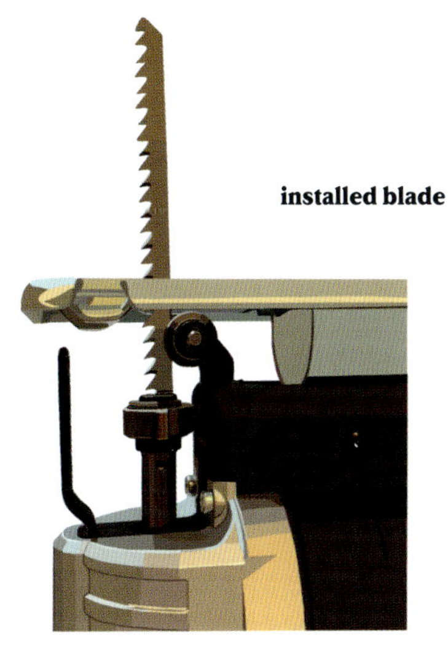

installed blade

Set the speed on the speed adjustment dial. Generally the harder the material, the slower the speed, and the softer the material the higher the speed. Read the manual for your particular saw to check what setting you need.

Now we're ready to cut. Connect the jigsaw to power, but keep it switched off, and rest the front of the base plate on the wood. Make sure the blade isn't touching the wood just yet. We need the blade to get up to speed before it comes into contact with the wood.

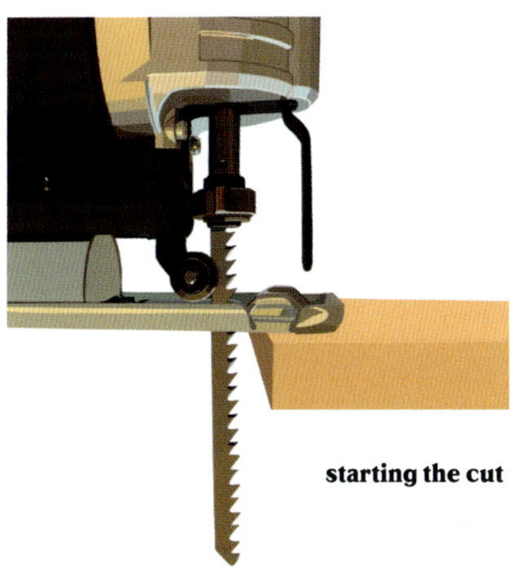

starting the cut

Press the trigger switch and wait a moment for the blade to get up to speed. For starting the cut, I recommend using about half pressure on the trigger so the blade is moving fast, but it isn't at full speed. Then gently push the saw forwards into the wood to begin cutting. Once you're into the wood, you can gradually up the pressure on the trigger to increase the speed. While you need to keep a gentle forwards pressure on the saw to move through the cut, be careful not to push too much – if you feel the saw struggling, it's likely that you're trying to move too fast. Follow the cut line, moving the saw to follow any curves. If you find yourself veering off the desired cut line, or feel a little out of control, ease up on the trigger a little to slow the blade down. The base plate should remain flat on top of the wood for the entirety of the cut.

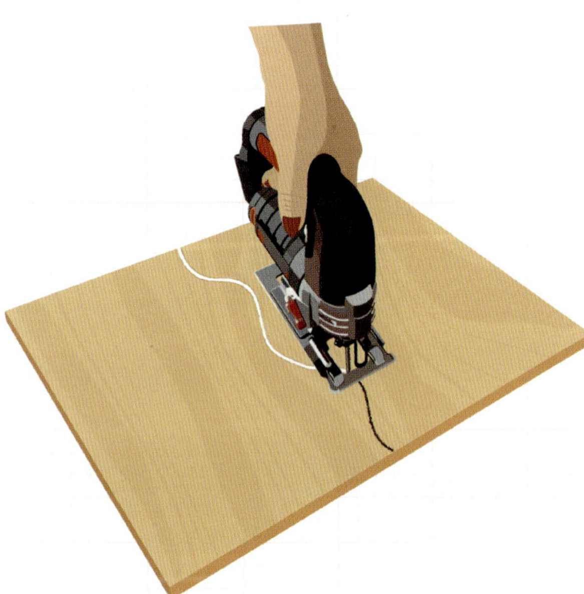

As you approach the end of the line, ease the pressure on the trigger a little to slow down the blade and ensure you have steady control of the tool as you complete the cut. The jigsaw blade will get hot during the cut, so be sure to let it cool down before removing it.

Cutting straight lines

While a jigsaw's stand-out characteristic is being able to cut curves, you can still use one to make straight cuts. The easiest way to do this is to clamp a straight guide onto the wood for the base plate to guide against as you make the cut. The guide can be anything with a straight edge like a length of wood, a speed square or a spirit level. A jigsaw blade has quite a bit of flex to it, so while straight cuts are possible, the flex of the blade can reduce the accuracy.

Tear out

As with all saws, you'll likely see some tear out when making a cut (see The Essentials: Cutting Wood). As jigsaws cut on an upstroke, you'll see tear out on the top side of the wood, so always cut with the good side facing down when you can. The easiest way to reduce tear out on the top side is to stick down painter's tape along the cut line.

Internal cuts

If you want to make an internal cut – that is, if you want to cut a shape out in the middle of the wood and not start from the edge – you can do this by using a starter hole. Drill a hole on the waste side of the shape, using a drill bit that's slightly bigger than the jigsaw blade.

Now you can slot the jigsaw blade in through the hole, power it on and cut around your guide line.

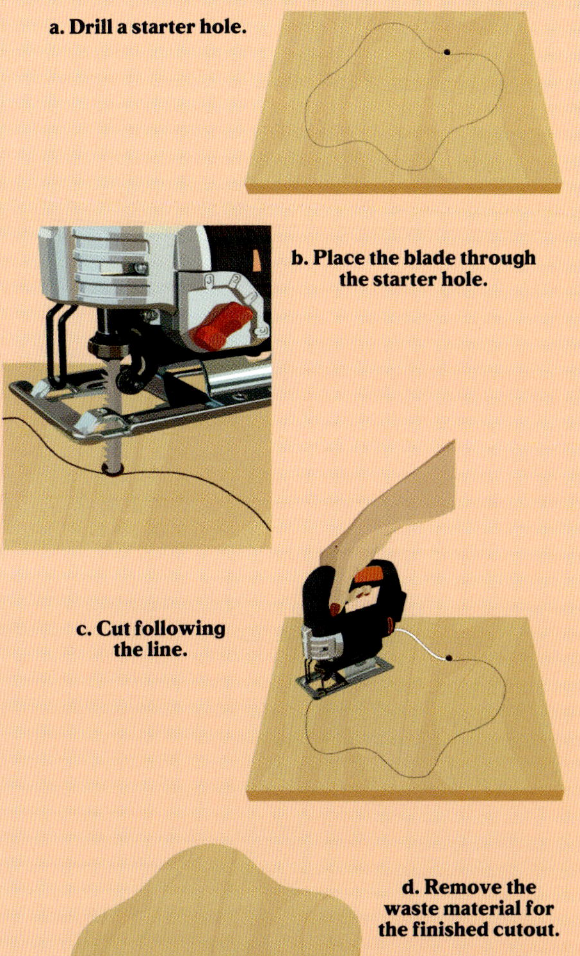

a. Drill a starter hole.

b. Place the blade through the starter hole.

c. Cut following the line.

d. Remove the waste material for the finished cutout.

Coping saw

If you're going down the hand-tool route, cutting curves and shapes can be achieved in much the same way as a jigsaw using a coping saw (see The Essentials: Cutting Wood). For internal cuts, you can drill a hole on the waste side of the cut line, then detach one end of the blade from the handle, slide it through the hole and reattach the blade.

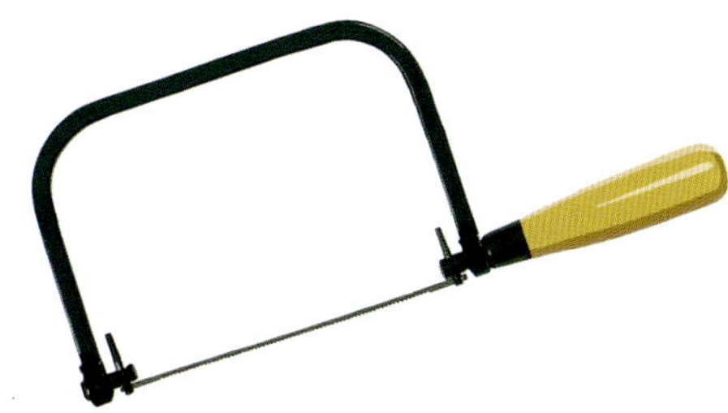

To sum up

- Ensure the space beneath the cut line is free from obstructions.
- Harder materials need a slower speed; softer materials need a higher speed.
- Internal cuts require a starter hole larger than the jigsaw blade.
- Be sure to read the user manual for your specific jigsaw and follow the manufacturer's instructions.

I love the possibilities a jigsaw provides. Cutting curves, wavy lines and organic shapes brings a whole new dimension to a project. There are some very affordable jigsaws available and as a jigsaw is also capable of making straight and angled cuts, it's a great budget-friendly option for beginners. If you haven't got your hands on a jigsaw yet, you don't have to miss out on the next projects – you can simply skip the parts that use a jigsaw, keeping the wood square.

PROJECT

The Shoe Rack

I'm obsessed with this design. It's simple to make but also incredibly functional and aesthetically pleasing – and it's easy to customise to fit your style. If you don't have a jigsaw, just skip step 2 and you'll have a square shoe rack instead of wiggles.

Tools:

- Jigsaw
- Sander
- Drill

Supplies:

- 15mm (5⁄8in) Forstner drill bit
- Painter's tape
- Wood glue
- Stain (optional)
- Clear coat (optional)

Cutting list:

- x2: 30 x 30 x 1.8cm (11¾ x 11¾ x ¾in)
- x4: 82 x 1.5 x 1.5cm (32¼ x 5⁄8 x 5⁄8in) round dowels

The length of the round dowels will dictate how wide the final shoe rack is – you can adjust this measurement to meet your needs.

Cut the wood to the cutting list and sand each piece up to 180 grit.

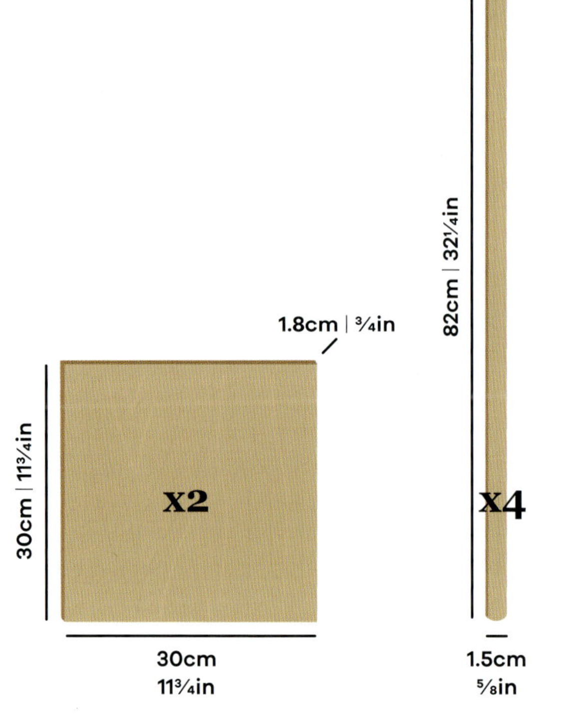

1

First, we need to tape the two 30cm (11¾in) squares on top of each other, ensuring the edges are aligned flush. We're going to keep these pieces taped together for the next few steps, so be sure to tape them well.

2

Next up is cutting the wiggly ends. To do this, draw your desired shape along the face of the board, close to the edge, then cut it out using the jigsaw. Having the two pieces taped together for this step means we're going to create the exact same wiggly shape on both pieces. I practiced drawing the wiggly by hand on a piece of paper until I was happy (it took more attempts than I wish to admit), then I copied it onto the wood.

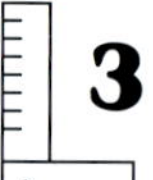

3

Now we need to mark the holes for drilling. Keeping the two pieces taped together, place the workpiece down on your worktop with the wiggly side to your left. Measure 4cm (1⅝in) from the bottom and draw a horizontal pencil line from right to left. Repeat at 18cm (7in) from the bottom. On each line, and measuring from the right-hand side, cross your horizontal with a short vertical line at 9cm (3½in) and 22cm (8⅝in). Where the lines intersect is where we'll drill the holes for the round dowels.

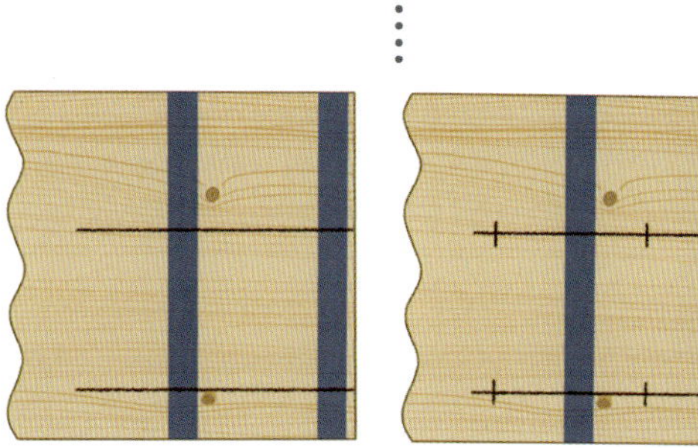

TIP

It's worth noting that I've based the placement of the dowels on the size of my shoes – if you have particularly small or large shoes in your household you may want to adjust the distance between the holes.

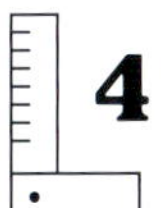

4

Using a 15mm (5⁄8in) Forstner bit, and with the two pieces still taped together, drill each hole all the way through. Be sure to place a piece of scrap wood underneath so you don't drill into your worktop.

Remove all of the tape to separate the two pieces and then take some time to hand sand the wiggly edges up to 180 grit.

5

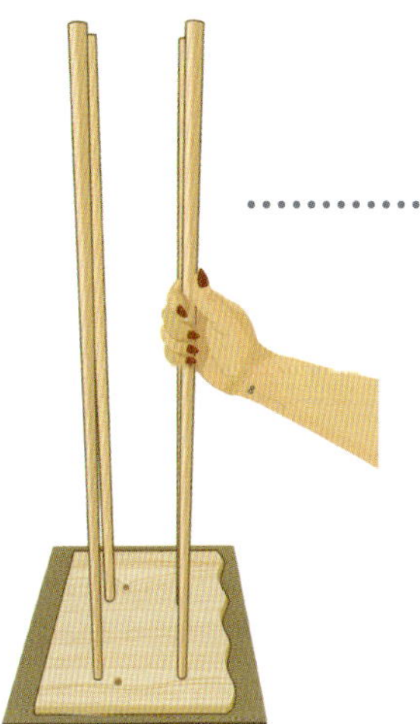

Using a small brush or toothpick, apply some glue to the inside edges of each hole, then place in the dowels. I found it easiest to lay one piece flat on the ground and push the dowels in until they were flush with the floor, but if you're doing it this way, lay a piece of paper underneath so you don't get any glue on your floor. Flip the piece over and push the dowels into the second piece. Remove any glue squeeze out with a damp cloth.

Once the glue is dry, give the piece a final sand to ensure any glue is removed and the dowels are flush in the holes. The last step is to add whatever finish you'd like. I stained mine in a dark oak colour and sealed it with a few coats of varnish.

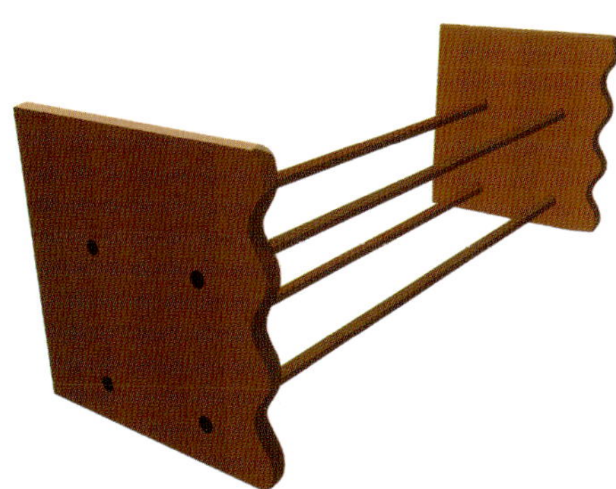

SWITCH IT UP

If wiggly lines aren't your thing, you can adjust this design however you like. For a sleek, minimal look, leave the pieces square. Or cut an arched shape for a softer look. You could also stack a few on top of each other, attaching them securely, to create a taller rack with more shelves. Go wild.

The Mirror

With this design, the shelf pieces slot into the spaces in between the decorative strips on the backboard and hold firm without adhesive – so you can change it up whenever you want, and add as many shelves as you like. If you don't have a jigsaw, just keep the backboard square.

Tools:

- Jigsaw
- Drill
- Sander

Supplies:

- 20cm (7¾in) diameter mirror
- Sticky tabs
- Wood glue
- Clamps
- Screws
- Stain (optional)
- Clear coat (optional)

Cutting list:

- x1: 44 x 30 x 1.8cm (17⅜ x 11¾ x ¾in)
- x14: 30 x 1.8 x 0.8cm (11¾ x ¾ x ¼in)
- x1: 12 x 30 x 1.8cm (4¾ x 11¾ x ¾in)
- x1: 18 x 4.4 x 1.8cm (7 x 1¾ x ¾in)
- x1: 12 x 4.4 x 1.8cm (4¾ x 1¾ x ¾in)
- x1: 8 x 4.4 x 1.8cm (3⅛ x 1¾ x ¾in)

Cut the wood to the cutting list and sand each piece to 180 grit.

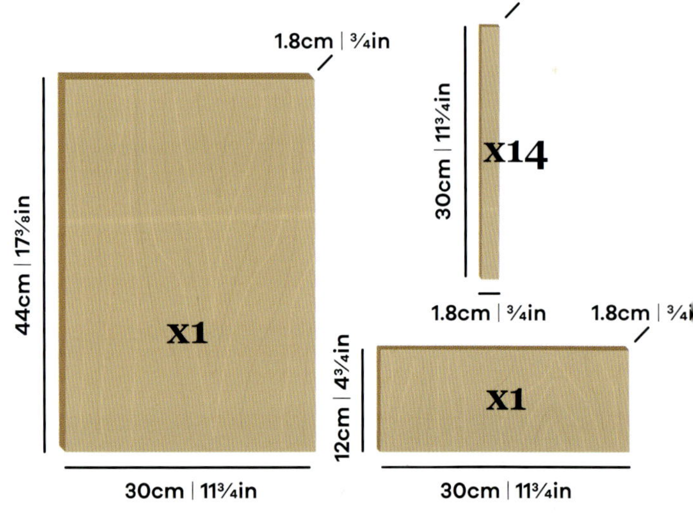

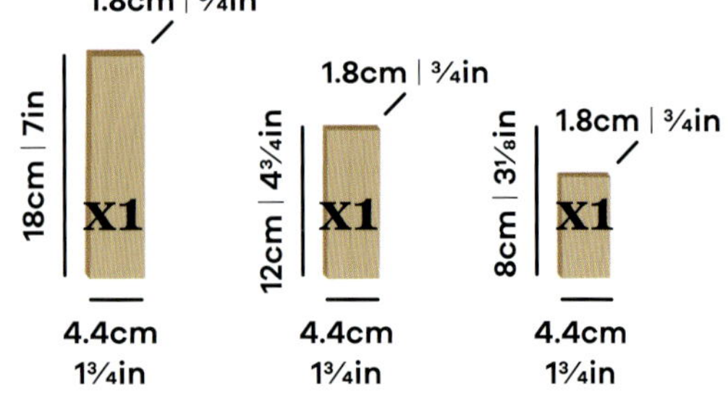

These three 4.4cm (1¾in) wide pieces are the shelf pieces. Cut as many as you want to whatever length you'd like.

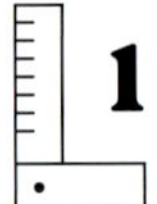

First, we'll glue the thin strips onto the backboard. Grab the 44cm (17⅜in) piece and lay it flat. Glue one of the 30 x 1.8cm (11¾ x ¾in) strips on top of the backboard, ensuring it's flush with the top edge, and clamp it in place until it's dry.

Now using the 4.4cm (1¾in) shelf pieces as spacers between the strips, glue a few strips down at a time. Allow them to dry before proceeding with the next few strips. Repeat until all strips have been glued into position. Place something heavy on top to clamp the strips down until the glue is dry.

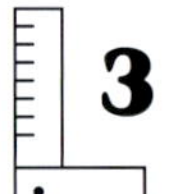

Once the glue is dry, flip the board over and draw a semicircle on the back, marking where we're going to cut with the jigsaw to make the arch shape. I used the pin and string method for this, attaching a pin and a pencil to opposite ends of a piece of string, pushing the pin into the centre of the upper part of the board, then holding the string taut and using it to guide the pencil around to draw a semi-circle. You could also use a plate or other circular object to draw around.

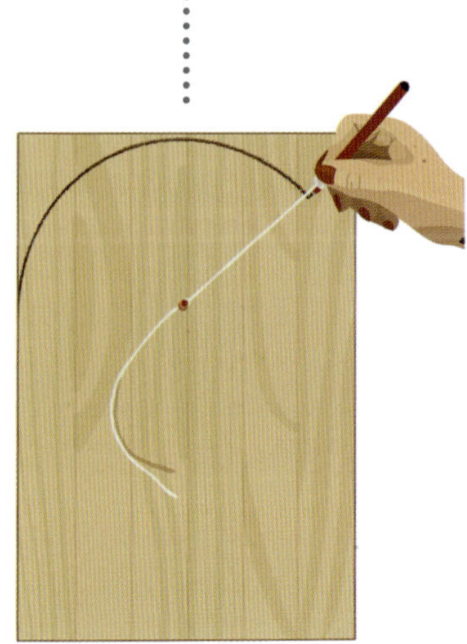

TIP

It's important to note that adding stain and clear coat to the project once it's assembled is going to add a fraction more thickness to the wood, so you don't want to position the strips too tightly against the shelf spacers in step 2. If you plan to use a thick finish such as varnish or poly, fold a piece of paper in half and use that along with the shelf piece as your spacer.

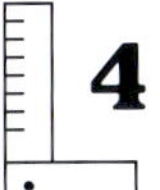

4

Proceed to cut out the curved shape using the jigsaw, then sand the exposed edges up to 180 grit.

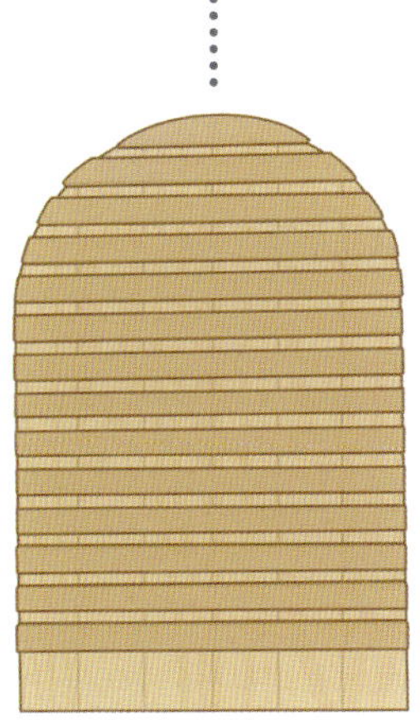

5

Now it's on to attaching the 12 x 30cm (4¾ x 11¾) base. Clamp the two pieces together, then drill and countersink the pilot holes before driving in the screws.

Complete the workpiece and shelf pieces in your chosen finish. I stained mine in a pine colour and added a few thin coats of varnish. It's important not to have too much finish build up in between the slats (see Tip), otherwise the shelves won't slot in and out easily, so be mindful to keep the coats thin and evenly covered.

Add a few sticky tabs onto the backboard and stick down the mirror. Now slot the shelf pieces in between the strips wherever you want them.

SWITCH IT UP

You can keep the backboard square if you're not into the arch look, or you can skip the mirror and just use this project for shelving.

The Upcycle

Not every project needs to be built from scratch. Upcycling is a great way to add your own style to an existing piece as well as save it from landfill.

Solid wood

Solid wood can be expensive to buy new, but there's an abundance of good-quality bargains to be found in second-hand shops. These can be sanded back raw, then refinished, allowing the piece to evolve with your taste. Most of my furniture was once light wood, but when I became drawn to darker tones, I didn't replace it – I simply sanded it all back and stained it with my new favourite shade. Wood does need to be completely raw in order to be stained, so be sure to remove any existing finish thoroughly. Start at 80 grit, and work through up to 180 grit.

Accents

Another great way to personalise existing furniture is with wooden accents. I'm obsessed with slatted furniture at the moment. Adding strips of wood to drawer fronts adds interest and texture. You can use flat strips, half round moulding or D-shape moulding. Subtle flairs can also transform a piece, like adding scalloped details to the base of a dresser, or adding box moulding to wardrobe doors.

Paint

Painting furniture is an easy way to bring your personal style to an existing piece of furniture. I like to keep a good amount of wood visible, but I love a colour-drenched look such as painting the bottom half of a nightstand in a single solid colour while leaving the top half of the wood untouched. Painting the bottom half of table legs is a great way to add a small pop of colour. If you're feeling really adventurous, go wild and paint a geometric pattern on a dining table or an abstract mural on a bookshelf.

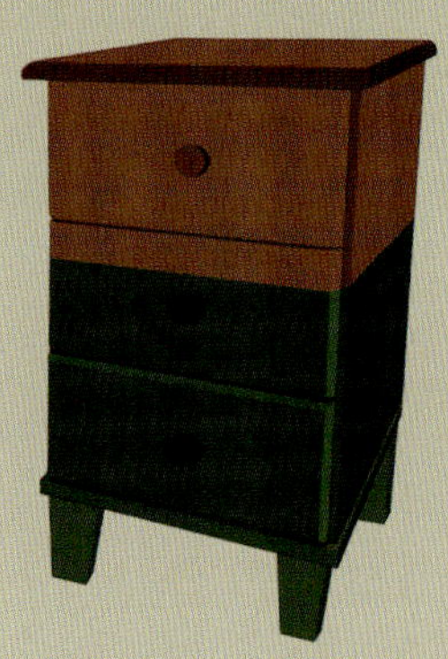

About the Router

Learning how to use a router was my woodworking Everest. I owned mine for several years before I used it – it terrified me and tutorials just left me more confused...

One day my tattoo artist offered a trade swap: make her something in return for a tattoo. The thing she wanted me to make required a router, but I wasn't about to give up this opportunity – so it was time to learn. Imagine my surprise when I realised it wasn't anywhere near as scary or complicated as I thought. It's now one of my favourite tools, and I use it all the time.

I got a snowglobe tattoo, by the way.

What is a router?

A router is a power tool that spins a router bit at high speed to cut, shape and trim wood. There are lots of different types of router bits, allowing for a variety of uses.

There are a few different types of routers – we'll talk about plunge routers later in the chapter, but for now we'll focus on fixed-base and palm routers. The only real difference is that a fixed-base router is larger and more powerful, while a palm router is more compact and less powerful, but usually more affordable. Both are operated in the same way.

- **Base plate** – this is the part of the tool that rests on the wood while cutting.
- **Collet** – the collet is where the router bit is installed.
- **Depth adjustment** – this adjusts how much of the router bit protrudes from the base plate.
- **Power switch** – this powers the router on and off.
- **Router bit** – this is what cuts the wood.
- **Speed adjustment** – this adjusts the speed at which the router bit spins.

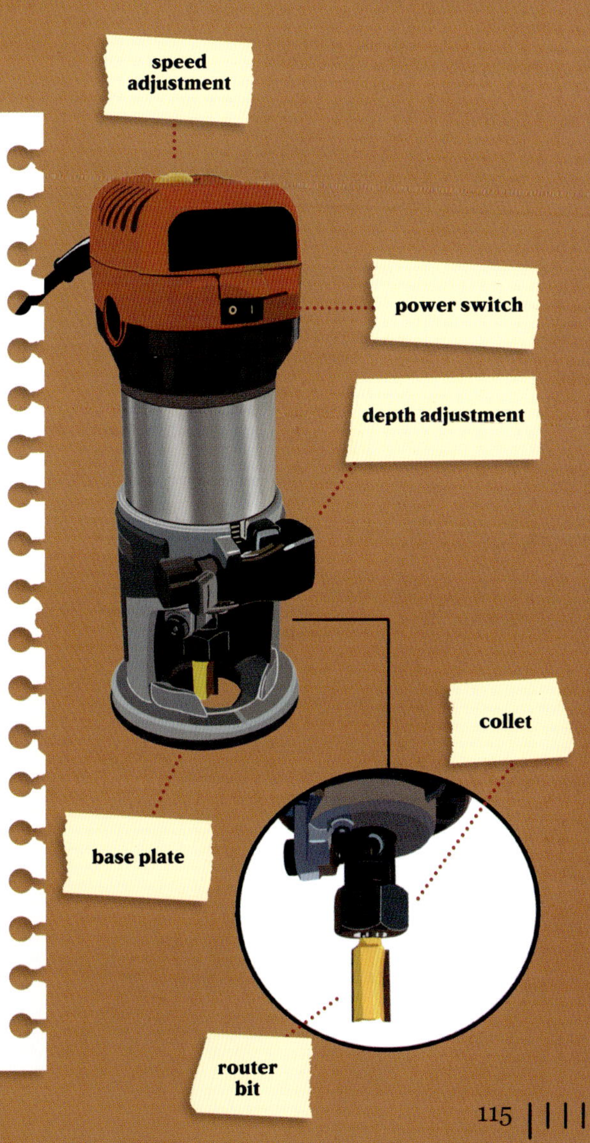

Router bits

The variety of router bits available – and what we can create with them – is what makes this tool so exciting. There are far too many to list here, so I'll cover a handful of the most common ones. I strongly recommend looking up other router bits, as some of the decorative ones are really cool.

Straight bit – the most commonly used bit is the straight bit, which cuts channels into the wood. Straight bits are used to achieve all sorts of things, especially dado joints, where a groove is cut into one piece of wood for another piece of wood to slot into.

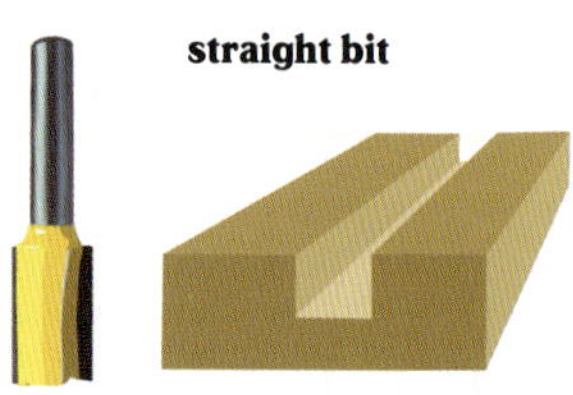

Flush trim bit – this can be used to trim the edge of a piece of material flush with another piece. It has a bearing that glides against one surface and cuts the adjoining surface to match.

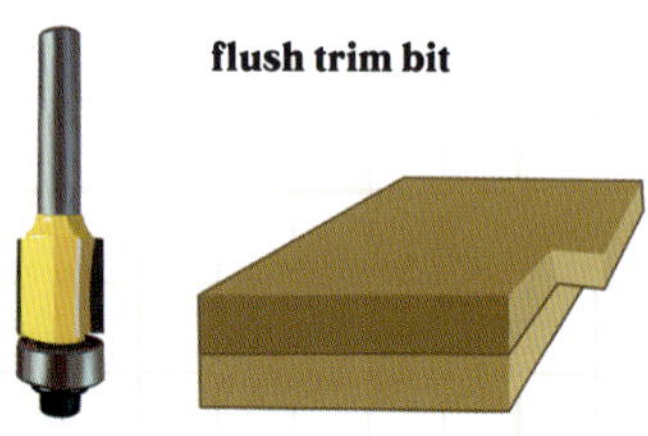

Roundover bit – This is my favourite bit to use. It cuts away the sharp corners of wood to create a rounded edge instead.

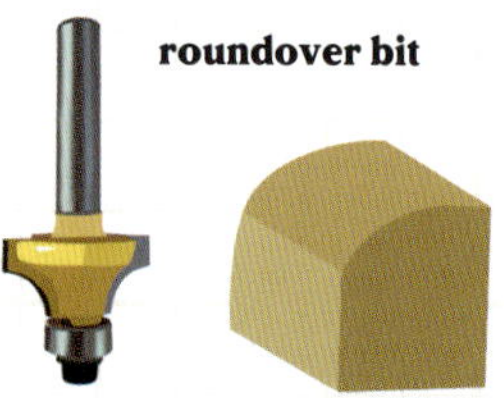

Chamfer bit – this is used to cut away the sharp corners of the wood to create a sloped finish on the edge.

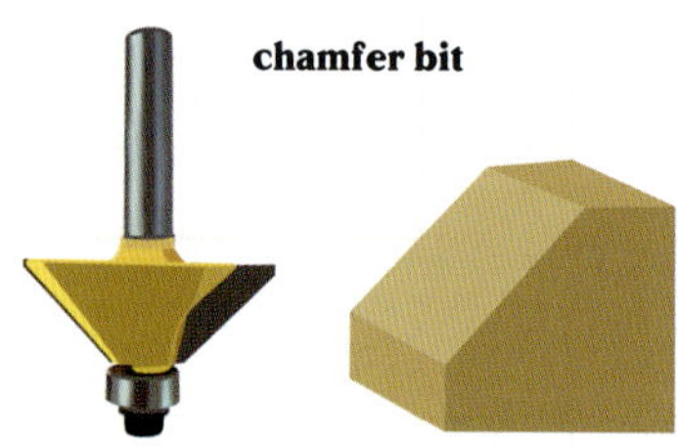

Cove box bit – this decorative bit creates half round grooves in the surface of the wood.

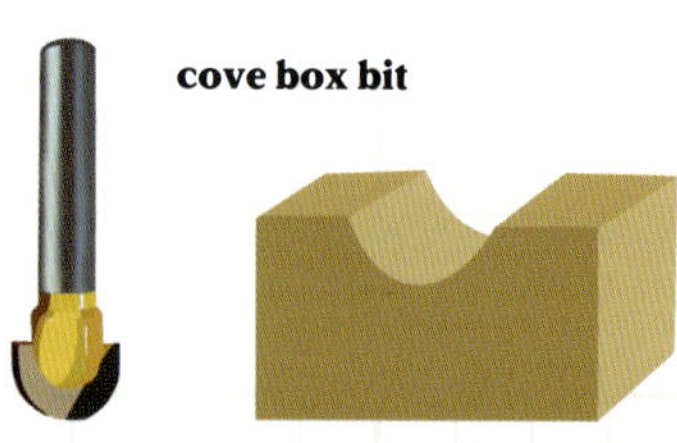

Shank size

It's worth noting that bits have two different shank size options: ¼in and ½in. Which one you need will be dependent on what size your router can take. Palm routers can usually only take ¼in bits, while fixed base routers can usually manage both.

How to use a router

To use a router, first install the router bit. Ensure the tool is switched off and disconnected from power, loosen the collet, insert the bit, then tighten the collet again. The collet is the part of the router that spins when powered on, so it needs to be held stationary to tighten or loosen it. Some routers have a locking button that holds the collet in place and you use a spanner to loosen or tighten it. Other routers have a two spanner system – one holds the collet in place and the other adjusts it. Be sure to follow the user manual for your specific router.

Next, set the depth – this adjusts how much of the bit sticks out of the base plate and, therefore, how deep a cut it makes in the wood. Don't make a deep cut in one pass, as this can cause the wood to burn and also puts too much stress on the router. How deep you can cut in one pass will be covered in your user manual, but it's usually around 3mm (⅛in). To create a deeper cut, start with a shallow cut, switch the router off, increase the depth a little and pass over the cut again. Continue to adjust gradually until you reach the desired depth.

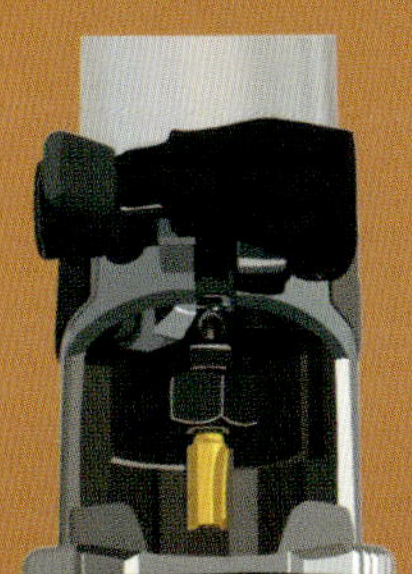

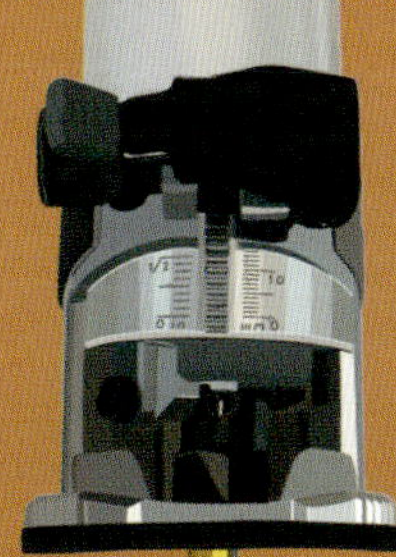

setting the depth

A speed adjustment dial sets the speed of the router. Refer to the user manual for the correct speed, as it depends on the router, the material and the bit you're using. Generally, the larger the bit, the lower the speed.

Ensure the workpiece is securely clamped to your work surface, then rest the base plate on the wood – don't let the bit touch the wood yet. Turn the router on and give it a few seconds to get up to full speed. If the router bit comes into contact with the wood before this, it'll cause kickback, so be sure to give it a moment.

Now ease the router forwards into the wood and start to cut.

starting the cut

Cut moving from left to right, or anticlockwise. This is so you're cutting in the opposite direction to the spinning of the bit, which stops the router pulling itself along and gives you more control. Keep both hands firmly on the router during operation.

cutting

Once the cut is complete, power off and – this is really important – wait for the bit to stop spinning before setting the router down on the work surface. Once it's completely still, you can place it down safely. Bits get hot, so allow it to cool down before removing it.

Shaping edges

A router bit that shapes the edges of the wood, such as a roundover or chamfer, is operated in much the same way as one that cuts into the face grain. The only difference is once you're up to full speed, you push the router into the wood until the bearing on the bit makes contact with the edge. You won't need to visually check this, you'll feel it. Then you can guide the router along the edge of the workpiece, keeping the bearing in contact with the edge of the wood at all times.

Fences and guides

As with most handheld tools, if you want to cut in a straight line with a router it's best to use a fence or guide. Most routers come with a fence that attaches directly to them. It consists of a straight edge that glides along the edge of the wood and a sliding mechanism that adjusts the distance between the router bit and the edge of the wood.

Alternatively, you can clamp anything with a straight edge onto the material, such as a piece of scrap wood, to guide the router against, just like with a circular saw.

Router burn

You may experience some scorch marks on the wood when using a router. This can be due to a number of things: the router speed is set too high, you're trying to cut too deep in one pass, or the router is moving too slowly on the material.

Check the required speed based on your router and the router bit. Generally, the larger the bit the lower the speed. Remember, if you need to make a deep cut, do it in several passes, cutting a little more deeply each time. You should aim to cut about 3mm (⅛in) at a time.

It can be hard to get your speed right when moving the router across the material. You want to go slowly enough so the router bit can cut cleanly through the wood without causing "chatter marks" (little scratches or lines in the wood instead of a clean surface), but you need to go fast enough that there isn't a buildup of heat that will cause the wood to scorch. This is really one of those occasions where you'll learn what's best the more you use the tool.

I still find myself making scorch marks from time to time, so don't worry if you do. If you don't mind the look of the scorch marks, just leave them – they'll add character. If you want to remove them, lightly sand them away, or increase the router bit depth by just the tiniest fraction and pass over the cut one more time.

Plunge cuts

A plunge cut is when the cut starts somewhere in the middle of the wood rather than at the edge. Usually, you start to make a cut with the router base plate rested on the edge of the wood, then allow the router bit to reach full speed before entering into the wood. Obviously, if we want to make a cut in the middle of the wood, this method isn't going to work.

This is where plunge routers come in. A plunge router has a spring-loaded base that suspends the bit above the surface of the workpiece. Then, with the router powered on and the bit spinning at full speed, it can be plunged down into the wood to the required depth. You can then continue the cut as usual, and the bit can be released back up at the end of the cut.

A plunge router is ideal for plunge cuts, but they are bulkier and a bit more expensive than the other two types. Most fixed-base routers have plunge-base accessories available that can be attached to the router base to assist with plunge cuts.

It's also possible to make a plunge cut with a fixed-base router without additional accessories. This technique involves resting the base plate on the wood at an angle, so the bit isn't touching the wood, then powering on the router and slowly bringing the base plate down until it's flat on the wood surface. The cut can then be made as usual. This is a simple way to make a plunge cut, but it's not something I'd recommend for beginners. It requires a decent level of comfort and control, so put that in your back pocket until you've spent some time with the tool.

To sum up

- Keep both hands firmly on the router during operation.
- Don't cut too deep in one pass, aim for around 3mm (⅛in) at a time.
- Cut moving from left to right, or anticlockwise.
- Make sure you read the user manual for your specific router and always follow the manufacturer's instructions.

Honestly, I wouldn't necessarily class a router as a beginner's tool. I wanted to include it here because people tell me all the time how intimidated they are by it, just like I was at the start. It's truly nothing to be scared of and it's so versatile, but don't feel like it's something you need to invest in straight away. The next projects use a router, but if you're not ready to dive into the world of routers just yet, I've included alternatives so you don't have to miss out.

PROJECT

The Lap Desk

Whether you're working, gaming or writing, everything's better from the comfort of your bed. This little lap desk can help with just that. If you don't have a router, I've provided alternatives in the steps.

Tools:

- Saw
- Sander
- Router
- Drill

Supplies:

- 6mm (¼in) router roundover bit
- 12mm (½in) router straight bit
- x8: 2cm (⅜in) right angle brackets
- Wood glue
- Screws
- Clamps
- Stain (optional)
- Clear coat (optional)

Cutting list:

- x1: 55 x 30 x 1.8cm (21⅝ x 11¾ x ¾in)
- x4: 25 x 3.4 x 3.4cm (9⅞ x 1⅜ x 1⅜in)
- x4: 19 x 3.4 x 3.4cm (7½ x 1⅜ x 1⅜in)

Cut the wood to the cutting list and sand each piece up to 180 grit.

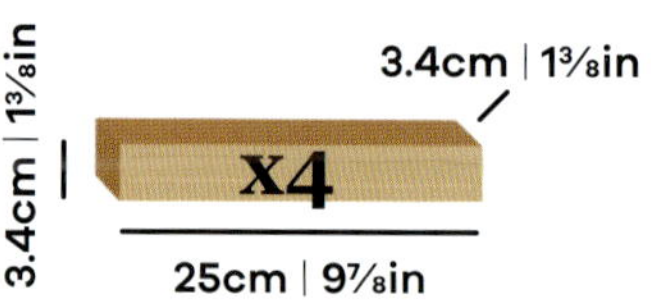

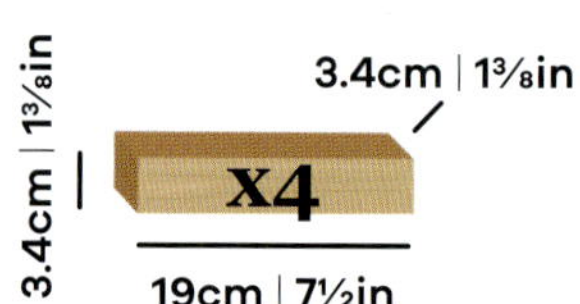

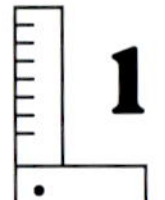

To make the legs of the desk, create a square by placing two 19 x 3.4cm (7½ x 1⅜in) pieces in between two 25 x 3.4cm (9⅞ x 1⅜in) pieces, aligning the edges. Add some wood glue, clamp the pieces in place, drill and countersink two pilot holes on each end, then drive in some screws. Repeat with the other pieces so you have two leg squares.

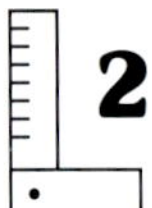

If you have a router, you can use a roundover bit or a chamfer bit to soften the sharp edges on the legs. I used a 6mm (¼in) roundover bit around the outer and inner edges to create a soft rounded finish. If you don't have a router, leave the edges as is.

I cut a groove into the desktop as a tablet holder – there's a few different methods for this depending on what tool you're using.

If you have a router, cut the groove all the way across using a 12mm (½in) straight bit. Clamp a fence in place to cut the groove 3.5cm (1⅜in) from the front edge. The total depth of the groove needs to be 1.4cm (½in), so start by cutting 3mm (⅛in) deep, then increase the depth and pass over the cut again. Continue to do this until the cut is 1.4cm (½in) deep.

If you have a plunge router, you can cut the groove 7cm (2¾in) in from each side.

If you don't have a router at all, use small strips of wood and glue them to the surface to create a faux groove. Or you can forget the groove and leave the wood as is.

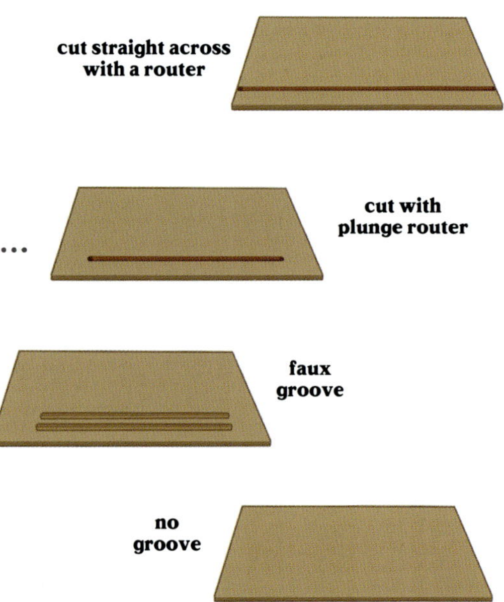

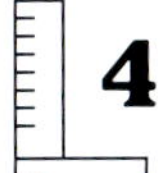

4

Use the 6mm (¼in) roundover bit on the edges of the desktop too. If you don't have a router, you can just skip this.

If you've routed the edges and groove, give those areas a quick sand up to 180 grit. Now finish all the pieces in your chosen finish. I stained mine in a light pine and sealed it with matte varnish.

5

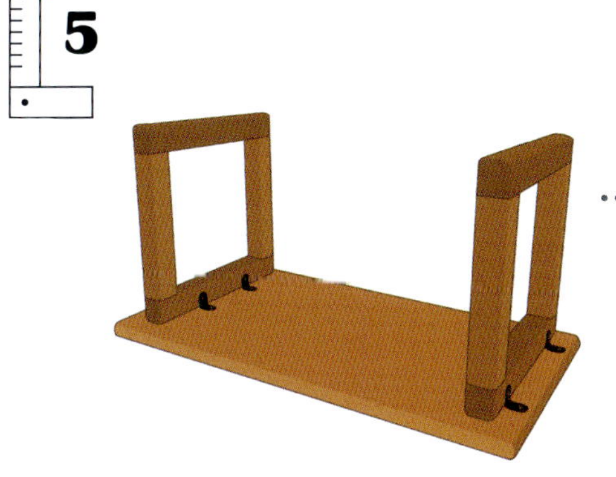

Then it's on to attaching the legs. Place the legs on the underside of the desktop, approx 3cm (1⅛in) in from each edge. Position the right-angle brackets with two on the outside of each leg and two on the inside of each leg as shown. Use a pencil to mark the placement of the fixing holes, then remove the brackets and drill the pilot holes. Place the brackets back into place and drive screws into the pilot holes to secure the legs to the desktop.

And that's it, your lap desk is complete.

SWITCH IT UP

Change up the design however you want! You could use a jigsaw to cut the desktop into an lozenge shape, or you could forget about the legs and make a longer version to use as a bath board.

PROJECT

The Pen Tray

This simple pen tray uses a cove box bit to create rounded grooves in the wood for a sleek final look. If you don't have a router, don't worry, you can still make this project by making fake grooves with scotia moulding (see Switch it Up).

Tools:

- Saw
- Sander
- Router

Supplies:

- 12mm (½in) router cove box bit
- A straight edge (like a piece of scrap wood)
- Clamps
- Stain (optional)
- Clear coat (optional)

Cutting list:

- x1: 30 x 15 x 1.8cm (11¾ x 6 x ¾in)

Cut the wood to the cutting list and sand each piece up to 180 grit.

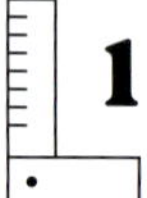

While our final design is going to be smaller when we're finished, we'll start with this larger piece so we have space for clamping it.

Starting approx 10cm (3⅞in) in from one end of the board, draw five lines spaced 1.2cm (½in) apart.

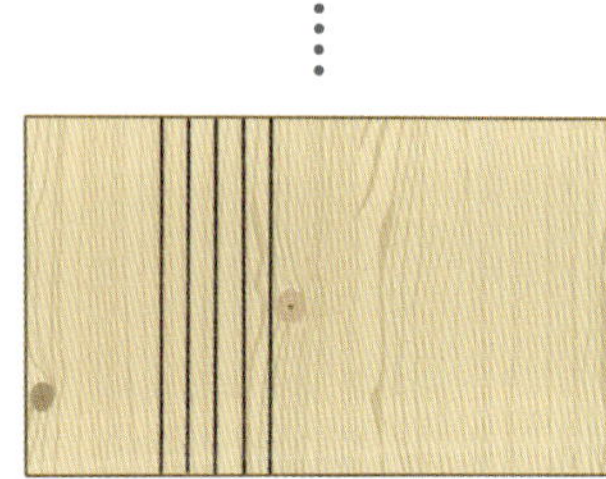

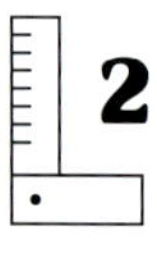

Line the straight edge up to the last line to guide the router, clamping it securely in place.

Install the cove box bit into the router and set the depth to cut approx 3mm (⅛in) deep. Glide the base plate against the straight edge as you complete the cut.

3

Turn the router off, move the straight edge to the next line, clamp it into place and route the next line. Continue with this until all five lines have been routed.

4

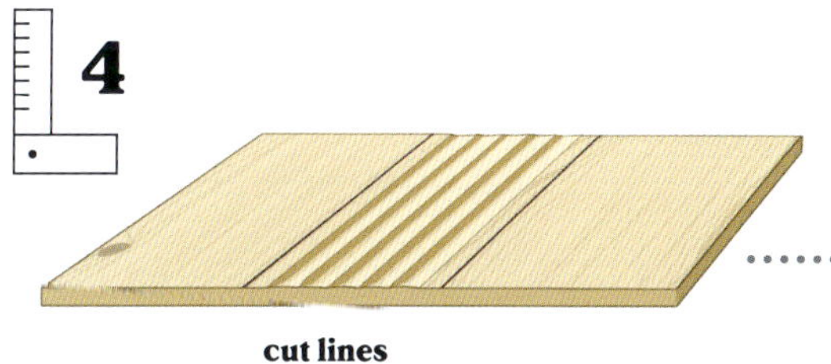

cut lines

The next step is to cut the workpiece down to size. Draw a cut line 1cm (½in) from the outer routed line at each side, then cut off the excess wood. Sand the newly exposed wood up to 180 grit, then sand the routed grooves by hand.

Finish the piece as you want – I really like the simplicity of raw wood, so I skipped the stain and finished it with some wax instead.

SWITCH IT UP

The number of decorative router bits out there opens this project up to so many possibilities –try using a V-groove bit to create triangular cutouts for a sharper look. To achieve the grooves without a router, get some scotia moulding and glue it onto the wood to create the groove effect.

The Jigs

A jig is essentially any template that increases efficiency, speed or accuracy. Usually used for repetitive tasks, jigs can help with things like drilling a neat line of holes or for clamping.

You can buy premade jigs, but many can be made using MDF or scrap wood. There's no master list of jigs you'll need, as it's all dependent on what you're making. If you find yourself repeating a task or if you want to be more precise, think about what you could make to help. We've already looked at using a stop block for making multiple cuts (see The Essentials: Cutting Wood), but here are a couple of more examples to fire your imagination.

Clamping

If you don't have a right angle or corner clamp, make a simple clamping jig from MDF. It's as simple as drilling a hole in the centre of a small square, then cutting a 90 degree section out. The two pieces can then be placed above and below the corner joint with a clamp to secure them together. The drilled hole prevents the jig making direct contact with the joint seam, so the jig won't get glued to the workpiece.

Repetitive drilling

You know those stand-alone bookshelves that have evenly spaced holes along the inside for adjusting the height of the shelves? How would you drill those holes yourself? You could manually measure and mark each hole placement, but it will be quicker and more accurate to make a simple drilling jig. Drill three or four evenly spaced holes into a block of scrap wood. Place it on your workpiece and insert the drill bit into each hole to drill. Once you've drilled the last hole, move the jig along the wood, aligning the first hole in the jig with the hole just drilled, then continue to drill through the guide holes. This will result in dozens of evenly spaced holes with no need to measure each one.

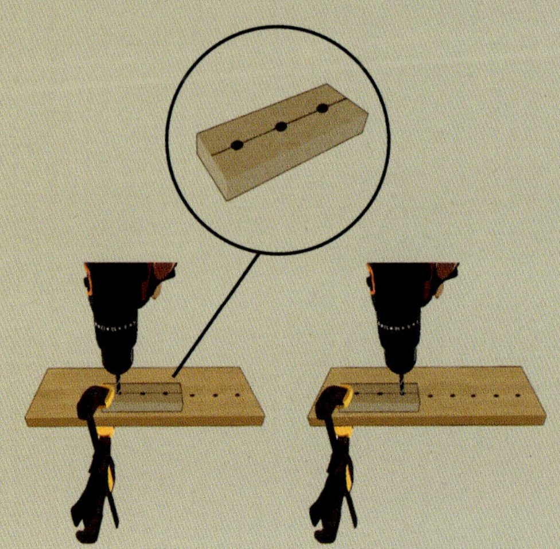

About Circles

Using circles in projects is one of my favourite things to do. Whether it's part of a shelf, a mirror or a lamp, there's just something about a wooden circle that fills my heart with joy. Learning how to cut a circle will open up a whole new world of possibilities for your projects.

What is a circle?

I know you know what a circle is, of course. But, before we look at the methods used for cutting a circle, let's remind ourselves of the important measurements. When it comes to a woodworking project, you're likely to decide what size circle you want based on the diameter, but the cutting methods we'll cover are based on the radius, so let's get familiar with these measurements.

- **Circumference** – the perimeter of the circle.
- **Diameter** – the distance across the circle through the centre.
- **Radius** – the distance from the centre point to the edge of the circle.

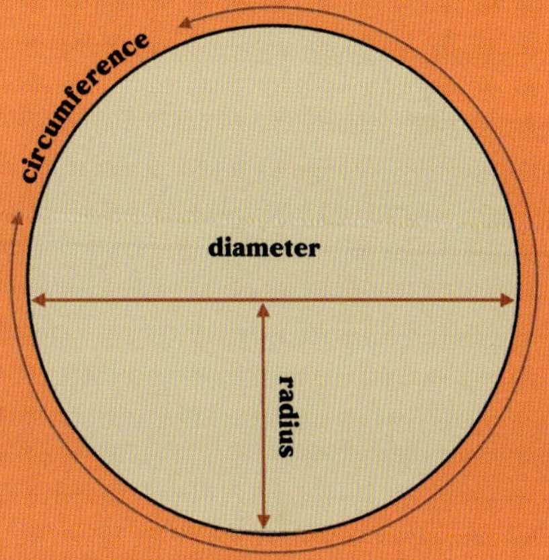

The radius is always half of the diameter. So if you want a 30cm (12in) circle, the diameter is 30cm (12in) and the radius is 15cm (6in).

If you ever need to find the centre of an existing circle, you can do so using a pencil and ruler. Draw three lines from edge to edge on the circle (a). It doesn't matter where the lines are, or even if they're the same length, but it'll be easier if the length of each is easy to halve. Now find the centre of each line and draw a perpendicular line through each one (b). Where these lines intersect is the centre.

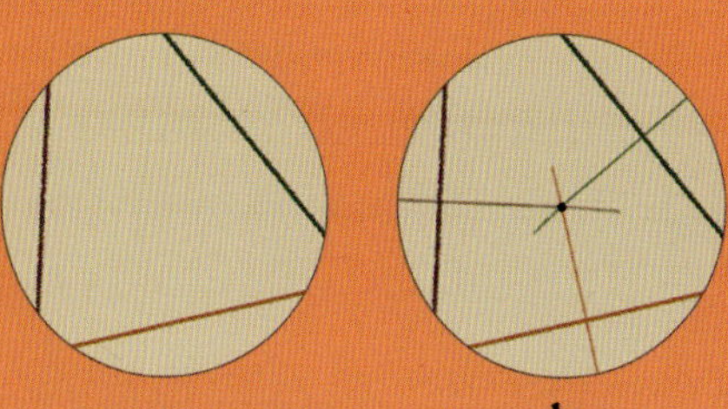

How to cut a circle

There are a lot of different ways to cut a circle from wood. In fact, I'd bet with enough research you could find a method to cut a circle with practically any woodworking tool. I would argue the easiest ways to do it are with either a jigsaw or a plunge router. Let's look at the techniques for these next.

Jigsaw

First draw the circle to be cut. You can draw around a plate or cup, or use the pin and string method as follows. Push a drawing pin into the centre of the wood. Then attach one end of a piece of string to the pin and the other to a pencil. Now draw a perfect circle by keeping the string taut and rotating the pencil around the pin. The length of the string will dictate the radius of the circle.

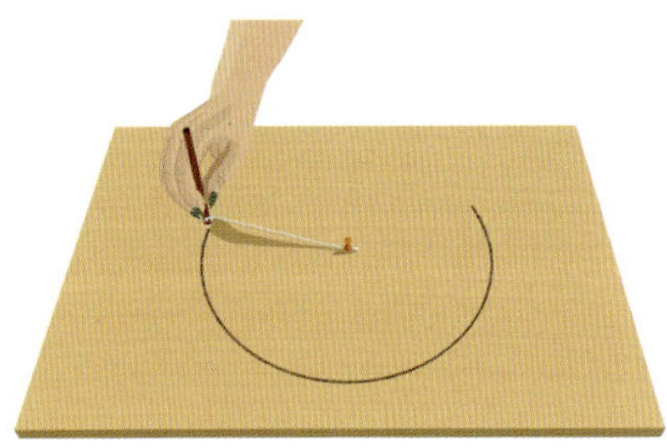

Once you have the circle marked out, you can use a jigsaw to cut it out by following the marked line by hand. It's as simple as that. Once the cut is complete, sand the circle's edge up to 180 grit. I recommend sanding by hand so you can keep the shape consistent – with the power of an electric sander, it can be easy to accidentally misshape the circle. Hand sanding can also be used to refine the circle if you veered off the cut line during cutting.

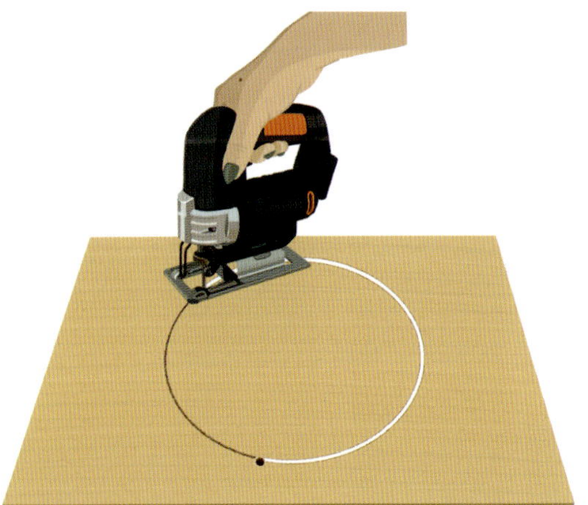

Plunge router

To cut a circle with a plunge router, you'll need a circle cutting jig – it's the method I use the most. You can make a jig yourself using scrap wood or MDF (we'll look at this in a moment), or you can buy one – choose a jig for your specific router model, or get a universal jig where you drill the mounting holes yourself, which means they're compatible with most routers.

When attaching a jig to a router, you'll first need to remove the existing plate that's screwed into the router's base. Then attach the jig to the router base using screws through the mounting holes.

Each circle cutting jig is different, so be sure to follow the manufacturer's instructions, but let's discuss the basics, looking at one example.

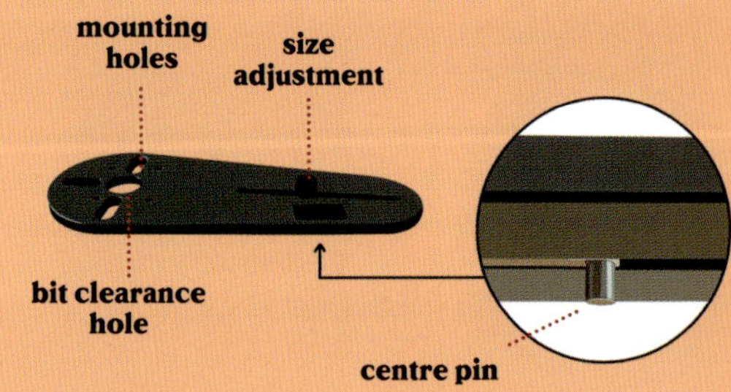

- **Bit clearance hole** – The router bit will extend through this hole to cut the material.
- **Centre pin** – a hole is drilled into the centre of the wood. The centre pin sits in the hole to anchor the jig to the wood so it can spin around to make the cut.
- **Mounting holes** – the base of the router is secured to the jig here using screws.
- **Size adjustment** – this adjusts the distance between the centre pin and the router bit, setting the radius of the circle.

Drill a hole in the centre of the wood for the centre pin to sit in. Use the size adjustment to set the desired radius of the circle. Now set the cutting depth on the plunge router. As always, it's best to cut 3mm (⅛in) at a time, increasing the depth with each pass, until your cut is complete.

Place the pin in the centre hole and ensure the jig is flat on the wood surface. Turn the router on, plunge the router bit into the wood and spin the jig around on the centre pin to cut the perfect circle. Once the cut is complete, hand sand the circle's edge up to 180 grit.

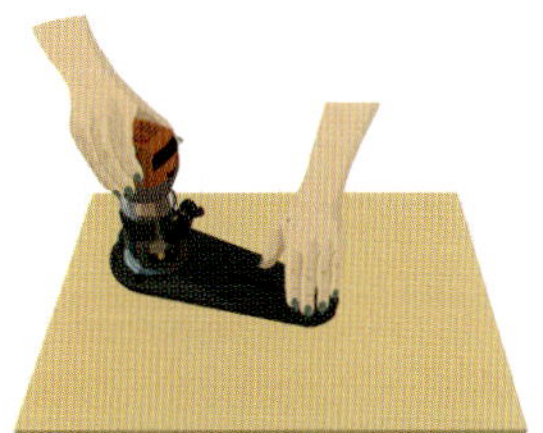

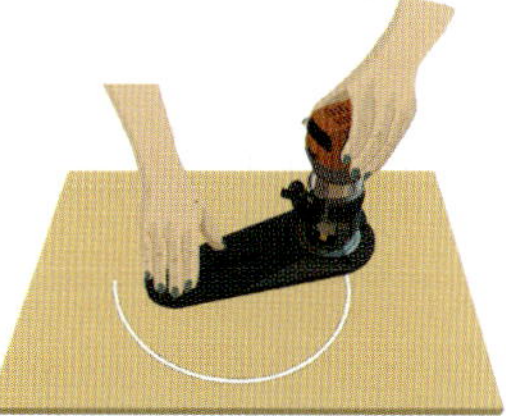

Hand tools

There's a range of hand tools that can be used to cut a circle. I'd suggest using the jigsaw method to cut the circle with a coping saw. Hand sand the circle to smooth the edges and clean up the shape if you find you've strayed from the cut line.

Handmade circle jigs

A circle cutting jig is a guide that attaches to one end of the jigsaw or router, anchoring a central point for the jig to spin around on for precise circle cutting. Here's how to make a simple jig yourself for your jigsaw or router.

Attach the tool to the end of a strip of scrap wood or MDF, with a cutout for the bit or blade to go through. Drill a hole in the jig for the centre point. Now you can hammer a nail into the hole and use that as the anchor to spin the jig around as you make the cut. Drill several holes along the wood for making smaller and larger circles.

To sum up:

- The radius of a circle is half of the diameter.
- Use the pin and string method to draw a circle.
- A circle cutting jig needs a centre point for the jig to spin around.

Using a jigsaw to cut a circle is arguably the simplest method as it uses the least amount of equipment. A router and a circle cutting jig is the most precise method. That being said, if you don't have the tools to cut a circle, or you're just not ready to tackle it yet, you can buy pre-cut circles in a variety of sizes. Also, most projects that use circles (like the two that follow), can usually be made with square wood instead, so there's no need to miss out.

The Circle Stand

Give your most prized possession a new home. Whether it's your favourite plant, a one-of-a-kind vase or a thrift-store antique, this stand is the perfect way to elevate and display beautiful things in your home.

Tools:

- Saw
- Sander
- Drill

Supplies:

- x4: 22mm (⅞in) right angle brackets
- x2: 22mm (⅞in) flat brackets
- Painter's tape
- Stain (optional)
- Clear coat (optional)
- Paint (optional)

Cutting list:

- x4: 25 x 1.5 x 1.5cm (9⅞ x ⅝ x ⅝in)
- x1: 20.5 x 1.5 x 1.5cm (8 x ⅝ x ⅝in)
- x2: 9.5 x 1.5 x 1.5cm (3¾ x ⅝ x ⅝in)
- x1: 20cm diameter x 1.8cm (7⅞in diameter x ¾in) circle

Cut the wood to the cutting list and sand each piece up to 180 grit. If you don't want to cut a circle, buy one pre-cut, or use a 20 x 20cm (7⅞ x 7⅞in) square instead.

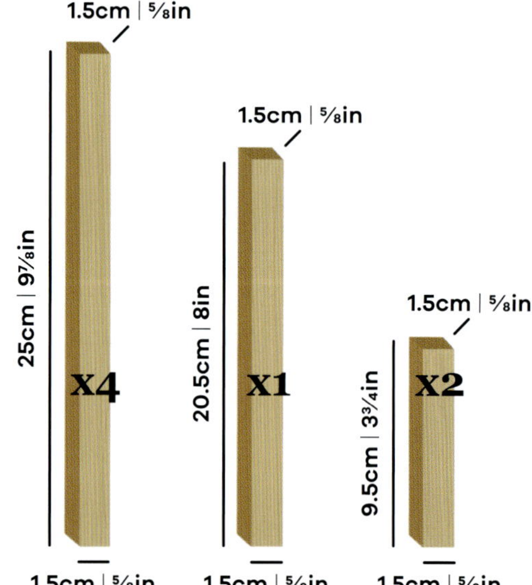

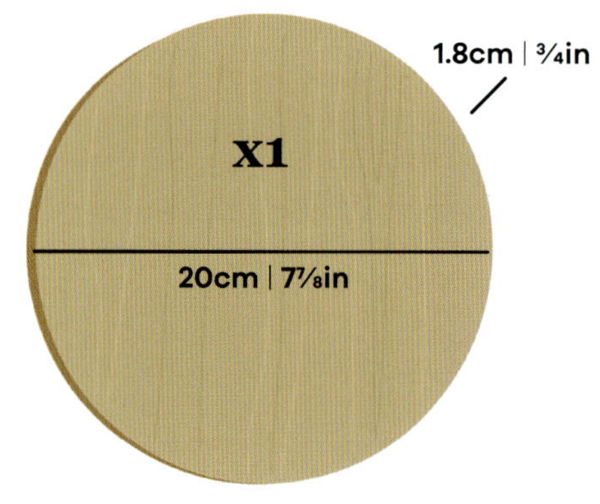

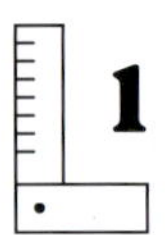

1

To create the cross base, butt the 9.5cm (3¾in) pieces against the middle of the 20.5cm (8in) piece and lay flat brackets across each joint as shown. Mark the hole placements, remove the brackets and drill pilot holes on the marked spots. Place the brackets back and drive screws into the pilot holes.

Place a right-angle bracket onto each end of the cross base, with the flat side of the bracket aligned flush with the end of the wood, then mark the holes with a pencil. Remove the brackets and drill the pilot holes on the marked spots. Place the brackets back and drive screws in to secure them.

2

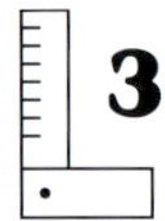

3

Next, line up the four 25cm (9⅞in) pieces so we can mark the holes that need drilling for the other end of the brackets. Add a piece of painter's tape to keep them aligned. Measure 12cm (4¾in) from the top and draw a horizontal line across all four pieces. Mark the centre of the line on each piece with a short vertical line.

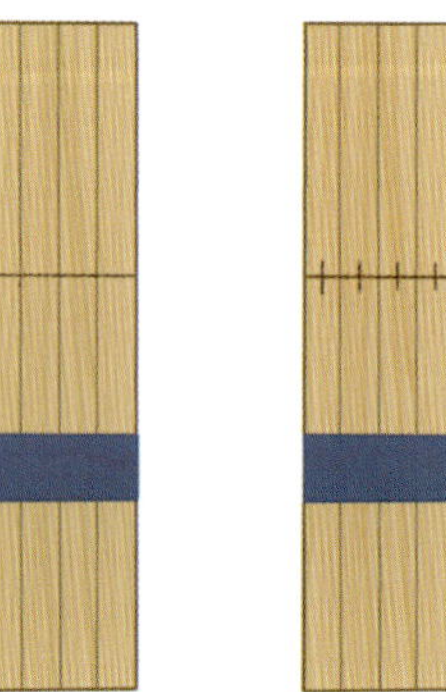

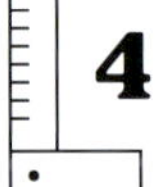

4

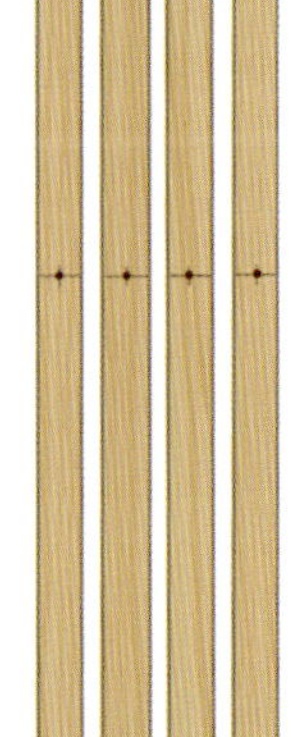

Where the lines intersect is where you'll place the pilot holes. Drill the pilot holes and remove any excess pencil with an eraser or sandpaper.

5 Now attach the cross base to the 25cm (9 ⅞in) pieces by driving screws down through each bracket and into the pilot holes.

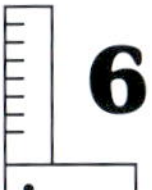

6

Apply your desired finish to both the stand and the circle. Now you can place the circle into the stand and the project is complete. It should be stable enough to leave the circle unattached, but if you have any small beings in your home who might make it their mission to knock things over (I'm thinking cats specifically but children probably fit that description, too) you can drive a few screws through the bottom of the cross base and into the circle to secure it.

I stained my stand and circle in a dark oak and finished with a few coats of varnish. I also decided to add a pop of colour with some colour blocking on the legs.

SWITCH IT UP

You can make this using a square instead of the of circle, or you can double up and attach two circles for an extra shelf.

PROJECT

The Circle Shelf

Back when I had an Etsy store, this was my most popular item. It was also my first viral video, so I guess I have the circle shelf to thank for getting my work seen and allowing me to share this journey with you. If you don't have the ability to cut a circle, remember you can buy one pre-cut.

Tools:

- Saw
- Sander
- Drill

Supplies:

- x3: 22mm (⅞in) square cup hooks
- Hanging hardware
- Painter's tape
- Wood glue
- Screws
- Stain (optional)
- Clear coat (optional)
- Paint (optional)

Cutting list:

- x1: 15cm diameter x 2cm (5⅞ diameter x ¾in) circle
- x1: 15 x 4.4 x 1.2cm (5⅞in x 1¾ x ½in)

Cut the wood to the cutting list and sand each piece up to 180 grit.

2cm | ¾in

x1

15cm | 5⅞in

1.2cm | ½in

15cm | 5⅞in

x1

4.4cm | 1¾in

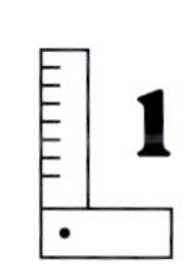
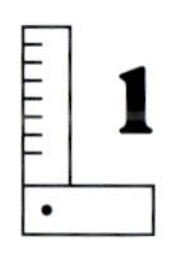

However you cut your circle, you should be left with some sort of pin mark in the centre, which is going to help us align the shelf. Add some glue to the back edge of the 15 x 4.4cm (5⅞in x 1¾in) piece and glue it to the circle, ensuring it covers the centre point and using your fingers to align it flush with the circle's edges. Add some tape to hold the shelf in place while the glue dries.

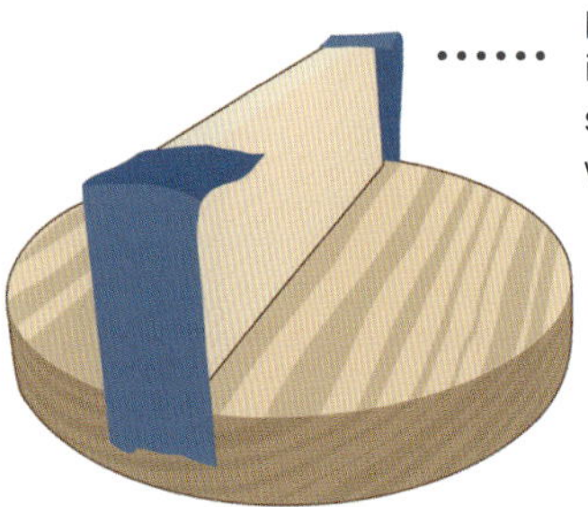

2

As this glued joint has such a small surface, we'll add some extra hardware to strengthen the joint. Drill and countersink two pilot holes through the back and drive in some screws.

Now mark three holes across the front for the hooks. I marked one in the centre then added another at either side, 3.5cm (1⅜in) from the centre hole. Drill the pilot holes on the marks.

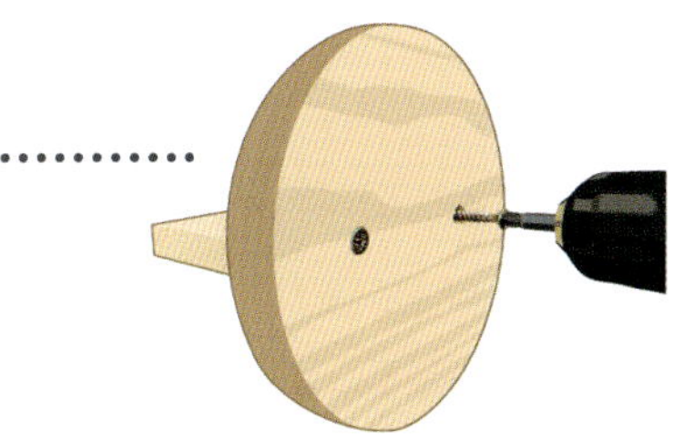

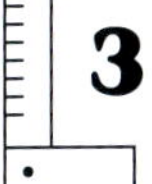

3

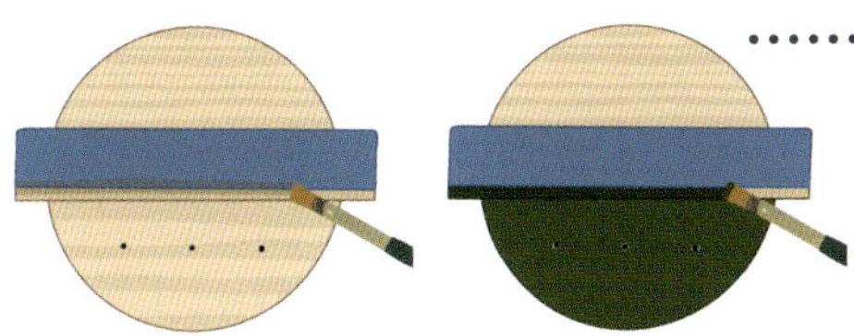

Before adding the hooks, take a moment to add your desired finish. I kept the wood unstained and added a green colour block across the bottom half, using painter's tape to create a crisp clean line, and sealed the whole thing with a few coats of varnish. You can use something small like a toothpick to clear out any paint or finish that gathers in the hook holes.

4

Now screw the cup hooks into the pre-drilled holes by hand. Finish by adding your chosen hanger to the back (see The Wall Fixtures for your best options).

And that's it – you're now the proud owner of a beautiful circle shelf.

About Wood Movement

This is a topic that intimidated me until recently. I would get lost down a rabbit hole of equations and calculations for finding the exact levels of movement to expect, and it all felt far too technical. But once I got my head around it, I realised how simple it was. So now I'm going to break it down for you.

What is wood movement?

Wood movement is only relevant to solid – and not manufactured – wood. As we all know, the trees we are privileged to live alongside are thirsty things, drinking water from the ground through their roots. Well, that doesn't really change when trees start their second life with us as wood. Wood is still thirsty or, more technically, it is hygroscopic. Instead of drawing water from the earth, wood absorbs it from the air. The moisture content of wood changes constantly throughout its life, fluctuating as the seasons change.

Like a sponge, wood expands when its moisture content is high and shrinks when it's low. This is wood movement. It's a gradual change that you won't notice happening, but have you ever had a door that sticks for half of the year, but is fine for the other half? That's wood movement in motion, due to the humidity levels in summer vs winter. There's no way to prevent wood movement; even if a water resistant finish is applied, wood still moves.

The fluctuations in wood barely affect the length of the board (along the grain) – it's the width of the board (across the grain) where the movement happens most.

So why do we care about wood movement? Well, we care because not accounting for it can cause joints to fail and cracks to appear. The last thing we want to do is create a beautiful piece of work only to have it ruined when the joints fail over time. Trust me – the first table I ever built was a coffee table for my brother, but I didn't account for wood movement and within a year one of the joints was busted. But there are things we can do. Simple things. We can't eliminate wood movement – so let's see how to work with it.

The problem with wood movement

We know wood movement happens across the width of the board, not so much on the length. When this movement is restricted, it causes stress on the wood and can lead to cracks appearing or joints failing. This happens when joints are made with the grains going in different directions.

Let's look at an example of a bad joint. As you can see, the bottom board wants to expand widthways (across the grain). The top board has been joined with its grain going the other way, and it isn't going to budge in its length because wood movement is minimal along the grain. So when the bottom board wants to expand or contract across the grain, the top board will prevent it from doing so. This will cause stress on the wood and lead to the wood cracking or the joint coming apart.

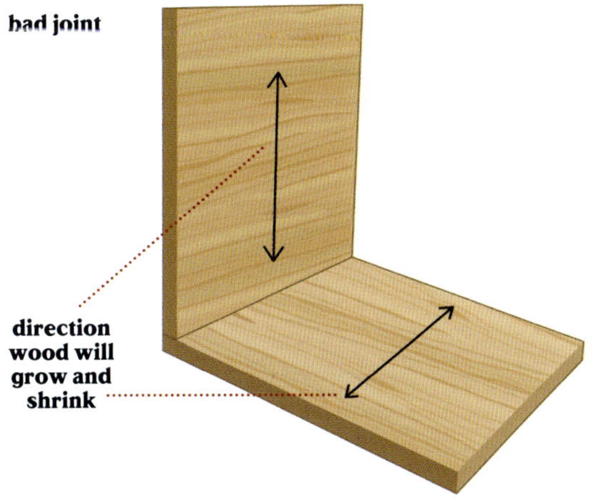

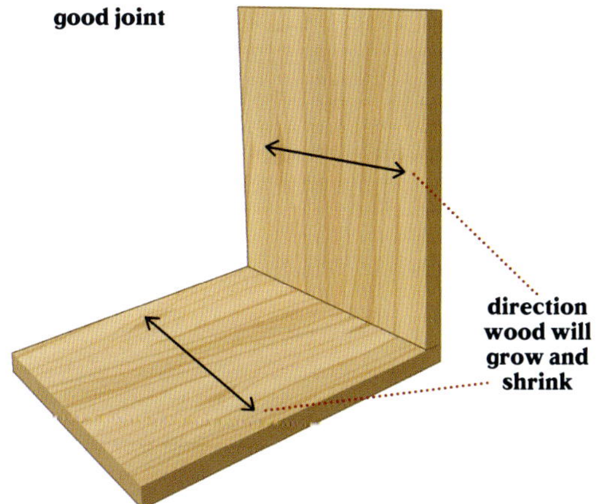

If we use the same set up, but simply rotate the top board so the grain runs in the same direction as the bottom board, then both boards can expand and contract with each other. Grains running in the same direction work harmoniously together – it's that simple.

So when creating any project, pay attention to the direction of the grain and ensure it remains harmonious.

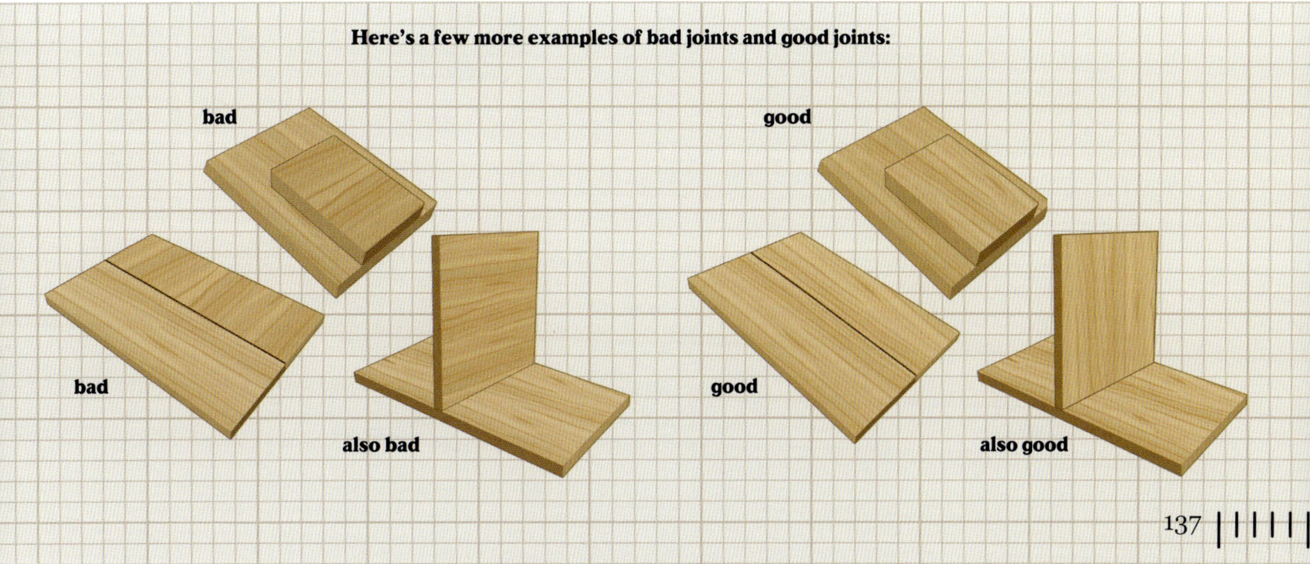

When harmonious grain isn't possible

While a lot of projects can be built using the concept of harmonious grain, it isn't always possible. In these cases, we have to take extra steps. A good example is for a table.

A table tends to consist of two parts: the table top, and the apron and legs. Aprons help support the tabletop and assist with attaching the legs. However, if the apron were to be attached to the tabletop with glue or screws, it would restrict the wood movement of the tabletop.

To account for wood movement, we need to use movement-friendly attachment methods.

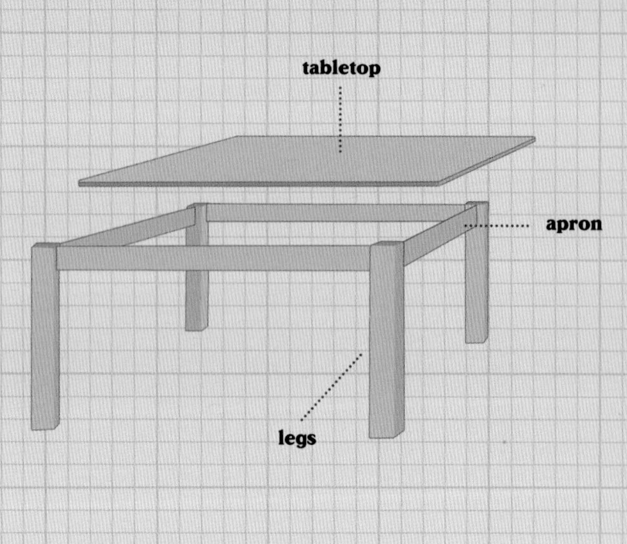

Z clips

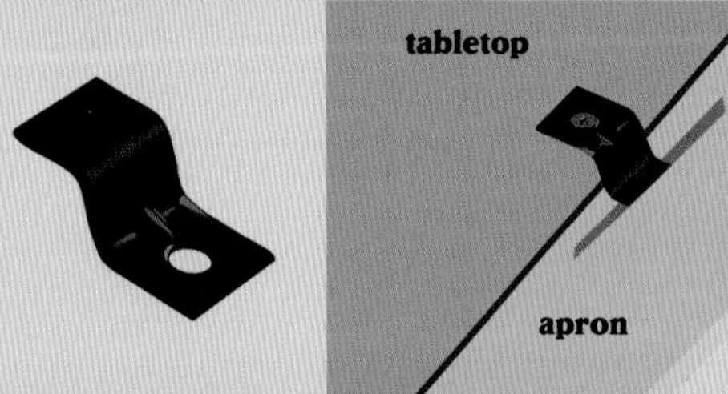

One of the most common methods is using Z clips. Z clips are installed by cutting a slot on the inside edge of the apron that's wider than the Z clip. One end of the clip is then inserted into the slot but not attached, and the other end is attached to the underside of the tabletop with a screw. As the wood moves, the Z clip has room to move across the slot, thus allowing for movement. A router and slot cutting bit is required to create the slots.

Figure eight fasteners

My favourite hardware to use is a figure eight fastener. Because of the shape of this fastener, it can swivel side to side with the tabletop as it moves, thus allowing for movement. One side is attached flush to the top side of the apron with a screw (a) and the other side is attached to the underside of the tabletop with a screw (b).

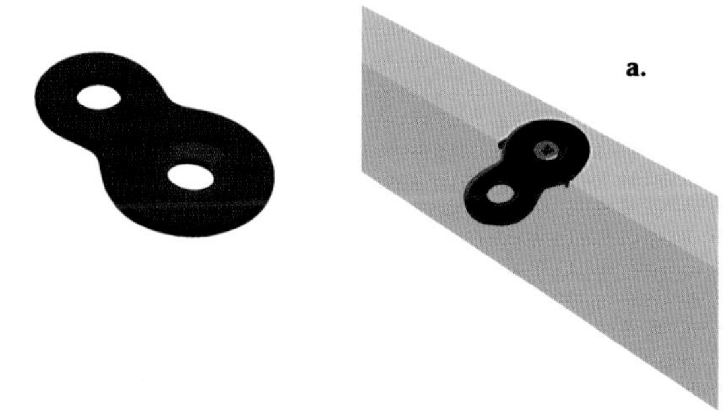

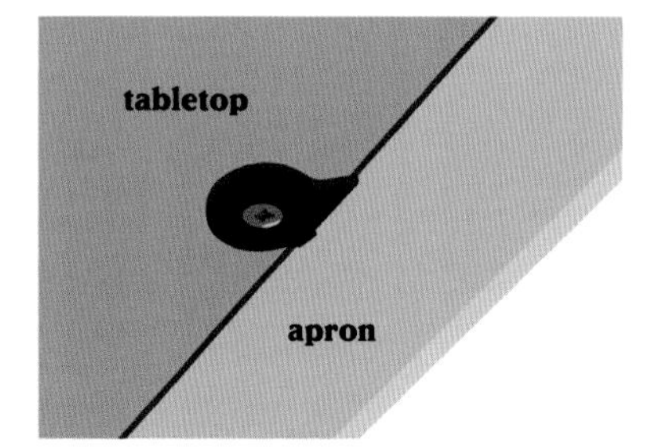

Installing figure eight fasteners

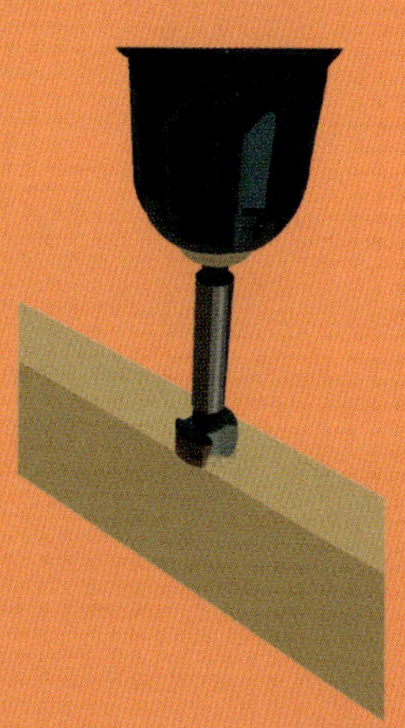

Installing figure eight fasteners requires just a drill, a Forstner bit and a chisel, so it's one of the simplest methods in my opinion. First, drill a shallow hole into the top of the apron for the fastener to sit in flush with the wood. Some figure eight fasteners have loops that are the same size, while others have a smaller and a larger loop. If you're working with the latter, the larger side should be attached to the apron, with the smaller loop attaching to the tabletop.

Use a Forstner bit that's the same size as the loop. Place the Forstner bit on the top side of the apron, overlapping slightly with the inside edge.

Once the hole is drilled, the ears will need to be removed with a chisel. The ears are the small excesses of wood leftover on the inside edge. These are easy to cut away with a chisel, or even a strong craft knife if you're working with softwood.

As we need to ensure the fastener will sit perfectly flush with the wood, I recommend drilling a small amount at a time, removing the ears, then placing the figure eight fastener in to check the depth. If it's not quite flush, drill a little more.

Once done, drill a pilot hole for the mounting screw on the centre spot left by the Forstner bit, then screw the fastener in place. Ensure the screw is snug, but not too tight – the fastener needs to be able to move with the wood. The best way to get this right is to tighten the screw as you usually would, then take a quarter turn back to loosen it just enough to allow for wood movement.

Once all the fasteners are attached to the apron, flip the tabletop over so that the underside faces up. Place the apron on top, mark the holes of the fasteners on the tabletop, then remove the apron. Drill the pilot holes, then put the apron back and drive in the screws.

Now as the tabletop expands and contracts, the fasteners can rotate with the movement.

Fasteners and wood grain

The angle at which the fasteners are installed on the tabletop is important. Fasteners installed on the top and bottom of the grain (i.e. along the grain) can be set straight, as these can swivel side to side with the movement of the wood as it expands and contracts across the grain.

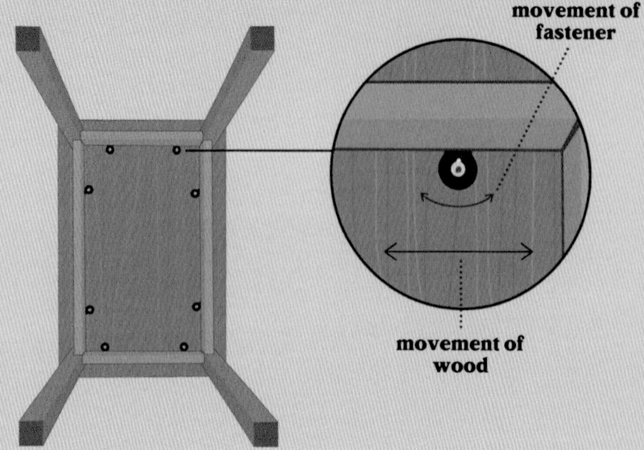

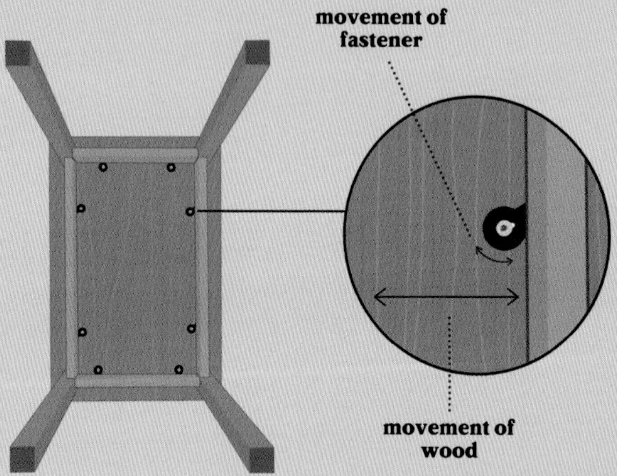

However, for the fasteners installed across the grain, the direction of the wood movement will be pushing and pulling on them, but the fasteners can't move in that direction. In this instance, when the fasteners have been installed in the apron, pivot them to a slight angle before attaching them to the tabletop. This will allow the fasteners to rotate with the direction of the wood movement.

TIP

How many fasteners you need will depend on the size of the table. There's no specific rule, but they have pretty good holding power so there's no need to go overboard. A few on each side will be enough. If the table is particularly large then you can add a few extra for stability.

How much does wood move?

All wood moves. No matter how small it is, it will shrink and grow with seasonal changes. But it's worth noting that wood movement is very minimal, so you'll usually find it doesn't cause much of an issue on smaller projects. You can look back through the book and see a few examples of projects where we haven't used harmonious grain. There's always a small risk that these joints can fail or the wood can crack, but the movement is so minimal on smaller pieces of wood that it's unlikely to happen.

How much a piece of wood will move is dependent not only on the size, but on the species, how the board was sawn from the tree and humidity levels. The change in humidity where you live has an impact. Wood that doesn't move much where I live may move a lot where you live. But to give you an example, based on my location and working with pine, a piece of wood that's 4cm (1⅝in) wide will only grow or shrink up to about 0.05mm (1⁄32in). Movement this small is very unlikely to cause any issues even if we don't use harmonious grain. A piece of wood that's 50cm (19⅝in) wide, however, could grow or shrink as much as 7mm (¼in). In this case, the movement is significant enough to cause stress to the wood.

The amount of movement is across the entirety of the board – whether it's a single piece of wood or several narrower pieces joined together, the amount of movement will be the same.

Some woodworkers will argue that no matter the size of the wood, techniques should always be in place to account for wood movement. Others will argue it's only when a board is wider than 10cm (4in), or even 30cm (11¾in), before you need to worry. I'm not going to claim who is right or wrong. If we were to err on the side of caution, ensuring that we use harmonious grain whenever possible and movement-friendly techniques when that's not possible will remove any risk of failure. I plan all my projects to use harmonious grain as a priority. On the occasions where harmonious grain just isn't possible, I don't worry about it if it's less than 10cm (4in) wide. If the wood measures between 10cm (4in) wide and 20cm (7 ¾in) wide, I'll try to account for movement, but if I can't rework the design, I'll take the risk. Anything wider than that is when I start considering other techniques.

If you're interested in looking into wood movement further, there are calculators available online that will work out exactly how much a piece of wood will move.

To sum up

- Wood movement happens across the width of the board (across the grain).
- Joining wood with the grains running in the same direction allows for wood movement.
- Joining wood with the grain running in opposite directions will restrict wood movement.
- For figure eight fasteners, install one loop flush in the apron and attach the other loop to the underside of the tabletop.
- Figure eight fasteners installed on the sides of the tabletop, across the grain, should be installed at an angle.

Wood movement may feel like a technical subject but when you understand the basics of why and how wood moves, it's pretty simple to understand how to work with it. Focus on using harmonious grain throughout your projects, and when that isn't possible, use movement-friendly techniques. Now that's said, let's make a table!

PROJECT

The Table

Building an entire table may not seem like a beginner's project, but it really is. I steered clear of building furniture for a long time because I felt it was outside my abilities, but it's actually a fairly simple process. We'll use the skills you've picked up throughout the book, plus some figure eight fasteners to account for movement of the tabletop.

Tools:

- Saw
- Sander
- Drill
- Pocket hole jig
- Chisel

Supplies:

- 20mm (¾in) Forstner bit
- x8: 20mm (¾in) figure eight fasteners
- Pocket hole screws
- Wood glue
- Clamps
- Stain (optional)
- Clear coat (optional)
- Paint (optional)

Cutting list:

- x1: 58 x 40 x 1.8cm (22⅞ x 15¾ x ¾in)
- x2: 46.5 x 4.4 x 1.8cm (18¼ x 1¾ x ¾in)
- x4: 40 x 3.4 x 3.4cm (15¾ x 1⅜ x 1⅜in)
- x2: 28.5 x 4.4 x 1.8cm (11¼ x 1¾ x ¾in)
- x48: 4.4 x 1.5 x 1.5cm (1¾ x ⅝ x ⅝in) (optional)

Cut the wood to the cutting list and sand each piece up to 180 grit.

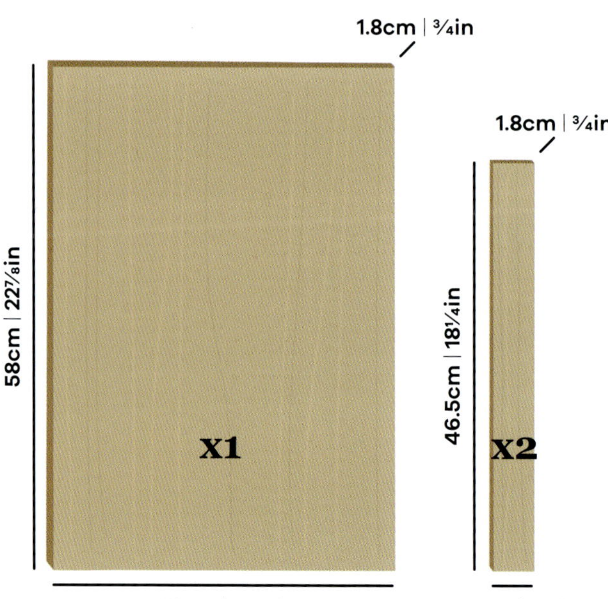

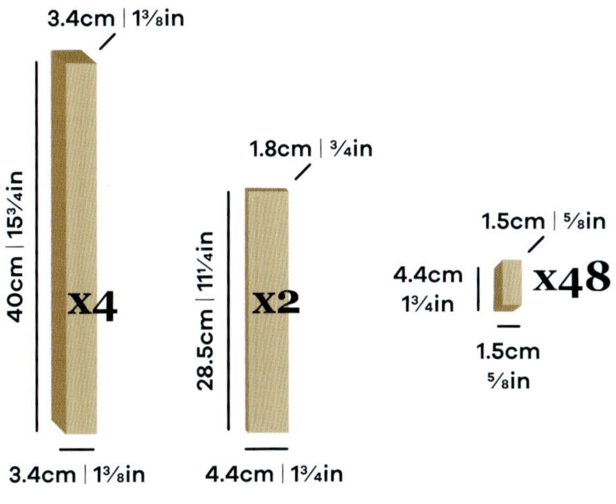

TIP

The 48 small blocks are for decorating the apron and are purely aesthetic. You may notice the grain direction of the apron is not harmonious with that of the blocks – we talked before about how minimal the wood movement is on small pieces like these, so I was happy to take a risk. If you want to take the risk too, please come join me on the dark side. Or feel free to skip them.

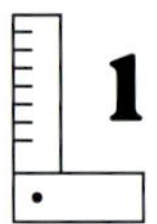

Drill two pocket holes into both ends of the two 46.5 x 4.4cm (18¼ x 1¾in) pieces and the two 28.5 x 4.4cm (11¼ x 1¾in) pieces. These are our aprons. If you don't have a pocket hole jig, attach the aprons using dowels.

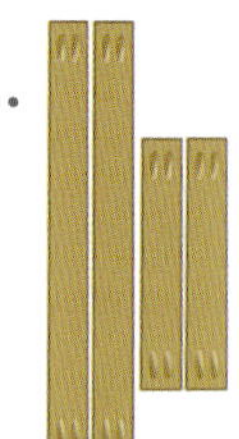

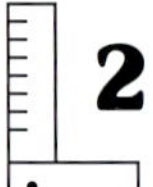

The 40 x 3.4cm (15¾ x 1⅜in) pieces will be our legs. To attach them to the apron at the correct height, use some off cuts from the 1.5 x 1.5cm (⅝ x ⅝in) pieces, placing them underneath one of the shorter apron pieces to lift it off the work surface. Now grab two leg pieces and align them at either side of the apron piece, ensuring the top edges are flush. The legs should lay flat on the work surface. If you're not using blocks on this project, you don't need to prop the apron as high – a thin bit of cardboard under the apron will lift it enough to make sure the screw enters the leg at the right angle. Drive in the pocket hole screws to secure them together. Repeat with the other short apron.

Now to attach the longer aprons. Place some 1.5 x 1.5cm (⅝ x ⅝in) pieces (or cardboard) underneath a long apron, then align the two assembled apron/leg pieces at either side, with the top edges flush. Drive in the pocket hole screws to secure them.

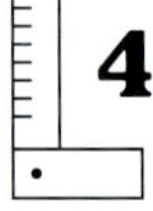

Repeat the same with the remaining apron piece, again placing some support (off cut pieces or cardboard) beneath the apron. Now you have a completed apron and legs.

If using, it's time to glue the 4.4 x 1.5cm (1¾ x ⅝in) blocks to the apron (if not, skip ahead to step 7). I suggest using your 1.5 x 1.5cm (⅝ x ⅝in) cut off pieces again here as spacers. Place a spacer on one end against the leg, then glue the first block down. Pop another spacer in and glue on the next. Keep going until all the blocks have been glued – nine for the shorter aprons and 15 for the longer ones.

To clamp the blocks in place whilst the glue dries, place a length of scrap wood across the front of the blocks and apply some clamps.

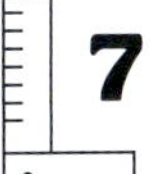

It's time to apply your desired stain and finish. I used a medium tone stain and finished it with a few coats of matte varnish. I also painted the space between each of the blocks on the apron with dark red. Stain and clear coat the 58 x 40cm (22⅞ x 15¾in) tabletop, too.

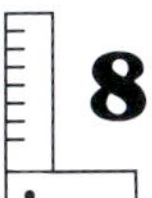

We're going to install two figure eight fasteners on each apron – exact placement isn't important. Using the 20mm (¾in) Forstner bit, drill holes into the apron, ensuring they're deep enough for the fasteners to sit flush. Remove the ears with a chisel. Drill the pilot holes and attach the fasteners with screws. The fasteners on the short side of the apron should be installed on the tabletop straight, but to account for the movement of the tabletop, the fasteners on the long side should be manually rotated to an angle.

The last step is to attach the figure eight fasteners to the tabletop. Lay the apron down on the underside of the tabletop so each leg is approx 2.3cm (⅞in) in from the edges. Mark the fixing holes with a pencil. Remove the apron and drill the pilot holes on the marks. Place the apron back and drive in the screws.

That's it! You made an entire table! It's as simple as that.

SWITCH IT UP

Now you know the basics of table making, you can adjust the design however you want. Make a short one with chunky legs for a side table, or paint the legs to add some character.

About Design

We all design differently. People often tell me they have the skills to make things but struggle coming up with ideas. I'm the opposite: a million ideas, mediocre skills. Whether you want to explore your creativity, or see yourself as more of a technical thinker, I want to share my design process with you. What works for me might not work for you, but I hope it opens your mind to new ways of thinking, imagining and creating.

What is design

Design isn't just about looks, it's also about functionality. For me, practicality and aesthetics take equal priority. But, if I had to choose, practicality takes precedence. It's not fun to make something you love only to find it doesn't function properly or work in the given space. Before I start to design anything, I ask myself:

- What is the purpose or function of this design?
- What size does it need to be to meet my needs and fit into the space?
- What features does it need to include to ensure it's usable and practical?
- What do I want it to look like?

Let's say I want to design a TV stand. A good place to start is with measurements. How tall should it be so the TV is at optimal viewing height? How wide should it be to fit into the space?

Once I have the basic measurements, I think about my other needs. Having a shelf is great, but closed storage can help keep things from looking messy, so I'll add some cupboard doors. Will I have room to open the doors? Are sliding doors a better option than hinged ones, or doors that open upwards instead of outwards?

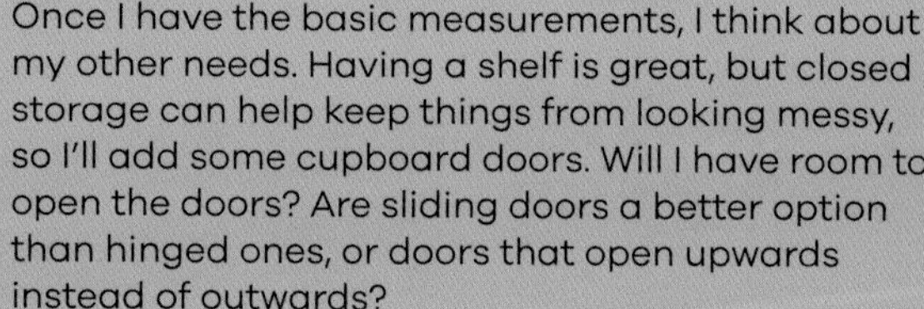

Once the design meets the functional needs, I can come back to the aesthetics. I think solid doors can look too heavy, so maybe I'll do a window cutout and add a sheet of frosted acrylic.

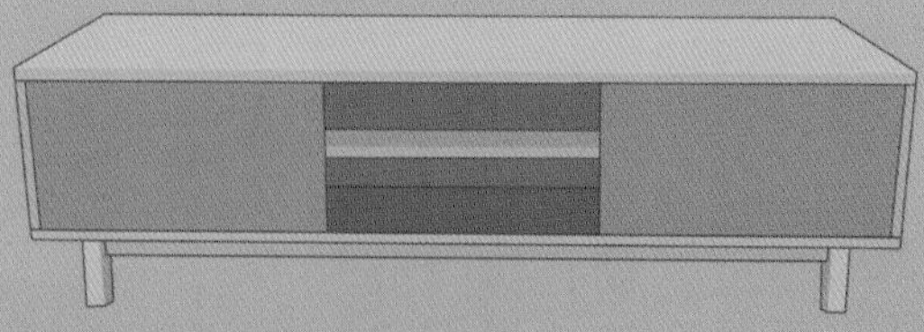

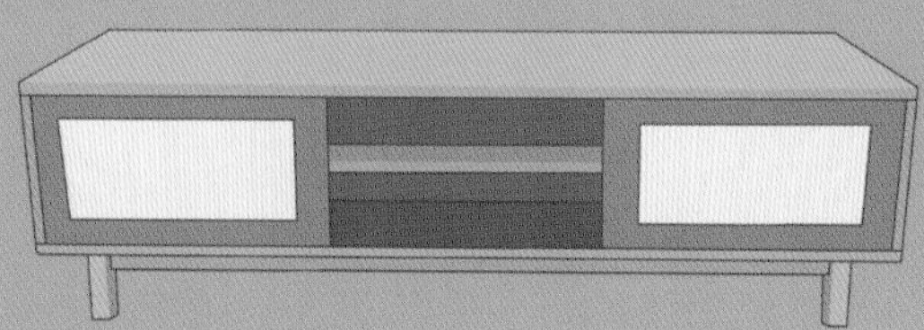

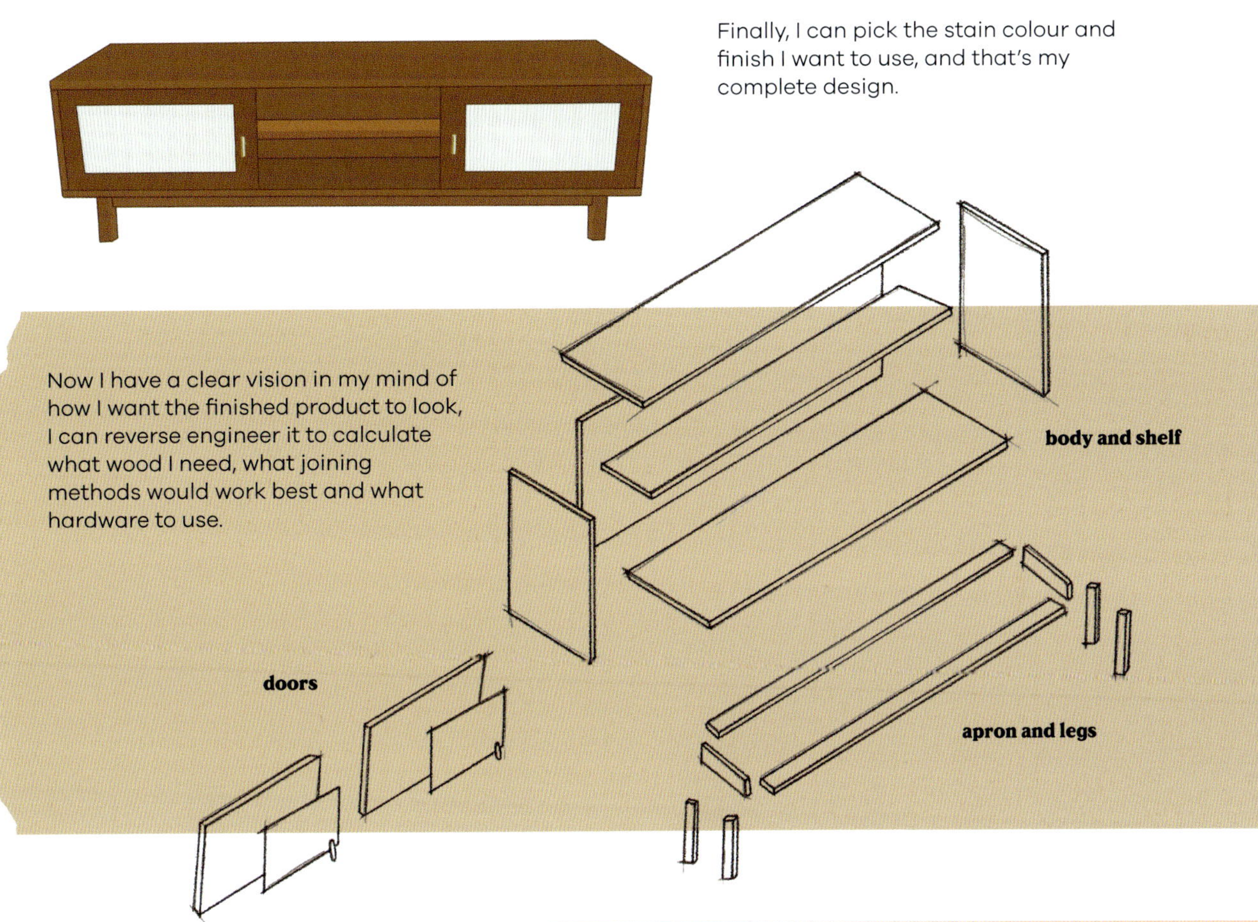

Finally, I can pick the stain colour and finish I want to use, and that's my complete design.

Now I have a clear vision in my mind of how I want the finished product to look, I can reverse engineer it to calculate what wood I need, what joining methods would work best and what hardware to use.

How to draw it up

There's a lot of software out there you can use to draw up designs, but I tend to use simple pen and paper. Or, more often these days, I draw it up on my tablet. What you use is up to you, but don't feel like you need expensive software and extensive knowledge. For some simple designs I won't even draw it up – the design is clear enough in my mind. Drawing up a design is just a visual aid for you to finalise the look of the build, make notes of the measurements and start to think about how to execute it.

How design begins

I find my creative process starts from one of three places. One: problem solving. Two: seeing something I like. Three: setting limitations.

Problem solving

Having a problem that needs to be solved is the birthplace of great ideas. An example of this is the side table I made for my new sofa, a design that evolved with each new problem (or opportunity!) that arose.

I got an electric recliner sofa (dreamy!) with the control buttons on the side. But my existing side table was too tall and covered the buttons. So my problem was accessing the buttons, and the solution was a shorter table. That's pretty simple, but it created a new problem...

The new table felt too short to rest my cup of tea on. A new problem needs a new solution, so I decided to add a second tier, half the size, for extra height without blocking the buttons. I played with a few different design ideas before settling on a solid top and side, with a half round cutout for fun.

solution 1: shorten table

solution 2: add a second tier

Thinking about the practical aspects of the second tier, I realised how annoying it would be if something small rolled underneath and I'd have to feel around to find it. I decided to add a hinge so I could lift it up for access.

solution 3: hinge the top tier

Once I had the final design, I broke it down to figure out what wood I needed and how best to join it together.

Problem solving is how I design most of my projects. Whether it's a two tiered side table, a cable organiser, or a magnetic knife rack. Find a problem, then think of a solution.

Inspiration

We probably all see things we like and wonder if we can make it ourselves. This is a good place to find inspiration. I don't recommend copying someone else's work directly, rather use it as a starting point.

Join me in an entirely made up scenario. I'm walking down the street, hot chocolate in hand, peering into shop windows, when something catches my eye. It's a mirror mounted on wood, with hooks beneath to hang keys – perfect for the empty space near my front door. That's when the thought hits me: "I could make that".

Now I have a starting point for my design. What would make it work better for me? I could adjust the size to fit my space. I'd prefer a round mirror. And I'd like a shelf for my glasses. I'll add some slats and stain it in my favourite colour. And here's the final design. You can see how different it is from the original.

inspiration

final design

You can be inspired by the shape of a building, the colour of a dress or the texture of a clay pot and use those elements in your design. One time, I was accidentally inspired by the water tap at my office. I came up with a cute idea for a lamp and then, a few days after making it, I was filling up my water bottle at the office when it suddenly dawned on me: the lamp was the exact same shape and size as the tap. Inspiration is everywhere.

Limitation

This is a process I use when I'm lacking inspiration and I want to kick start the process. Sometimes creativity can really flourish when it's limited by time, materials or style.

Every woodworking project will leave you with off cuts to add to your scrap pile. When inspiration is at a low, I like to challenge myself to make something using these scraps. I'll play around with the off cuts until I get an idea. Sometimes I make something great, sometimes it's terrible, but that's not the point. What matters is the challenge and reigniting my creative spark.

Time is another limitation that can help you find inspiration. 'Crazy eights' is a design exercise that uses time constraints to encourage new ideas without overthinking – give yourself eight minutes to come up with eight new design ideas.

Let's say you want to make a bench, but you're stuck on the design. Grab some paper and divide it into eight sections. Set an eight minute timer and draw a different design in each box. The goal is to throw designs onto the paper without too much thought. Get weird with it. The designs don't have to be possible or practical.

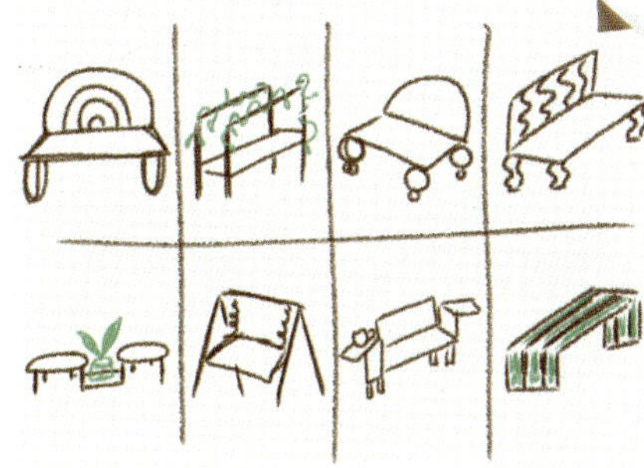

Now review your designs. Maybe there's one you love, in which case you can develop the idea fully. Maybe two of them pique your interest: draw four more designs inspired by each one. Keep going, always on a time restriction, until you have a clearer idea of what you want. Then focus on developing that design with no time restriction.

Take a break

If all else fails, take a break. I'm a big fan of letting things percolate – once I have a rough idea, I let my subconscious mull it over. I trust my brain to work on it while I'm busy with life. After a few days, or even weeks, I come back to the design to see if I have a clearer picture in my mind. I usually do.

To sum up

- Design is about practicality, functionality and aesthetics.
- Have a starting point: problem solving, inspiration, limitation.
- Use "crazy eights" to encourage new ideas.

I truly believe that being creative is something you can learn. While we're busy with life's demands, our creative muscles can become dormant. Flex those muscles. Give your imagination permission to explore without judgement. Learn from mistakes, celebrate successes. Let your inner designer wander free, and see what they come up with.

PROJECT

The Sideboard

This project incorporates my favourite elements. Slats, lots of wood, the colour green. What would you change to better suit your taste? Maybe you'd prefer an oval top, or maybe a more solid, blocky look. Maybe you'd prefer it short and wide, or tall and narrow. Or maybe it's perfect for you, in which case, you're welcome. Let's make a sideboard.

Tools:

- Saw
- Sander
- Drill
- Pocket hole jig
- Chisel

Supplies:

- x4: 32mm x 6mm (1 ¼ x ¼in) shelf pins
- x8: 20mm (¾in) figure eight fasteners
- 20mm (¾in) Forstner bit
- 6mm (¼in) drill bit
- Pocket hole screws
- Screws or small nails
- Wood glue
- Clamps (or weights)
- Stain (optional)
- Clear coat (optional)
- Paint (optional)

Cutting list:

- x1: 65 x 49 x 0.3cm (25 ½ x 19 ¼ x ⅛in) MDF
- x2 : 70 x 30 x 1.8cm (27 ½ x 11 ¾ x ¾in)
- x1: 65 x 27 x 1.8cm (25 ½ x 10 ⅝ x ¾in)
- x2: 59.5 x 4.4 x 1.8cm (23 ⅜ x 1 ¾ x ¾in)
- x46: 46 x 1.8 x 0.6cm (18 ⅛ x ¾ x ¼in) D-shape moulding
- x2: 46 x 30 x 1.8cm (18 ⅛ x 11 ¾ x ¾in)
- x2: 46 x 9 x 1.8cm (18 ⅛ x 3 ½ x ¾in)
- x2: 19.5 x 4.4 x 1.8cm (7 ⅝ x 1 ¾ x ¾in)
- x4: 10 x 3.4 x 3.4cm (3 ⅞ x 1 ⅜ x 1 ⅜in)

Cut the wood to the cutting list and sand each piece up to 180 grit.

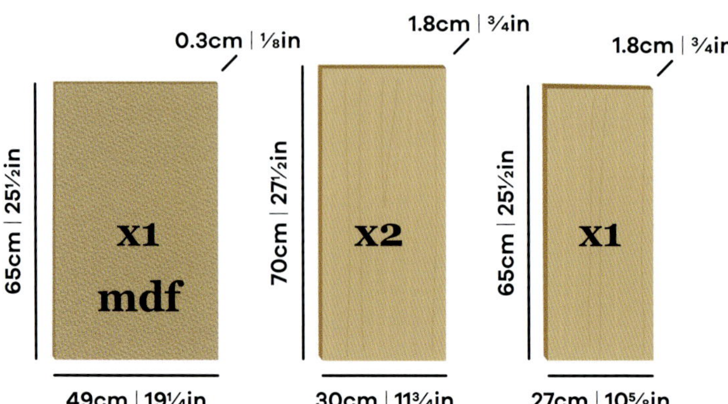

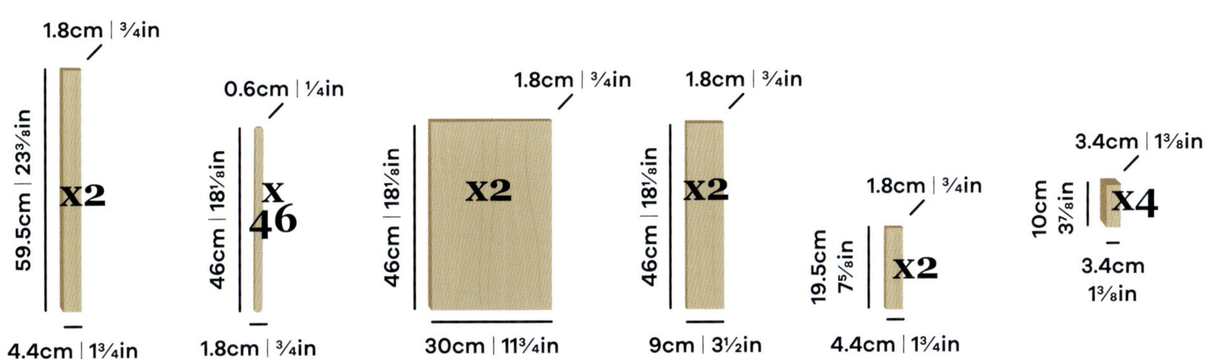
1.8cm | ¾in
59.5cm | 23⅜in
x2
4.4cm | 1¾in
0.6cm | ¼in
46cm | 18⅛in
x 46
1.8cm | ¾in
1.8cm | ¾in
46cm | 18⅛in
x2
30cm | 11¾in
1.8cm | ¾in
46cm | 18⅛in
x2
9cm | 3½in
1.8cm | ¾in
19.5cm
7⅝in
x2
4.4cm | 1¾in
3.4cm | 1⅜in
10cm
3⅞in
x4
3.4cm
1⅜in

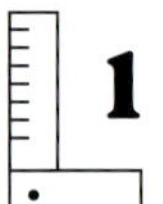

First up, let's assemble the apron and legs. Drill two pocket holes into both ends of the 59.5cm (23⅜in) and 19.5cm (7⅝in) pieces. These are our aprons.

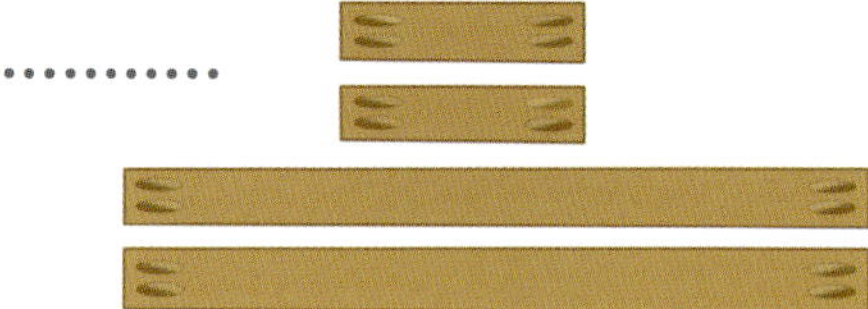

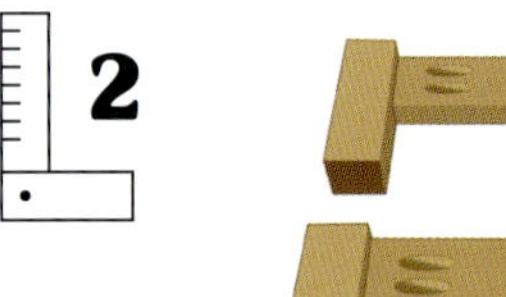

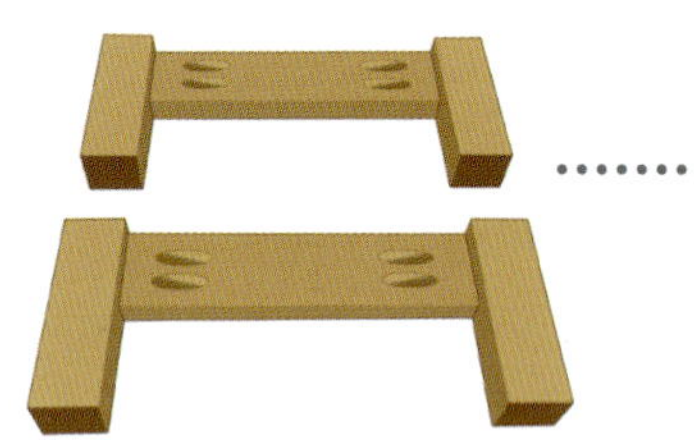

The four 10 x 3.4cm (3⅞ x 1⅜in) pieces are the legs. To attach the legs to the apron at the correct height, place a thin piece of cardboard underneath a shorter apron to lift it off the work surface. Now grab two leg pieces and align them either side of the apron, flat on the work surface, and drive in the pocket hole screws. Repeat with the remaining short apron.

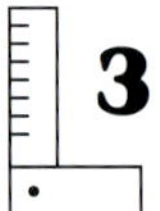

Now align those pieces with a longer apron, using the cardboard to lift the apron a little from the work surface, and drive in the pocket hole screws. Repeat with the remaining apron. We now have a completed apron and legs.

4

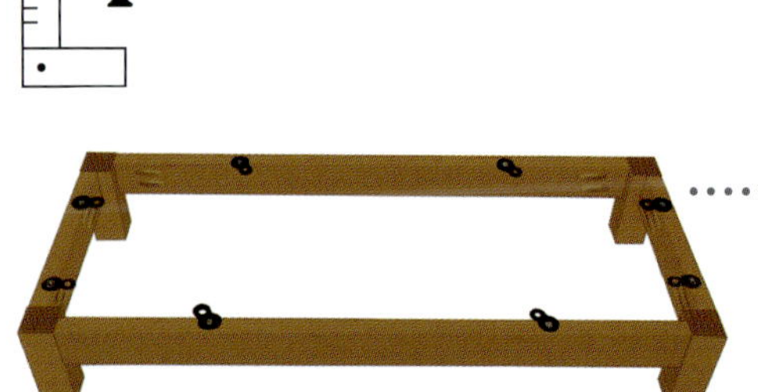

We'll be using figure eight fasteners on the apron to attach it to the base of the sideboard. First, stain and clear coat the apron and legs. Once dry, install two figure eight fasteners on each apron – exact placement isn't important. Use the 20mm (¾in) Forstner bit to drill the holes then remove the ears with a chisel. Drill the pilot holes and drive in the screws to attach the fasteners. Manually rotate the fasteners on the long aprons so they're at an angle to account for the direction of wood movement once assembled.

Now set the apron and legs aside while we build the body of the sideboard. First, the side panels.

5

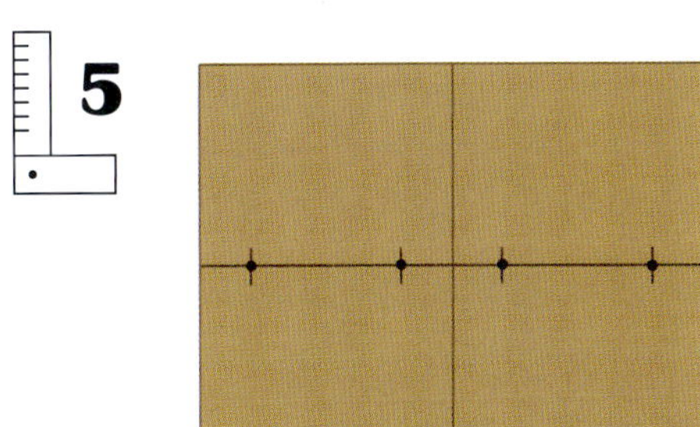

Line up the two 46 x 30cm (18⅛ x 11¾in) pieces side by side. For both pieces, measure 23cm (9in) down from the top and draw a horizontal line right across. Draw short vertical lines across the horizontal line, 6cm (2⅜) in from each edge. Where the lines intersect is where we'll drill the holes for the shelf support pins.

Using a drill bit the same diameter as the shelf pins, drill holes deep enough for the pins to sit in. My shelf pins are 6mm (¼in) in diameter so I used a 6mm (¼in) drill bit. The part of the pin that sits in the wood is 14mm (½in) long, so I drilled the holes 14mm (½in) deep. We'll insert the pins near the end of assembly; for now we're just making the holes.

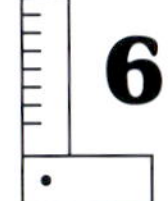

6

On the same side as the shelf pin holes, drill three pocket holes along the top and bottom of each board – one in the centre and the other two 5cm (2in) in from the edges. We'll use the pocket holes to attach the panels to the base and tabletop when we assemble the sideboard.

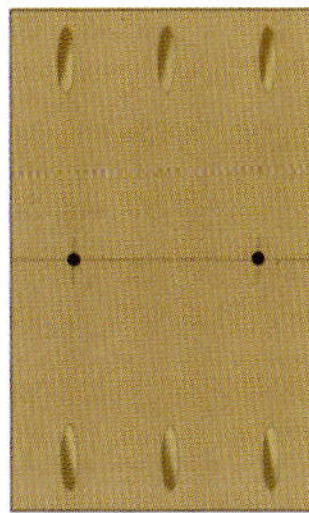

7

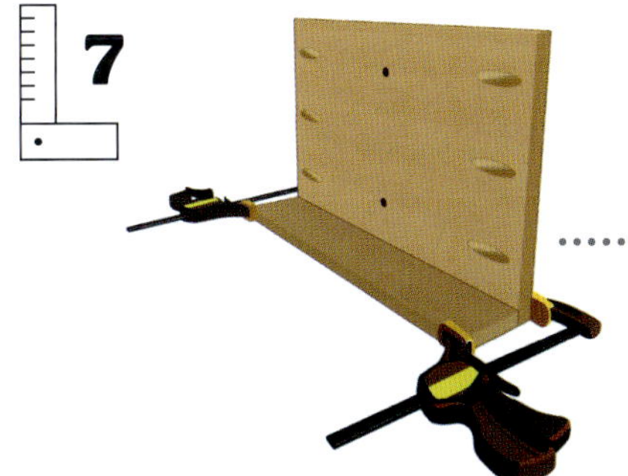

The next step is to attach each side panel to a smaller panel for the front of the sideboard. Butt a 46 x 9cm (18⅛ x 3½in) piece against a side panel, on the same side as the pocket holes and shelf pin holes. Ensure the ends are aligned, and add clamps to secure them together.

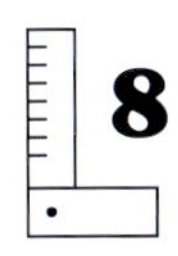

8

Drill and countersink four pilot holes and drive the screws in to attach the pieces together.

9

Repeat Steps 7 and 8 with the remaining 46 x 9cm (18⅛ x 3½in) piece and the other side panel.

10

Now it's time to attach the D-shape moulding to the panels. I found it easiest to lay the panel down over the edge of the worktop. Add glue to the surface of the panel and place the moulding down. Start gluing from the end with the joint and work your way to the other end, removing any glue squeeze out as you go.

11

Thin moulding like this often isn't very accurate in width, so if yours are a little narrower or a little wider than 1.8cm (¾in) it may take either 16 or 17 pieces to cover the panel. Don't worry if there's a little bit of wood left uncovered at the end. This will be at the back so it won't be noticeable. Once it's all in place, put some weights, or anything heavy, on top to clamp the moulding in place while the glue dries.

12

Once the glue is dry, turn the piece around on the worktop to glue the moulding to the shorter side. Use weights again to clamp them down. This side should fit around six pieces of moulding.

13

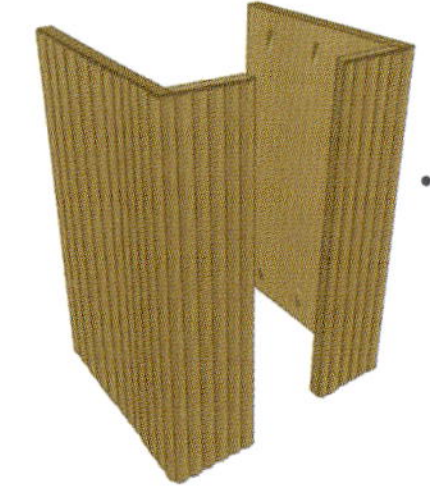

Repeat to cover the side and front of the second panel. Once the glue is dry, give the moulding a light hand sand with 180 grit to make sure the surface is clear of any dry glue.

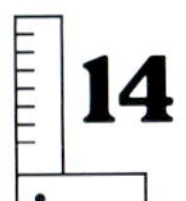

14

Before we move on to assembly, you could stain and clear coat all of the project pieces now. The assembly doesn't require any further glue, so you don't have to worry about stain preventing the glue from bonding. However, if you want to be able to sand the piece after assembly, then leave the stain and top coat until afterwards. This part of the process is totally up to you.

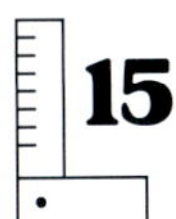

15

Now we're on to the assembly. Place the side/front panel pieces on top of each end of a 70 x 30cm (27½ x 11¾in) piece. The side and front of the panels should align flush with the base piece. The back of the panels will overhang the back of the base piece a little bit. Drive some pocket hole screws through the previously drilled pocket holes.

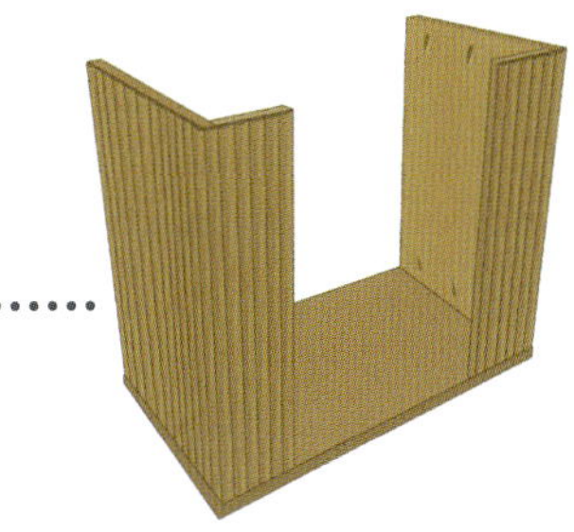

16

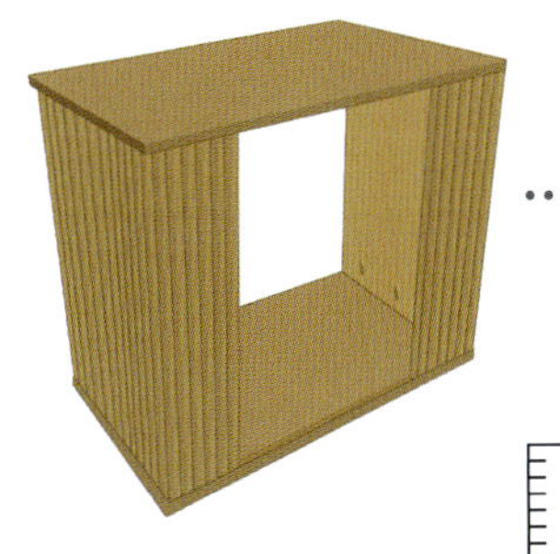

Now flip the whole thing over and place it on top of the remaining 70 x 30cm (27½ x 11¾in) piece. The alignment should be the same as before – the front and sides should align flush, with the back overhanging a little bit. Attach it with pocket hole screws.

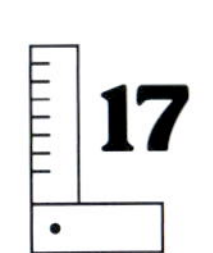

17

If you haven't done so yet, stain and clear coat the whole piece, plus the 65 x 27cm (25½ x 10⅝in) piece – this will be the shelf. The 65 x 49cm (25½ x 19¼in) MDF is going to be the backing of the sideboard. MDF doesn't take stain well so I recommend painting it. If you're not a fan of a lot of colour, paint it a colour similar to the wood tone.

18

Once the finish is dry, it's time to attach the apron and legs. Lay the apron and legs upside down on the base of the sideboard. The legs should be approx 1.8cm (¾in) in from each edge. Mark the fixing holes for the figure eights, then remove the apron and drill the pilot holes. Place the apron back onto the base and drive in the screws.

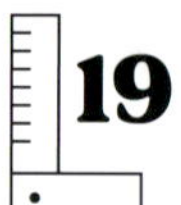

Flip the sideboard over onto its legs so it's upright. Place a shelf support pin into each of the pre-drilled holes.

20

Place the shelf onto the support pins. You'll need to go through the back of the sideboard to insert the shelf, as the front panels will prevent it from fitting through the front way.

The last step is to attach the MDF to the back. It should fit in between the side panels. Use small nails or screws to attach it to the top and base of the sideboard.

And just like that, the sideboard is complete. Whether you adjust the design to better suit your aesthetic, or keep it as is, I hope this build will help you realise that not only is building furniture possible, but it's as easy as just deciding to do it. So bring character, style and fun into your home by creating. It might not come out perfect, mine certainly didn't, but perfection isn't something we should be chasing. Joy is.

The Next Chapter

Here we are – the last chapter of the book, but the next chapter for you. Armed with the knowledge and confidence I hope you found in these pages, you can go out into the world and start the next chapter on your journey.

Woodworking is what you make of it. It's an art. It's a hobby. It's a solution. It's therapy. You get to take everything you've learned here and start carving out your own path to find what woodworking means to you.

At the risk of sounding way too sentimental, woodworking has changed my life. It's shown me how capable and creative I am. It gave me purpose when I was lost. It gave me confidence when I was insecure. It gave me joy when I needed it most. But it hasn't always been easy. Woodworking has traditionally felt like a hyper masculine space, and I didn't always feel like I fitted into that. In fact, for many years I didn't refer to myself as a woodworker, because I wasn't sure if I was good enough, or technical enough, or creative enough. But then I realised that if you work with wood, it's woodworking. It doesn't matter if you're making small things or big things, if you're using butt joints or dovetail joints, if the final piece is wobbly or wonky or not the way you imagined. It's all woodworking. And I can only hope that by sharing the knowledge I've gained over the years, you too can realise this space belongs to all of us. Art has long been dominated by the outcasts and the underestimated, and it's time that spilled over into woodworking, too. You and me. We belong here.

OKAY LOVE YOU BYE

About the Author

Annabelle is a self-taught woodworker who has been working with wood for almost a decade. From her workshop in the attic, she has accumulated a huge online following (@annabellejune_) building anything that pops into her head, and has an unrelenting urge to show everyone she meets that they can do it too! Her approach to woodworking focuses less on refining traditional or complex skills and more on bringing your vision to life in the simplest way possible. She focuses on the joy of woodworking, the beauty of creating something with your hands and the rejection of perfectionism. This is her first book.

Index

A DAVID AND CHARLES BOOK

David and Charles is an imprint of David and Charles, Ltd, Suite A, Tourism House, Pynes Hill, Exeter, EX2 5WS

EU GPSR Authorised Representative: Logos Europe, 9 rue Nicolas Poussin, 17000, La Rochelle, France Email: Contact@logoseurope.eu

First published in the UK and USA in 2026

A catalogue record for this book is available from the British Library.

ISBN-13: 9781446315736 paperback
ISBN-13: 9781446315743 EPUB

This book has been printed on paper from approved suppliers and made from pulp from sustainable sources.

Printed in China through Asia Pacific Offset for: David and Charles, Ltd, Suite A, Tourism House, Pynes Hill, Exeter, EX2 5WS

10 9 8 7 6 5 4 3 2

Publishing Director: Ame Verso
Managing Editor: Jeni Chown
Editor: Victoria Allen
Project Editor: Claire Coakley
Design and Art Direction: Jess Pearson
Pre-press Designer: Susan Reansbury
Illustrations: Kathrine Buckland
Photography: Jason Jenkins
Production Manager: Beverley Richardson

David and Charles publishes high-quality books on a wide range of subjects. For more information visit www.davidandcharles.com.

Share your makes with us on social media using #dandcbooks and follow us on Facebook and Instagram by searching for @dandcbooks.

Layout of the digital edition of this book may vary depending on reader hardware and display settings.

Thanks

I've always dreamt of writing the acknowledgements in my own book one day, and now I'm here it's hard to know what to say. This book wasn't made possible by just one person, it's the culmination of love, support and hard work from all the people in my life over the years. My online community who have been with me every step of the way. Thank you for cheering me on through every success and mistake, and reminding me over and over again why I do this work. My loved ones who never had a doubt I would get here one day. Thank you for sharing in my excitement and pretending not to be bored when I ramble on about woodworking. The whole team who made this book possible; Ame, Jess, Claire, Victoria and Jason. Thank you for taking a chance on me, investing in my passion, and believing in this book.

But above all, I want to thank my sister. Words will never be enough but they're all I have. Thank you for being my best friend. Thank you for making me brave. Thank you for being you. It is the greatest honour to share this book, and life, with you. We did it!

Colman's
Mustard
IRWIN
20
30